To

_____

From

_____

Date

_____

365 Spirit-Lifting Devotions for Mothers

ISBN-10: 0-8249-4525-5
ISBN-13: 978-0-8249-4525-1

Published by Guideposts
16 East 34th Street
New York, New York 10016
Guideposts.org

. Distributed by Ideals Publications, a Guideposts company
2630 Elm Hill Pike, Suite 100
Nashville, TN 37214

Guideposts and *Ideals* are registered trademarks of Guideposts.

Acknowledgments
Every attempt has been made to credit the sources of copyrighted material used in this book. If any such acknowledgment has been inadvertently omitted or miscredited, receipt of such information would be appreciated.

Unless otherwise noted, Scripture references are from The Holy Bible, King James Version (KJV). Other Scriptures are taken from The Holy Bible, New International Version®, NIV® Copyright © 1973, 1978, 1984, 2011 by Biblica, Inc.™ Used by permission of Zondervan. All rights reserved worldwide. The New King James Version (NKJV). Copyright © 1982 by Thomas Nelson, Inc. Used by permission. The New American Standard Bible® (NASB), Copyright © 1960, 1962, 1963, 1968, 1971, 1972, 1973, 1975, 1977, 1995 by The Lockman Foundation. Used by permission. *The Living Bible* (TLB) © 1971. Used by permission of Tyndale House Publishers, Inc., Carol Stream, Illinois 60188. *The Message (*MSG*).* Copyright © 1993, 1994, 1995, 1996, 2000, 2001, 2002 by Eugene Peterson. Used by permission of NavPress, Colorado Springs, CO. Revised Standard Version of the Bible (RSV), copyright 1952, 1971 by the Division of Christian Education of the National Council of the Churches of Christ in the United States of America. Used by permission. The Holy Bible, New Living Translation (NLT), copyright 1996, 2004, 2007 by Tyndale House Foundation. Used by permission of Tyndale House Publishers, Inc., Carol Stream, Illinois 60188. Used by permission. All rights reserved.

Cover design, interior design, and typeset by Thinkpen Design, Inc.
www.thinkpendesign.com

Printed and bound in China

10 9 8 7 6 5 4 3 2 1

DAILY GUIDEPOSTS

365 SPIRIT-LIFTING

DEVOTIONS

Mothers FOR

Guideposts

INTRODUCTION

As a mother comforts her child, so will I comfort you.
—ISAIAH 66:13 NIV

365 Spirit-Lifting Devotions for Mothers IS A BOOK FOR US—FOR
MOTHERS, STEPMOMS, MOTHERS-IN-LAW, GRANDMOTHERS, EVEN STAY-
AT-HOME, CARETAKING DADS, AS WELL AS THE SPECIAL PEOPLE WHO FILL
IN AS A MOTHER. AS GUIDEPOSTS WRITER MARY ANN O'ROARK PUTS
IT, "IN SITUATIONS WHERE A HELPING HAND OR A LOVING GESTURE IS
NEEDED, I AM SOMEONE'S MOTHER."

*I*n *365 Spirit-Lifting Devotions for Mothers,* we share, reminisce, and
encourage other mothers as they move through the many stages of
mothering: the sleep-deprivation of new motherhood, the early years from
toddler to middle school, the fears for sometimes troubled, older children,
engagement-and-wedding planning, facing the empty nest—in short, our ex-
periences through the countless joys and challenges of motherhood.

Drawing on the life lessons of a generation of writers, *365 Spirit-Lifting
Devotions for Mothers* commemorates small steps and milestones and offers
comfort and joy through the wisdom that mothers pass on to—and receive
from—their children.

Learn how the mothers of Ray Charles and Enrico Caruso believed in their
sons' abilities when no one else did. Travel with Marion Bond West and her
mother as they bring a baby gift to her black babysitter in the racially segregated
South of 1942. Join Marci Alborghetti as she wonders how Mary, a simple
peasant girl, reacted to the expensive gifts the Magi brought her newborn son.
Be lifted by Patricia Pusey's prayerful strength while she tends her cerebral-palsy
afflicted daughter.

These and other stories will fill you with affection and admiration for all
mothers, including yourself. Eric Fellman sums it up best: "We may pray to 'Our
Father,' but the face of God we see, the hand of God we clutch, and the heart of
God we trust, belong to our mothers."

January

January 1

Thou hast beset me behind and before, and laid thine hand upon me.
—PSALM 139:5

*S*omething delightful interfered with my agenda for New Year's Day. I had been up way too late the night before, so I thought that I would settle in for a relaxing day of snacking and watching parades and college bowl football games. Our daughter Kelly and her husband Brett planned to come over. I eagerly looked forward to a Scrabble rematch with Brett around our kitchen table.

When they arrived in the afternoon, Kelly had a set of borrowed cross-country skis with her. It was a brilliant day to be outdoors. Under a crisp blue sky, dazzling ice crystals caught the sun across the snowy fields. There was nothing to do but bundle up and join my daughter for my maiden voyage on my new snowshoes!

As we made our way side by side through the unmarred glittering snow, I glanced back at our tracks and called to Kelly, "Hey, look! Yours are smooth and straight and dainty on skis, and mine are chunky and clumpy and uneven with my snowshoes." She smiled as we resumed our gliding and trudging up a slight incline, faces toward the sun.

"We're breaking trail into the new year!" Kelly exclaimed.

Yes, we were, this frisky daughter of mine and I. She was twenty-three; I was forty-eight. Of course our "tracks in the snow" would look different. Maybe at some spots in our lives we'd even cross over, and I would be the graceful glider and she the slower plodder. We all break trail differently, some with more ease than others. But the thrill of it is, with Jesus Christ—the Beginner and Finisher of our faith—the job gets done.

I took another look back at our double trail in the snow. I'm sure I saw a third set of tracks.

Jesus, Lord of time and space, You go behind and before
and beside me as I enter this new year. Thank You.
—CAROL KNAPP

JANUARY 2

Offer the sacrifices of righteousness, and put your trust in the Lord.
—PSALM 4:5

*I*t was late. I sat in the dark at my computer, playing a mindless game while I tried to let the day's events settle. My son John came out of his room. He'd had a hard day and a long week battling irritability and anxiety. Now he wanted to talk. I girded myself for a long, trying conversation. "Mom, I noticed that all of the Christmas presents we give you are practical things," John began.

Taken off guard, I nodded. When did my eleven-year-old become observant? For years I've economized at Christmas by asking for wooden spoons, rubber scrapers, bath mats, and other household essentials. Until now, none of the children had noticed. "What would you want if we could afford something really nice?"

"Oh, I don't know," I replied casually but with an inner twinge. "I haven't thought about it for years."

"Well, what do you like to do besides take care of us?" John pursued.

I was silent, thinking. There isn't often room in my day for considering what I like to do. I searched my memory for what I'd enjoyed "pre-children." "I like to read a lot. I like to visit art museums and go for walks in the woods," I began. "I like talking about books and eating Thai food with your father. I like having quiet time alone." A list of things I hadn't done for a long time poured out.

John said nothing. Then, "Are you sorry you had children, Mom?" I turned to him, so he could see the fierce conviction in my eyes. "No, honey. Absolutely not. I wouldn't trade this for anything."

Jesus, even when a sacrifice is made freely,
it's not without cost. Don't let me take Yours for granted.
—JULIA ATTAWAY

JANUARY 3

They shall feed every one in his place.
—JEREMIAH 6:3

$\mathcal{P}$ hyllis, my next-door neighbor's mother, always wore an apron. That's because she was always cooking: rolling out pie crusts for the firefighters in her picturesque New Hampshire town, shaping dozens of her famous mountain cookies for bake sales, or simmering Boston baked beans for church suppers. If food was needed, Phyllis was there. When her daughter Janice invited me over for cookouts, supposedly Phyllis's day off, I'd enjoy the conversation—and Phyllis's creamy potato salad with a yummy extra something. That woman just *had* to cook.

Now Phyllis knew that I felt lonely living on the lake in the winter, especially during that first empty-nest year following my daughter Trina's graduation. So during the darkest evenings of the year, Phyllis included me at her table for a proper Sunday dinner: meat, potatoes, gravy, several vegetables, and two desserts, a true labor of love whipped up by a woman nearly eighty years old and too diabetic to eat most of it. Yet how she nourished so many of us!

Then one July afternoon, God suddenly called Phyllis home. Janice found her mother near the door of the sun porch, wearing her apron. In her hand were crumbs of bread; she had been on her way to feed the birds.

> *Lord, thank You for the ways dear Phyllis nourished me.*
> *Use me to carry on her pantry ministry.*
> —GAIL THORELL SCHILLING

January 4

If we hope for what we do not yet have, we wait for it patiently.
—Romans 8:25 niv

My five-year-old grandson Drake is allergic to peanuts. We found this out a few years ago when his first peanut-butter sandwich was followed by his first trip to the emergency room. The doctor told us that there was a small chance Drake might outgrow this allergy. We've all prayed that might be the case, but we've also educated Drake about his "problem" and taught him that he cannot eat everything others may be eating.

Last month Drake was retested. His three-year-old brother Brock was tested for nut allergies too. The week before the procedure, Drake was smiling and wiggling with excitement. "Nina, I'm going to have a test and I might not be allergic. If I'm not allergic, I'm coming to your house to eat peanut butter!" But when the nurse called with the results, Drake was still allergic to nuts. Brock, however, was not.

A few days ago, the boys and I were heading home from preschool. From the backseat, Drake said, "Nina, can you guess who's not allergic to nuts? No, it's not me. It's Brock!" I glanced in the rearview mirror to see Drake pointing to Brock, a big smile on his face. We drove in silence for a few minutes before Drake continued. "I will be tested again when I am six. Maybe I will not be allergic that time. And then, Nina, I will come to your house and eat peanut butter."

Hope—pure, unadulterated hope. Drake was happy knowing that his desire could still come to pass. He would wait expectantly. And in the meantime, he'd celebrate his brother's good fortune.

I'm going to try (again) this year to do as the Apostle Paul admonishes: to hope, to believe and to wait—patiently. It shouldn't be too hard. After all, I have Drake to show me how it's done.

> *Father, I wait for Your perfect timing in my life.*
> —Mary Lou Carney

While we look not at the things which are seen,
but at the things which are not seen.
—2 CORINTHIANS 4:18

*E*verything I saw indicated that my son Jeremy was heading in the wrong direction—again. Long-standing addictions resurfaced, along with risky living and foolish spending, and he had stopped taking medication for his bipolar disorder. He ignored the family and refused our phone calls.

Finally, I went to see him. The door of his apartment was unlocked, and I burst in. It was like looking into a corner of hell—Jeremy was in a rage, totally out of control. As he bellowed, "Get out!" I turned and left, defeated and almost without hope.

Outside his apartment distant church bells I'd never heard before softly chimed a familiar hymn: "Crown him with many crowns, the Lamb upon his throne...." I forced myself to look up into the amazing blue sky and prayed. "Lord, I choose to believe You have a plan to redeem him." It wasn't an easy prayer. I'm not certain I believed it. Day after day, month after month, as Jeremy's circumstances became worse, I struggled not to let them control my thoughts. I remembered, instead, the clear chiming of the bells and tried to believe they rang for Jeremy's recovery.

Nearly a year later, Jeremy knelt at the altar as a small band of believers gathered around him. Bit by bit he moved into another dimension, physically and spiritually, leaving behind a lifestyle that had almost killed him. Before my eyes he became a man of integrity, purpose, and righteousness.

I'd been given everything that I'd barely hoped for—and more.

Father, no matter what the outward circumstances,
help me look toward what I can't yet see.
—MARION BOND WEST

JANUARY 6

Nations shall come to your light, and kings to the brightness of your rising.
—ISAIAH 60:3 RSV

I often wonder what happened to the gifts of the Magi. After a particularly moving Epiphany service, I like to think about the people those gifts may have touched.

How did Mary, Jesus' young mother, view that sudden unexpected wealth? Had she been awestruck? Had she expected it? Had she put it aside, planning some day to use it for Jesus' studies with a rabbi, or for the family she hoped—like any mother—He would have? What of Joseph? Had he been forced to use some of it on the flight to Egypt and, later, on their return to Nazareth? Had the people he'd paid to help them found themselves blessed by some miracle or shining memory?

Usually, I put away my manger on Epiphany, but this year I'll leave it up a little longer. Maybe all year. It makes me think. What did that awestruck young shepherd tell his wife the next morning? Did that wealthy astrologer kneeling before a penniless Child treat his own servants differently when he returned home? And, if he did, did they, in turn, become gentler with their own families?

What wondrous questions come to your mind when considering Christ's life?

> *Lord, as I imagine how Your every act affected others,*
> *help my acts, in their small ways, to do the same.*
> —MARCI ALBORGHETTI

And as the bridegroom rejoiceth over the bride, so shall thy God rejoice over thee.
—ISAIAH 62:5

"Mom, we're engaged!" Kendall's words tumbled out of the telephone late one afternoon. Little did she know that I'd been waiting all day for her call, because I knew she was getting engaged that day. One week earlier, her then-boyfriend David Parkhurst flew to Colorado and took Lynn and me to dinner to ask our blessing on his intention to propose to Kendall. His gesture, and the sacrifices he made to carry it out, not only endeared him to us, but gave us the privilege of anticipating this phone call.

David actually surprised us. He didn't tell us the reason for the dinner, instead saying something about his parents flying through Denver and they had arranged for a layover so the four of us could meet for the first time. The plan was to get together at a restaurant at 6:30 on a Friday evening. When we showed up, the maitre d' greeted us warmly. "Your table is ready," he said, "and a young man is here waiting for you." Lynn and I looked at each other with the first inkling of what might be unfolding. Sure enough, when we got to our table, there was David—only David.

"Your parents aren't coming, are they?" I asked as I gave him a hug.

"No," he grinned, "it's just me."

For the next couple of hours, the three of us talked and prayed and ate and laughed and, of course, I cried as he told us why he loved Kendall and wanted to marry her. We joyfully gave him our blessing, and he shared with us his plan for proposing to Kendall the next weekend. That's why I expected her phone call on this day.

As Kendall overflowed with excitement on the telephone, I overflowed with gratitude for a future son-in-law who cared enough to carry out that ageless tradition of asking for our daughter's hand, which included us in their circle of love on this day.

> *Thank You, Lord, for the way an engagement*
> *enlarges and enriches a whole family.*
> —CAROL KUYKENDALL

My mouth shall speak wisdom; the meditation of my heart shall be understanding. I will incline my ear to a proverb.
—PSALM 49:3–4 RSV

*D*on't get me wrong, I love dishwashers, microwave ovens, and all the gadgets that make life easier, but there are times I'm nostalgic for the sweet moments during my growing-up years when Mother and I did the dishes by hand. It was an unhurried time, a time to linger. Often it was a joking, laughing time, or a time to sing lilting favorites like "When Irish Eyes Are Smiling" and "It's a Long Way to Tipperary." Mostly though, it was a talking time.

Aprons on, we would stand at the kitchen sink together. I washed, my hands tingling in foamy hot suds, while Mother dried. In between there was chatter, interspersed with the homilies by which Mum gently guided my attitudes and developed my values. She had a reservoir of what I came to call her "dishpan proverbs." If a pot wasn't washed properly, it was handed back with "If something's worth doing, it's worth doing well!" When I got my first job, frittered away my paychecks, and was constantly short of cash, I heard, "Spend more than you earn, and you're sinking your boat!" There was no gossiping with Mum. "Rise above it!" she'd say. "Say something nice or don't say anything at all!"

During my dating years, littered with emotional hurts, Mum would frequently frown and clatter the cups as she stacked them. "It takes quite a bit of sorting out to find out just whom you don't want to be with, before finding out whom you do!" she'd say. Much teary-eyed sorting out finally brought me a love, steadfast and true, that has lasted for more than forty years.

I've raised my own family on Mother's "dishpan proverbs." Pulled from the kitchen sink, they are wisdom much remembered and passed along. In a muddle? Life twisted up? Come on in, we'll do the dishes and sort it out. You wash, I'll dry.

Help me to remember, Lord, that wisdom can be found even in the sharing of a simple task.
—FAY ANGUS

Blessed be God, even the Father of our Lord Jesus Christ, the Father of mercies, and the God of all comfort; Who comforteth us in all our tribulation.
—2 Corinthians 1:3, 4

It has always seemed odd to me that during her lifetime my mother never seemed to be what you'd call "religious." She saw to it that her three sons always went to Sunday school, while church for her was a Christmas Eve-and-Easter thing—except I do recall that the moment she heard the news of the D-Day invasion she got right into her car and drove around until she found a church whose doors were open. There were a number of times that I had the feeling, and it was only that, that Mother was praying. But I never asked her about this.

In her late fifties Mother developed cancer, and during the last, long months of this illness she was in severe pain. Generally I would go to see her before my work day would begin, and then again in the evening. I'd sit with her, my eyes glancing from a bottle whose tablets provided her only relief, to her face, which was beautiful and strained and resolute, somehow. Often in my own concern and frustration, I'd feel like cursing. *Yet, why doesn't she?* I'd wonder. I was impressed by her curious equanimity.

One evening, in a silence, our eyes met, and I knew that Mother was reading the questions in my mind. She reached out for my hand and when she could feel its warmth she said something that has reassured me ever since.

"God," she told me in a low voice, "never said He'd keep us from trouble, but He did promise to help us in trouble. And He does, you know, He does."

I know You'll be there, Lord, when I cry out.
—Van Varner

For the things which are seen are temporal;
but the things which are not seen are eternal.
—2 CORINTHIANS 4:18

O ur children Ross and Maria love to watch home videos of when they were very small. Maria, now seven, especially enjoys seeing her twelve-year-old brother as a baby. They laugh at how he waddles around and falls down or chases the dog and squeals. The last one they watched, of Ross's third birthday, is a favorite.

"There's the big bug," Ross said, watching himself unwrap the year's best-loved gift. "I wonder what happened to that thing?" While the kids laughed about a boy who'd wanted a big, ugly bug for his birthday, I felt a little sad. All he'd wanted that year was a toy bug, and we searched everywhere for the right one. But now, like so many other things that once mattered so much, it had disappeared, either given away or settled to the bottom of a junk drawer.

"All those treasures forgotten," I said to my husband Paul, thinking that I don't need more reminders that my kids are growing up.

"Yeah," he said, "but remember how much that ugly bug meant to him? That's what matters."

As I thought about it, I understood. No matter how much our children may have loved a special toy or stuffed animal, those things simply don't last. The gifts that matter are the ones we can't hold in our hands. Love, trust, joy, faith, self-confidence—the gifts I have prayed for God to help me impart to my children. Those are the things Ross and Maria hold on to tightly and take with them everywhere they go.

Now when I find those former treasures in the junk drawer, they serve as gentle reminders. While my children are growing up, they're not abandoning their real treasures, but taking along the best of all we've given them.

Teach me, God, to enjoy the passage of time as another of Your eternal gifts.
—GINA BRIDGEMAN

I desire to do your will, O my God; your law is within my heart.
—PSALM 40:8 NIV

"Mom, make my hair extra neat today. François is teaching, and he doesn't like messy buns."

I dutifully sprayed on a little more water and twisted Mary's hair a bit tighter. I find it funny that Mary is aware of the preferences of her various ballet teachers. Then again, it's funny that I know anything at all about putting up hair.

Before I had a daughter in ballet I knew nothing about buns. Hair wasn't on my radar; I would have happily gone through life clueless about the subtle distinctions in using bobby pins and elastics. But life with children takes funny turns, and I find myself at middle age with a remarkable amount of knowledge about things I never imagined I'd know.

I know about learning disabilities and cleaning snake cages and organizing reenactments of the Revolutionary War. I can test for a broken bone and distract a nap-deprived toddler during rush hour. I know (sort of) what a vector is, and I've learned an astonishing and heartbreaking amount about anxiety disorders. None of these things were on my list of hoped-for accomplishments in life.

Yet somehow this pile of oddities has a lot to do with who I am today. I've grown more from doing what's been plopped in my path than I have from pursuing my own interests. In a way, that's as it should be. I see what I want, but God sees beyond that to what I need. There's a lot that goes into learning how to twist a bun into place.

Lord, whatever I want for myself, help me want what You want for me more.
—JULIA ATTAWAY

And let him that is athirst come.
—REVELATION 22:17

I was eight years old when the little gift catalogue came in the mail. "This ornamental poppy is the most amazing thing we have offered yet!" it boasted as it described the ten-cent, artificial plant whose bud would blossom into a scarlet poppy when dropped in water. *What a wonderful gift for my mother,* I thought. If only I could squeeze ten pennies from my tiny allowance without her finding out before her birthday.

Somehow I managed, but when the package came I was heartbroken. It looked anything but magical. The stem was kinked wire, and, no matter how hard I tried, I was unable to imagine the shapeless curl of paper at the end of the wire ever turning into anything resembling a bloom.

Almost tearfully, I wrapped the gift. "I paid a whole dime for it and it's not going to work," I said sadly when I presented it.

My mother smiled. "We don't know until we try."

We filled a jar with water and dropped in the worthless-looking trinket. And then the promised miracle happened! The wire stem straightened up like a real plant reaching for the light. One by one the perfectly shaped, opaque petals opened—slowly at first and then, as the paper absorbed water, in a burst of crimson glory. Later, after we'd thought the miracle was complete, fragile, fernlike leaves unfurled up and down the now-straight stem.

The ornamental poppy truly was a thing of beauty. All it needed was the magic of water. And that's all we need, too—the living water of Christ that brings out the glory in our drab lives. Only He can serve us "living water."

Through You, Lord, the beauty within me unfolds.
—JUNE MASTERS BACHER

*Be careful for nothing; but in every thing by prayer and supplication
with thanksgiving let your requests be made known unto God.*
—Philippians 4:6

om, ready for dominoes?"

"When I finish," I say, quickly looking up from the computer. I read the prayer submitted to OurPrayer.org and click the Approve button so that it posts on the site. OurPrayer.org is a Guideposts Web site where I blog, edit inspiring stories, and review prayers.

"Now?" Solomon taps the domino box on the computer table. I nod. As a work-from-home mom, finding a happy balance between work and play is an ongoing challenge. The kettle whistles, and I pour myself a cup of chamomile tea and grab a juice box for Solomon. This time of day, while Henry naps, is what Solomon calls SMT: Special Mommy Time.

Solomon rests his chin on the table as we select our dominoes. One by one the tiles turn into a long snake of black dominoes and white dots. As Solomon thinks over his next move, my thoughts drift to a prayer that's submitted every day by the same OurPrayer member: "Dear God, thank You for today." More than a decade ago, when I worked for a company that helped launch Web sites, we brainstormed the ways we thought the Internet would change the world. We spoke of advancements in entertainment and commerce; we never imagined people reaching out to each other online with love and support, one prayer at a time.

Sitting in a patch of sunlight with Solomon, I say a prayer of thanksgiving for the blessings in my life and for that special OurPrayer visitor who reminds me every day that today is a gift to cherish.

Dear God, thank You for today.
—Sabra Ciancanelli

January 14

Believe in the light.
—John 12:36

*R*ay Charles was one of the most influential soul singers of all time. His music, often upbeat, sometimes plaintive, could set my feet to tapping and rock my soul with emotion. Shortly after his death I saw the movie *Ray*. It showed how he began to go blind when he was seven years old and how his mother, a poor sharecropper in Florida, did all she could to help him overcome his disability. One scene in particular stood out in my mind.

Imagine this boy, now totally blind, walking into his cabin and falling to the floor. The audience sees him there, screaming out for his mother. She stands nearby, perfectly still; she knows instinctively that her son must overcome the darkness on his own.

Thinking he is alone, the boy slowly picks himself up off the floor. He moves toward the fireplace and feels the heat. From the open window he hears a horse and buggy passing by. He realizes he is going to be okay. His mother, hovering all the while, weeps and finally embraces her boy.

That scene reminded me of a night when I felt completely alone. I had thought that if I tried hard, God would make everything okay for me, but it hadn't worked out that way. I sat in my backyard in anguish, feeling totally abandoned. But now this memory took on a new dimension. I realized how God had been hovering near, feeling my pain, ready to embrace me with a hug. All I had to do was pay attention. All I needed to do was listen. And with Him by my side, I could pick myself up and feel my way to the light.

Father, in the dark times, keep me believing in the light.
—Brock Kidd

JANUARY 15

Give good gifts unto your children.
—MATTHEW 7:11

*I*f only we had a car, we could go see Jimmie and her new baby," I complained to my mother when I was about six. After my father died, Jimmie came to our house and cared for me while my mother worked. Mother beamed. "We can go, Mannie!" She polished my white sandals, dressed me in a pink sunsuit and sat me on the back of my new (secondhand) yellow bicycle. As Mother peddled, we bumped over the railroad tracks. I peeked around her to be sure our baby gift stayed in the basket.

Suddenly we seemed to enter a brown world. Brown close-together houses, which needed painting. Brown dirt yards swept smooth. Brown children laughing. The brown mailman waved to us, as did the women hanging out sheets. We saw Jimmie's mother; she came running to meet us and hugged us. Finally we saw Jimmie, lying in bed, holding her baby. Mother and Jimmie spoke in hushed tones while I marveled over the newborn. Jimmie opened the gift we'd brought, and I got to put the blue kimono on the baby.

Jimmie came back to care for me, bringing her sweet little son, and I pretended he was the little brother I longed for. When I got out my crayons, I reminded him to make the people in the coloring book brown and pink.

It was decades before I realized that my mother had also given me a remarkable gift that hot Southern summer day in 1942.

Father, help parents remember how simply children are taught life's lessons.
—MARION BOND WEST

JANUARY 16

O lord, thou hast searched me, and known me. Thou knowest my downsitting and mine uprising, thou understandest my thought afar off.

—PSALM 139:1–2

I was 20,000 feet in the air, my face pressed against the oval window of an airplane. Beyond, an infinite blueness blanketed the world with lonely space. My four-year-old son sat in my lap, his shaggy brown hair nestled against my shoulder.

The nose of the plane dipped. We began our descent. "In a moment we'll see a big city from the plane," I said.

We squeezed our faces into the little window and suddenly there it was, far, far below, gleaming in the sun like a child's miniature blocks. "Do you see the tiny people way down on the ground?" I asked. Bob nodded.

As he watched the ant-sized people, he asked, "Mama, is that what God sees when He looks down from heaven?"

A God's-eye view of the world? I thought of all the vastness God could see. A planet with four billion people, spinning in a universe with a hundred million galaxies. Suddenly, I felt small and insignificant...an ant-sized speck at the end of God's vision.

Bob tucked his head beneath my chin. His hair tickled my neck and some words of Jesus drifted to mind. "The very hairs of your head are all numbered" (Matthew 10:30). How could I forget? God deals up close and personally with every person. I turned to my son. "When God looks down on the world, He sees us so closely, He can count every hair on our heads. That's how special and near we are to Him."

"Wow!" Bob whispered, wide-eyed with wonder.

I smiled. That was my feeling, exactly.

When I feel tiny and insignificant, lost in the vastness of everything, remind me that in Your eyes, I am special.
—SUE MONK KIDD

Bless the Lord, O my soul...who heals all your diseases.
—PSALM 103:2–3 RSV

Several years ago, my son Chase went on a church ski trip. None of the other youth from our little church skied; they were on the trip to meet kids from other churches and maybe frolic in the powder. Not my son.

A couple of years earlier, he had convinced me to let him try ski lessons. Chase is a natural athlete and always game for adventure. Soon he was going up higher and higher mountains. Snowboarding was his choice, and I alternately covered my eyes and opened them to watch him swooshing downward, white powder flying behind him.

My daughter Lanea and I were about to go out for dinner when the phone rang. "He hit face first," the voice on the phone said. "It's not too bad. He's had a mild concussion." It was my worst nightmare. Chase's father had died of head injuries in an accident. Thank God Chase was alive!

I spoke to Chase at the hospital. "I'm fine. Stop worrying and go to dinner, Mom. I'm getting a ride home."

When Lanea and I got back from dinner, there was Chase, sitting at the computer. Half his face was bandaged, swollen beyond recognition, the outer layer of skin gone.

"Oh, Chase!" I cried.

He shrugged. "I told them not to tell you so you wouldn't worry. I'm okay, Mom," he said. But he wasn't okay. The wounds were deep and the doctors gave me directions to treat them like third degree burns. There could be infection and serious scarring.

We prayed. Trust God, I reminded myself.

Within days, spots of my son's own ebony pigment began to dot the pink wounds. Within a couple of weeks, he was back at school. Today, if you looked at my handsome son, you'd never know it happened. When I look at him, I see a miracle.

Lord, thank You for Your healing touch.
—SHARON FOSTER

For whom the Lord loveth He correcteth;
even as a father the son in whom he delighteth.
—PROVERBS 3: 12

Some years ago my daughter surprised her artist great-grandmother with a fistful of hastily colored pictures. Grandma looked them over carefully, then remarked gently, "You know, these aren't really pictures. They're more like scribbles!"

I had always greeted Rebecca's efforts with a casual "How pretty, dear," and was afraid her feelings would be hurt by Grandma's bluntness. But Rebecca took the criticism evenly. "I'm not too good at coloring," she admitted.

"You could be," Grandma told her. "Bring me your crayons and lots of paper."

The two, separated by more than 80 years, spent a happy hour exploring the world of color and design. Rebecca learned to color, and I learned a lesson, too: Criticism, offered in love and followed by constructive action, is far more valuable than empty praise.

Dear Lord, may I learn to give and receive criticism in Your spirit of love.
—PENNY V. SCHWAB

JANUARY 19

Follow that which is good, both among yourselves, and to all men.
—1 THESSALONIANS 5:15

*W*hen I rediscovered that wonderful childhood poem "The Cupboard" by Walter de la Mare, in an old poetry book, I had no idea what fun it would become for my five-year-old grandson Caleb and me. We were visiting my son in his new home. Phil had, to a child's mind, a "portal to another kingdom" in his kitchen—a tall white cupboard in which he stockpiled just about every kind of candy there is. Caleb would have cleaned him out if I hadn't declared, "I am in charge of the cupboard."

"I have a small fat grandmama," I quoted,
"With a very slippery knee,
And she's Keeper of the Cupboard,
With the key, key, key.
And when I'm very good, my dear,
As good as good can be,
There's Banbury Cakes, and Lollipops
For me, me, me."

I even had a small key with which I pretended to open the cupboard door.

Caleb, catching the spirit, eyes gleaming, recited, "When I'm very good... as good as good can be" every time he thought he should have a treat. Inserting the names of the goodies in Phil's stash, he'd say, "There's cherry twists and jelly beans for me, me, me."

Engaging our imaginations, Caleb and I created a great memory with that poem and my son's candy cupboard. The poem focused us on kindness and goodness in our daily interactions, because the secret of the cupboard isn't the key or the candy...the secret is in what *really* opens the cupboard door.

> *Jesus, Your goodness and kindness, imparted to me,*
> *Open eternal treasures to which You hold the key.*
> —CAROL KNAPP

The King will reply, "I tell you the truth, whatever you did
for one of the least of these brothers of mine, you did for me."
—MATTHEW 25:40 NIV

It was my third trip down the steep stairs in our two-hundred-year-old farmhouse. It was late, and I was very tired. The youngest of our seven children, eighteen-year-old Brittany, was fussing and needed attention—once again.

Brittany has cerebral palsy and can neither walk nor talk. She had undergone surgery to correct her severe scoliosis just six months earlier, and she was recovering very slowly. It seemed that nights were particularly difficult.

That evening, her inability to turn herself over to ease the strain on her still-healing spine muscles was causing her yet another uncomfortable sleep. She sighed her thanks as I gently turned her over and adjusted her covers, and before I left her room she was fast asleep.

I paused to observe Brittany in the dim light, and in that moment I forgot about how tired I was after months of interrupted sleep. The peaceful expression on her face caused me to feel blessed to have one of God's special children in my care.

Brittany's calls in the night allow me to hear the quieter voice of God, reminding me that I can be His hands to care for one of His angels.

Thank You, Lord, for using me where Your work needs to be done. Let me
always strive to share the comfort of Your love with those around me.
—PATRICIA PUSEY

You will be blessed when you come in and blessed when you go out.
—DEUTERONOMY 28:6 NIV

It was a day for rejoicing. Our son Chris was about to graduate from college. But by the time we claimed seats on the concrete steps on the crowded square at the University of Southern California, I felt stressed out from traffic, crowds, and jet lag. Suddenly Chris appeared carrying the uniform he needed to wear at his Army commissioning ceremony right after graduation.

"Mom," he said, "can you sew on some buttons? I didn't realize when I bought it that they weren't already sewn on." The uniform had come with a detached collection of shiny brass buttons sewn onto a short strip of material.

As Chris handed me a piece of thread and a tiny needle from a hotel emergency kit, I panicked. How am I supposed to do this sitting here on the steps? I don't even have a pair of scissors!

As Chris hurried off to line up, I looked down at my impossible job feeling like the whole day was careening toward disaster. Then a woman, who had obviously been through graduations before, walked by carrying a small hand-lettered poster. It read, "Too blessed to be stressed."

I took a deep breath, prayed, "Lord, help me" and examined the buttons on the strip of cloth. They were exactly as far apart as the button-holes! Between graduation and commissioning, I ran over to a nearby drugstore, got a package of safety pins and pinned the strip of buttons to the coat. Chris kept his coat tightly buttoned during commissioning and, thankfully, no one detected my less-than-regulation job.

The woman with the sign understood that even happy occasions bring with them a certain amount of stress. Luckily, the same God Who sends the big blessings is also the One Who gives us the grace to make it through the unexpected challenges of every big day.

Dear Lord, remind me that on the big days I need Your help more than ever.
—KAREN BARBER

*Always be prepared to give an answer to everyone
who asks you to give the reason for the hope that you have.*
—1 PETER 3:15 NIV

*W*hat matters most in a family these days?" a new mom asked our luncheon group, women of different ages and stages of life. Her question sort of hung there, suspended in silence over the table. It's the kind of question that doesn't have a quick answer because there are so many possibilities.

The momentary silence was soon filled up by conversation that headed in a different direction, yet I continued to ponder her question. As a new mom, I used to wonder the same thing. But within five years, my husband Lynn and I had three children, and we hardly had time to pause and consider what mattered most. We simply did the best we could in the midst of our busy circumstances.

Now our children are grown, and we just celebrated the arrival of our first grandchild. I have more of life to look back on and a new reason to consider what matters most to our family and what I'd like to pass on to the next generation.

So as this new year begins, I'm carrying that question with me as I stir-fry some chicken for dinner, take a bunch of pictures off our refrigerator door and put them in our photo album, or stop everything I'm doing simply to sit and hold my new granddaughter. And I'm enjoying the process of thinking about all the possible answers.

*Lord, as I think about all the things that matter most to our family,
help me to remember what matters most to You in the light of eternity.*
—CAROL KUYKENDALL

JANUARY 23

And our daughters will be like pillars.
—PSALM 144:12 NIV

*M*y dad was an impulsive man. When I was twelve years old, he asked if I wanted to go to work with him one holiday morning. This would be the first time I had gotten to go with him by myself.

Dad was an engineer at the Nationwide Insurance building in downtown Columbus, Ohio. He took one of us with him only on holidays when no one else was in the building. We got to explore basements, huge boiler systems, executive offices, and the rooftop. All of us returned home and bragged to our brothers and sisters about how far we had leaned over the edge, shouting to the pedestrians on the sidewalks far below.

I finished my morning newspaper route in time to leave the house with Dad while everyone else was asleep. When my mother woke up, she didn't know where I was. She sent the rest of the family out to look for me, and to check all the porches for newspapers to see if I'd finished my route. Finally, she called my dad to let him know I was missing.

"You can stop crying. He's with me," my dad said. He didn't say anything for the rest of the lengthy call except, "You're right" and "I'm so sorry."

I watched Dad hang up the phone and knew there would be no fun, no exploring, and no rooftop. Then the phone rang again. The call was brief, but the transformation in my dad's mood was so miraculous I wondered if the call was from God.

It wasn't, but the message was. My sister Patti had phoned—without permission, I'm sure. "Mom still loves you, Daddy," she said.

Dear God, thank You for sisters—and daughters—whose love can work miracles.
—TIM WILLIAMS

And David danced before the Lord with all his might.
—2 SAMUEL 6:14

*M*y son is a dancer.

Chase is sixteen, and he is also a kickboxer, a football player, a musician, and a scholar. He is very handsome and enjoys an active social life. At a time in his life when most people his age would do anything to avoid any kind of embarrassment, he is a dancer—and I admire him for it. He is comfortable with who he is, with all of who he is.

He knows that dancing is not what most people expect when they meet him—all six feet and 196 pounds of him. But, when Chase dances, he is incredibly graceful, athletic, even inspiring. In his movements, I can feel him praising God.

His talent amazes me. But mostly, I admire him because he has the courage to embrace his gifts rather than deny them so that he will fit in or make others feel more comfortable. Rather than not being himself, he endures an occasional whisper or question.

But most times the comments are favorable, and sometimes wistful. When I've told other men about Chase's passion for dancing, they smile, nod, and seem to drift into bygone days. "I used to sing," they tell me. Or they recount how, long ago, they danced or sang or painted. They have confided to me that they stopped pursuing their talent because they were afraid of what other men might say or do.

Chase's courage and commitment also makes me question myself about what I might have left behind. How often, because I fear what people might say, have I denied a little bit of who I am and what I believe? Am I all that God has called me to be? Am I singing His praises in all the different ways He has called me to sing?

> *God, help me to lead a life that praises You fully.*
> *Help me to dance like David—and Chase.*
>
> —SHARON FOSTER

JANUARY 25

"As a mother comforts her child, so will I comfort you."
—ISAIAH 66:13 NI

When I pressed the button on my answering machine, Angela's voice came on with a youthful "I'm trying to be casual, but I'm really in a panic" urgency. "Hi, Mary Ann. It's Angela. I don't want to bother you but...."

Angela is the niece of a close friend. She's in her junior year at college. Now she was calling from her home in Massachusetts, and the gist of her message was this: She was scheduled to leave in two days for a semester abroad in Prague, and her visa hadn't arrived yet. Turned out it was still at the Czech Republic consulate in Manhattan; was there any way I could get it and express mail it to her so she could board the plane in forty-eight hours? She didn't want to put me out but....

It took some maneuvering and feverish phone calls, including a fax from Angela authorizing me to do the pickup, but finally we figured it out. I arrived at the Czech consulate minutes before closing and announced my mission at the front desk. A woman in a business suit strode out with a packet. "You are her mother?" she asked. For a second I was startled, because there it was again, that unexpected lurch of my heart. I'd never had children, and although the deepest disappointment had passed years ago, there were still moments when I felt a stab of regret.

"You're her mother?" the woman repeated.

"I wish I was," I said. "I'm just a close friend." And then in an instant another thought surfaced. For right here, right now, I am her mother. In situations where a helping hand or a loving gesture is needed, I am someone's mother. The thought had a good feel to it—and the regret was gone.

Holy Spirit, please keep my mind open to being a mother to others.
—MARY ANN O'ROARK

I prayed for this child.
—1 Samuel 1:27

*W*hen my sister teased me on the phone the other day that I was always our mother's favorite, I was prepared to deny it, as usual. Yes, I was the baby of the family. And, yes, I came along late in my mother's life. Her "surprise," she liked to say. Still, I always thought my siblings made too big a deal of it. And after so much time, I would think they'd be tired of teasing me. I mean, we're all adults now.

Besides, parents may love their children differently but never one more than another. "Oh no," my sister always says, "you were the apple of her eye!"

Was that really true? My sister and I have talked about it a lot, and when we get serious, she always says that without me my mother would never have survived the death of my brother Bobby, the second youngest child, four years my senior. "You know, when Bobby died, if Mom hadn't had another little boy to love, I don't know what she would have done. You were her godsend."

My sister is right: My mother probably gave me enough love for two kids. In fact, maybe that's just what she was trying to do.

Father, You make a gift of us to others. Thank You for letting me
be the little boy my mother needed to love twice as much.
—Edward Grinnan

A man cannot tell what shall be; and what shall be after him, who can tell him?
—ECCLESIASTES 10:14

*D*igital photography is amazing. I have no idea how it works, but I know that it does. The other day I found that I had 115 photographs of my grandson on my computer—and he was only seven weeks old!

His father wanted to compare them with baby pictures of himself, and the battered albums of my children's babyhoods were brought out. We played the "He looks just like..." game. It's lots of fun linking the generations, even if the resemblance is mostly imaginary.

There is only one photograph of me as a child: a very small, black-and-white picture taken when I was maybe three or four. My children can't understand that; they want to see the others. There are no others. Life was very different in the England of the 1950s as we struggled to recover from five years of war. Food was still rationed—oranges were an exotic luxury—and photography wasn't thought of.

We've come from black-and-white to living color. I've come from a small English village where I hoarded food coupons to New York City, one of the largest and most complex places in the world, with restaurants from almost any country you can name. How will digital photographs strike this baby when he's middle-aged? My imagination can't stretch that far.

> *Change is a part of every life, Lord. Let me greet it*
> *with an open mind and an open heart.*
> —BRIGITTE WEEKS

JANUARY 28

"But its leaves will be green, And it will not be anxious."
—JEREMIAH 17:8 NASB

*T*homas, our youngest, had forgotten my birthday. It was so unlike him. He was not quite sixteen when I turned forty-seven. Sure, he'd said "Happy birthday," but there was no homemade card or even a hug. Maybe he was too busy for his old mom.

On the day after my birthday, I woke up and lay in bed for a few minutes, remembering the births of our children. My mind moved on to the difficult teenage years of our two daughters, now in their twenties. Thomas' time is coming. How will I deal with that? His rebellion has probably started. See, I'm not important to him anymore.

Minutes later I heard, "Mom, can you come here?" I slid into my slippers and plodded to the kitchen. Thomas had gotten up early, clipped roses from the yard, put them in a vase, toasted and buttered me a bagel just the way I like it, and poured my orange juice. He even put out strawberry jelly and a spoon.

"Happy birthday, Mom. Sorry I forgot yesterday." He'd passed me in height over the last year, but he still gave me one of his best little-boy hugs.

"You're going to make a mighty fine husband," I said. Then I glanced out the open window and spotted the wild dogwood in full bloom. I heard the birds singing. They'd been at it since daybreak, but somehow I'd missed them.

God, no matter what the season, You send glimpses of heaven.
—JULIE GARMON

However, our God turned the curse into a blessing.
—NEHEMIAH 13:2 NKJV

Saturday was my parents' sixtieth wedding anniversary. My four siblings and I reserved the fellowship hall at their former church in Dallas for a come-and-go reception in their honor.

I prayed it would be more than a nice little reception. Since moving from Dallas to east Texas, Mother and Daddy had suffered several years of serious health problems in a new town with few friends. Mother deeply needed to reconnect with her old ones.

Unfortunately, that Friday our plans came unraveled. An ambulance ushered my father to a hospital fifteen miles away, and clouds threatened a rare snowstorm. *How can we go on with it?* I thought. Yet how could we not? Family members were already en route from five hundred miles away.

So not only did I talk to God about the snowstorm, I talked to the storm itself. I took authority over it; I rebuked it; I spoke peace to it in the name of Jesus. After all, He calmed a storm and He did say believers would do greater works than He did.

You can probably guess what happened.

It snowed all Friday night and most of Saturday—four inches. Mixed with my discouragement was this one mental reminder from God: Trust Me. I know how to bless my children.

We decided to go on with the reception without Dad and hoped somebody would show up. Amazingly, almost seventy people did! Our come-and-go turned into a come-and-stay; for three-and-a-half hours friends and family ate, talked, laughed, hugged my mom, and wrote notes to Daddy in the hospital.

God, indeed, knew how to bless His children. The glow of the evening stayed with Mother longer than the flowers they received. And the snow was a bonus that will continue to bless her every time she remembers how people loved them enough to come in spite of it.

Father, help me to trust that You know best how to bless Your children.
—LUCILE ALLEN

"He was lost and is found."
—LUKE 15:32 NIV

*M*y youngest son Kevin had moved into his own apartment. Although he lived just across town, I'd not seen him much. Maybe I'm having empty-nest syndrome, I reasoned. After all, he was the last of my four children to leave home. I tried calling. I tried leaving messages. "Kev," I'd say, "how come you don't return my calls?" or "How come you don't stop by?" or "Don't you know we miss you?"

Finally I tried what I should have tried first: I sat down at my desk in the study, bowed my head, and prayed. *I need Your words, Lord, because mine aren't working. Help me to say the right thing to my son. Amen.* I looked up and noticed the church bulletin on my desk. I'd scrawled a few thoughts on it while listening to the sermon that morning. It was based on one of my favorite Bible stories, the prodigal son, who is welcomed back into the family fold after going off on his own. I read my notes: "No stern sermons, no lectures, no guilt trips. His father, instead, had thrown him a party."

"Of course, Lord!" I said out loud. I called Kevin and left a simple message: "Hi, Kev. It's Mom. I'm cooking your favorites tonight: shrimp and sausage jambalaya, crawfish cornbread, and bread pudding. Come on by!"

That evening after dinner was over and the dishes were done and Kevin had gone back to his apartment, laden with leftovers, I prayed:

> *Father, thank You for the opportunity not just to listen*
> *to my favorite story, but to live it.*
> —MELODY BONNETTE

For he shall give his angels charge over thee, to keep thee in all thy ways.
—Psalm 91:11

I'm a worrier; I always have been. Unfortunately, I seem to have passed on this trait to my three-year-old son. Solomon fears monsters. Scary things live in his closet, and gorillas lurk in the attic, behind the couch or in his bedroom.

"They're in there, Mom," he says, pointing to his room. "Gorillas." The first time he announced the arrival of the primates, his big eyes were so intense, his tone so serious that I checked his room as much for myself as for him.

Each night we go through the same ritual. "Come with me," I say, entering his room. "See. There's nothing here. Just us."

Together we look in the closet. "Nope, no monsters." I look under the bed, behind the dresser. No gorillas.

His little head nods in agreement. "Nope, Mama. No gorillas in here."

One night I said, "See, Solomon, you're safe. There's no one in the house, but Mommy and Daddy and you."

"And the angels," he said.

"The angels?" I asked.

"The angels who keep the monsters and gorillas away."

Often when I'm in bed, my thoughts shift to the usual worries about things at the office, finances, and the future, but then I find myself thinking about Solomon's monsters. Aren't my worries the same? Fear of things that are for the most part figments of my imagination? As I close my eyes, I can feel the angels taking away the weight of my anxiety.

Lord, when worries are lurking in the dark corners of my mind,
remind me that You are always with me—and so are Your angels.
—Sabra Ciancanelli

February

FEBRUARY 1

Call unto me, and I will answer thee.
—JEREMIAH 33:3

*W*hen our daughter Amy Jo's marriage ended, she moved back in with us. She enrolled in a full-time master's program at a nearby university, but was feeling restless and unsure about the future. "You know," she said one night as she was setting the table, "I used to talk about going to law school. Remember?"

I did remember. She had only been about ten when she first brought it up. And although she'd mentioned it a few times during the years, it somehow had fallen by the wayside as she got a degree in communications, took a job, and got married. Now it was surfacing again.

"I remember," I said, "but I'm not sure if that's what you should do now or not." Silently, I wondered where she would get the money. "Just pray about it, honey," I said, turning back to the stove. The words sounded frail. Wasn't there something else she should be doing?

A few minutes later, Amy Jo came back into the kitchen, beaming. She spread out the Chicago Tribune on the table and pointed to a classified ad: "Wondering if law school is right for you? Work for us and decide!" It was a large law firm in Chicago, an easy train ride from where we lived. So Amy Jo took the job, working for a year as a court runner. She loved it! Then she took the admissions test and enrolled in Valparaiso University, where she's currently studying law.

I've always believed in answered prayer. But these days I'm looking for those answers in lots of places. My Bible, of course. But also in the "thought for the day" that appears on my e-mail. Or in the overheard wisdom of an older woman in line at the grocery talking—on a cell phone—to her daughter. And, yes, even in the newspaper. As for the financial problem of law school—Amy Jo is on full scholarship, which is something we both prayed about!

> *Open my eyes, Father, to the unique avenues*
> *You use to let Your answers reach me.*
> —MARY LOU CARNEY

FEBRUARY 2

His love is perfected in us.
—1 JOHN 4:12

The kitchen was filled with the scent of fresh-baked sugar cookies. Four-year-old Brock sat on a stool as I coaxed scalloped hearts from a round of rolled-out dough. His assignment was to add the little candies that would turn each cookie into an edible Valentine.

"Mom," he said, without glancing up, "you know what I'm gonna be when I grow up?"

"No, Brock, what are you going to be?"

"I'm gonna be a turner."

"A turner? What's a turner, honey?"

"Oh, first I'm gonna be a football player, then I'm gonna turn into a baseball player, then I'll turn into a fireman, then a cowboy. You know, Mama...a turner!"

In his book *Prayer Can Change Your Life*, written with Elaine St. Johns, Dr. William R. Parker says we are all moving in one direction or another, becoming the persons we will ultimately be. Some of us are focused on a life of good and move in that direction, others are "turners" and have no set focus, no destination. So, now, let's define our focus. Think far ahead, one generation, then two into the future. Imagine your grandchildren or your earthly heirs in their middle years, sitting around a table at some happy homecoming. For me, it sounds like this:

"And what was your grandmother like?" one of my great-grandchildren asks.

The answer to that question is the person I want to become: "She loved without condition, laughed a lot, relished life. She had a way of making you feel you were the most important person there ever was."

In the weeks ahead, let's begin our prayer practice by spending at least five minutes a day openly and honestly describing this best self to God. Share your dreams with God. There's nothing a Father would rather hear!

Father, I offer my best self to You. Use me to reflect Your love to others.
—PAM KIDD

FEBRUARY 3

How good is a timely word!
—PROVERBS 15:23 NIV

*I*f I could do it over again, I wouldn't yell," I told my daughters-in-law Patricia and Jerie. "I'm sure the main thing your husbands remember about childhood is me screaming at them."

It was the first time I'd voiced what had long been a genuine regret. I'd asked God's forgiveness, and our grown children didn't seem to resent me. Still, I knew my short temper had caused them misery. For instance, I was in "mid-yell" at Patrick for breaking a heavy bottle before I noticed blood pouring from the cut on his arm. I made Michael practice his 4-H talk six times in a row, harshly correcting tiny mistakes. And once, frustrated by her nighttime wandering, I tied Rebecca's door shut.

A few weeks after our conversation, Patricia brought up the subject again. "I asked Pat what he remembered about his childhood. He remembers you reading Ferdinand the Bull, and playing Uncle Wiggley, and the time his pig had babies and you sat in the barn with him all night." Then Jerie called. "Mike remembers you frying two chickens so he could have all he wanted, and letting him keep Dobie when he already had a dog." Rebecca remembered the yelling, but also playing "dress up" with my best clothes, and bedtime prayers.

Their kind words helped me do something I suspect many other parents need to do: Forgive ourselves for parenting mistakes. Once I did, I began to enjoy memories of happy times instead of being haunted by sad ones. I've had opportunities to share my experience with other parents: an airplane seatmate racked by guilt over her work schedule's effect on her daughter; a friend who'd broken her son's prized records when he refused to turn down the volume. And I've retold the story to Rebecca and Patricia and Jerie as they struggle to be the best parents possible.

Loving Father, thank You for helping my children remember the best of times!
—PENNEY SCHWAB

FEBRUARY 4

And oh, may this my glory be,
That Christ is not ashamed of me!
JOSEPH GRIGG, HYMN

When I was a little girl and Mama had dressed me for a special occasion, she always called from the door as I left, "Don't forget who you are!" That was her way of reminding me that, as her child, I should put forth my best manners and not embarrass her. So, when my own children came along, I passed the same words of warning on to them. Even into their teenage dating years I'd remind them as they left the house, "Don't forget who you are!"

Last summer Lindsay and Marcus were home from school. Dressed for a luncheon, I peeked in the kitchen as they labored over a pizza, and told them good-bye. Before I reached the car, the front door suddenly swooshed open behind me and Lindsay called out, "Hey, Mother! Don't forget who you are!" She closed the door quickly and I could hear their giggles.

I smiled as I drove away, but her words echoed in my head. "Who am I indeed?" I asked aloud. "Why, I'm a child of the King!"

Father, I'm proud to be Your child; help me always to make You proud of me.
—ORA LINDSAY GRAHAM

He guides me along right paths.
—PSALM 23:3 NLT

*M*y grandmother was dying of cancer. She looked so tiny, so frail as she lay in the hospital bed, so unlike the strong, self-reliant woman I'd seen on so many mornings, sitting at the kitchen table with a steamy cup of coffee.

I spent a few minutes talking with my mother and sister, then offered to stay in the room while they went downstairs for a break. Grandmother had had a restless night, and I knew that they were both exhausted from tending to her.

I pulled a chair close to the bed. Grandmother opened her eyes wide and looked at me, unable to speak. *Does she know who I am?* I wondered. I spoke to her quietly, but my words only seemed to upset her. *Lord,* I prayed, *give me words to calm her.*

I took Grandmother's hand and began to pray out loud the first words that came to me: "The Lord is my shepherd, I shall not want...."

By the end of the psalm, Grandmother was completely relaxed. Her breathing was quiet and even. I gently placed her hand back down on the bed. When my mother and sister returned, they were relieved to find her resting.

"What did you do?" Mom asked.

"Well, I didn't know what to do, so I recited the Twenty-third Psalm," I replied.

My mother looked surprised. "Did you know that the Twenty-third Psalm has always been her favorite Scripture?"

I didn't, but the Lord did.

Lord, when I have no words to speak, thank You for giving me Yours. Amen.
—MELODY BONNETTE

*For where two or three are gathered together in my name,
there am I in the midst of them.*
—MATTHEW 18:20

I often make big dinners for my extended family. We began calling these events "parties" for the little ones. "Nina, are we having a party tonight?" my grandson Drake would ask if I stopped by his house. And his little brother Brock would join in: "Party! Party!" Not long ago, I bought a little neon light. It spells out the word "party" in a rainbow of colors. Once everyone has arrived for dinner, the grandchildren gather 'round while I plug it in.

Last night my daughter Amy Jo called to see if I could take care of the boys for the evening. Drake and Brock and I dined alone on spaghetti and meatballs that I'd pulled out of the freezer. As we settled down at the table, Drake suddenly sat up and pointed. "The party light, Nina. We forgot the party light!"

"But it's just the three of us...," I began.

Drake smiled. "But it's still a party!"

So I plugged in the light. And in the autumn twilight it glowed soft and inviting. We ate in silence, the only sound was the slurping of spaghetti into small mouths. I think I sense God's presence most during these simple times, times when I find myself standing in a small oasis of gratitude. There I recognize how blessed I am, that I—and those I love—are not alone on this earthly trek.

Come, Sweet Jesus, into every moment of my life.
—MARY LOU CARNEY

"Prayer should be the key of the day and the lock of the night."
—Thomas Fuller

The thought of facing a night without a doctor's diagnosis and proper medication for my sick daughter finally outweighed my fear of driving on the icy, snow-banked streets. I tucked her under a blanket on the back seat, and while the engine warmed, bowed my head and asked God to give us protection. We made our way in complete safety.

Several days later when the illness and storm were long past, we again got into the car. This time without a moment's hesitation I warmed the engine and backed out into the street.

"Aren't we going to pray this time, Mama?" a little voice asked.

She caught me off guard. Instinctively I turn to God when worried or fearful. But when the crisis is over, how human it is to forget to include Him in the good times.

"Yes," I said to my daughter. "We are going to pray."

Forgive me for the times I forget, Lord. Help me to remember.
—Patti Phillips

Mine eyes are ever toward the Lord.
—PSALM 25:15

*M*y granddaughter Tirza recently turned one. During my daughter Kelly's pregnancy, I'd hoped for a brown-eyed girl. In my father's family the boys had brown eyes and the girls their mother's blue. I'd inherited my dad's darker eyes and passed them on to my daughter. I even purchased an elegant brown-eyed doll for Tirza before she was born and shared with the doll's designer my dream for a third-generation girl with chocolate eyes.

In the weeks after Tirza was born, I studied her eyes whenever I held her. They were a tantalizing mystery. While flirting with earth tones, that pesky blue wasn't giving in either. Finally Tirza's eyes cast their vote. Did brown win? Not exactly. But they sure weren't blue. They ended up slate gray with brown flecks. My wish hadn't been completely ignored!

Someday I'll tell Tirza the story of her grandma's thwarted dream. And I won't leave out the most important part: Brown, blue, green, or gray, as long as they look to Jesus, the Lord of Life, her eyes are the right color.

Jesus, Son of God, the eyes that see and love You are beautiful beyond telling.
—CAROL KNAPP

Trust no Future, howe'er pleasant!
Let the dead Past bury its dead!
Act—act in the living present!
Heart within, and God o'erhead!
HENRY WADSWORTH LONGFELLOW

*W*hen our daughter Karen was a baby, I could hardly wait for her to sit up by herself. When she could do that, I started urging her to crawl. When she'd mastered that, I began coaxing her to take her first few faltering steps. Then one day she walked out the door, down the street, and straight into the arms of her kindergarten teacher, while I stood in the doorway wondering where those baby years had gone.

I still jump at the future that way. Instead of savoring my breakfast coffee, I gulp it down so I'll have time for a second cup. Instead of relishing the warmth and stimulation of my shower, I'm planning what to wear that day. While I'm eating my meatloaf, I've got my eye on the lemon pie. All day, I seem to live just a step ahead of the present moment. But at a recent prayer retreat, we practiced trying to be really present in the now.

We started with our morning prayers. We centered our thoughts on God for the whole prayer period. Two minutes of steady presence, we found, were better than fifteen minutes of meandering mind. Since that time I've become aware that each moment has its own intensity—and reward—if I'll only give myself over to it.

Lord, this moment is a gift from You. Let me spend it wholly in Your presence.
—MARILYN MORGAN HELLEBERG

FEBRUARY 10

And he that watereth shall be watered also himself.
—PROVERBS 11:25

*M*y mother was a generous giver. When she passed away, she left little behind in the way of worldly goods. Her only heirloom was a stately, walnut hall tree she'd bought on one of her yard sale expeditions. Last fall my siblings and I heard that the historic Madie Carroll House, a museum in the Guyandotte community of Huntington, West Virginia, was looking for Victorian-era furnishings. We prayerfully decided to donate Mother's hall tree to it. Mother had taught first grade at Guyandotte Elementary in the 1940s and '50s, and we thought it would be a nice way to honor her.

I visited the museum when it was all decked out in holiday finery. Someone had hung a pine wreath from the top peg of Mother's hall tree. A docent was addressing a group of children. "Back in Victorian times, people didn't have closets," she told them. "They hung their coats and hats on hall trees just like this one." She pointed to a pair of curved arms at the center of it. "Right here's where they used to put their umbrellas. The metal dish at the bottom kept the water from hurting the wood."

A small girl with blonde pigtails reached out to touch the docent's hoopskirt. "I like learning about the olden days," she said.

Through our giving, Mother was still teaching. And like the gifts Mother gave while she was living, this one would go on and on and on.

Dear God, help me to place everything I own in Your capable hands.
—ROBERTA MESSNER

There is no fear in love.
—1 JOHN 4:18

For many years after my husband Larry and I were married, I was at odds with his mother. I longed for a good relationship with Laverne, but I felt she was too reserved, and intentionally kept me at a distance. I wanted the kind of closeness she had with her daughter Sherry, but it seemed I was always on the outside looking in.

I'm not much of a pack rat, but I do save all the letters we receive, and over the years I have collected thousands. When I decided to sort them, I was stunned to find that more than two hundred had come from Larry's mother. In them she had woven a tapestry of the life she had shared with Larry's dad in Michigan during the past twenty-five years. It had been a very long time since I had read the letters, and I was suddenly struck by the love and warmth expressed in them.

Laverne had shared the family's everyday activities, the younger kids' events at school, the births, deaths, and marriages of mutual friends and relatives, and the many birthday and Christmas celebrations that we had missed because we were too far away in North Carolina. Time and again, in subtle ways, she had singled me out in the letters, doing her best to make me feel special.

Why hadn't I been more aware of Laverne's intentions as the letters had trickled in one by one? My answer shamed me. I had been so focused on the things I felt she was not giving me that I had missed the great bounty of love being offered each time she wrote to us.

It was hard to write the long overdue letter of apology that my wonderful mother-in-law deserved, but she was gracious and forgiving. And today, I'm thankful to report, we finally have the relationship my heart has always longed for.

Father, I give thanks that even when my perceptions
are distorted, You still see me with eyes of love.
—LIBBIE ADAMS

FEBRUARY 12

Her children rise up and call her blessed.
—PROVERBS 31:28 RSV

*H*alf of what I think I know about mothers comes from having one. The other half comes from being married to one. In fact, I probably know more about my mother from being married to my sons' mother for twenty-two years. Here are the key things I've learned.

- Mothers are the people who take Jesus at His word when He says to forgive each other "seventy times seven."
- Mothers are the ones who still believe in you when everyone else begins to doubt.
- Never get between a mother and her cubs. Even if you are the father, you lose.
- The best gift you can give your children is to love their mother.
- A mother's prayers are more powerful than any force on earth or in heaven.
- A father may know best, but a mother cares best, and children will pick caring over knowing every time.
- We may pray to "Our Father," but the face of God we see, the hand of God we clutch, and the heart of God we trust belong to our mothers.

Lord, thanks for giving us mothers so that
we can see, hold and hear You more clearly.
—ERIC FELLMAN

Lord, thou hast been our dwelling place in all generations.
—PSALM 90:1

*I*t was my mother's eighty-third birthday, and I was not looking forward to visiting her.

She no longer could say for sure what year she was born. In the 1950s she had been a quiz show champion. Now you couldn't even get her going anymore on baseball or politics.

On the drive to see her at the group home where my siblings and I had recently moved her, my own memory troubled me. I thought of all the times she had wanted me to visit and I hadn't come: the Easter vacation in college when I went to Key West, the Thanksgiving night I went to a movie rather than help with the dishes, the extra days I couldn't spare after my father's funeral....

I was in a bad state when I arrived at the group home, although the fierce strength of her hug was a surprise coming from the stooped figure who greeted me. "My youngest," she announced to the other residents. We sat quietly together for a time when, suddenly, Mom said, "Remember my birthday when you played the trombone?"

I thought she was drifting into some irritating absurdity, and then a memory fell open. I must have been about nine, and I'd just taken up the trombone. It was a sad time for Mom. We'd lost my brother in a tragic death, my older sister and other brother were off to college, and my father was away that night on business. Just the two of us were celebrating with one candle and a homely little cake.

"Until you came down the stairs playing 'Happy Birthday' on your trombone, it was the worst birthday of my life. Now I think it might have been the best."

As my mother relapsed into silence, my bad state began to turn. *God makes certain memories strong for us,* I thought, *so that when our capacity to remember begins to fail, the best can still prevail for those times we need them most.* I felt a warm strength flow in the hug that came from my mother's frail and brittle arms. It is the strength of the spirit when the body fails, and of God bringing out the best in us.

> *God, help me not to dwell on my failings,*
> *but to build on the love and goodness in my life.*
> —EDWARD GRINNAN

FEBRUARY 14

And all thy children shall be taught of the Lord;
and great shall be the peace of thy children.

—ISAIAH 54:13

sther, our vivacious teenage daughter, burst into the kitchen after school one day in mid-February and waved something at me, singing out, "I got a rose!"

"That's nice," I said absentmindedly.

As a refugee sponsor for our church, my mind was mulling over the problems that needed to be solved before our refugee family arrived in a few days: find appropriate housing complete with furniture and appliances; stock the shelves with groceries; arrange for daily transportation to and from school, the doctor and church; and, since they wouldn't be able to speak English, arrange to take them shopping and introduce them to unfamiliar ways in their new country.

"'Bye, Mom," Esther yelled as she slammed through the back door. "I'll be back at eleven."

I watched her little green car shoot out of the driveway on its way to her after-school job. Suddenly, my mind snapped to attention. What was it she'd been so excited about?

Why, Valentine's Day! What was it she'd said? A rose? I hurried into her bedroom and picked up a small vase that cradled a perfect red rosebud. My daughter had received her very first rose from an admirer. She'd wanted to share her precious moment with me, and I let worries get in the way.

When my daughter came home from work that night, I was determined to do better. "Esther," I said, "tell me about the rose...."

Father, help me to remember that life is too short to zoom
past intimate moments with my children. Let me gather them,
savor them, and store them up for years ahead.

—HELEN GRACE LESCHEID

FEBRUARY 15

Love covers a multitude of sins.
—1 PETER 4:8 RSV

*S*ometimes I feel overwhelmed by the challenges of parenting. I especially struggle to control my temper. But on my refrigerator is a paper heart, pasted on red construction paper, to remind me of a lesson I learned one February.

That day I just lost it with my then-six-year-old daughter—about valentines, of all things! I insisted Elizabeth sign her name to the last three cards for her kindergarten class. "Elizabeth, there will be no time in the morning to finish before school, so please finish now."

Tears and refusals from Elizabeth. Loud demands from me. She had written her name seventeen times and simply couldn't sign three more. Yes, she could—and must. No, she couldn't—and wouldn't. Angrily, I sent her upstairs to get ready for bed. I tossed the valentines into the box and slammed cupboard doors while cleaning up the kitchen.

Then, clearing papers off the counter, I picked up a worksheet from Sunday school, a page of six hearts with jagged lines through them. Inside each heart was a Bible verse about love. The children could cut out the heart pieces, then match up the Scripture verses to paste them back together.

As I stared at the paper, the verse in the first heart pierced my own: "Love one another; as I have loved you" (John 13:34). How I'd failed to love Elizabeth as God loves me, so patient with my weaknesses, holding back His anger, understanding and giving constant help! I tiptoed upstairs to tuck her in. "Elizabeth, please forgive me for shouting at you," I said.

To my surprise, she murmured, "Oh, Mom, I'm sorry I didn't want to do what you wanted me to do." With a forgiving hug, our relationship was glued back together.

> *Dear God, when I've done something to break a relationship,*
> *help me to admit my mistakes and ask for forgiveness.*
> —MARY BROWN

FEBRUARY 16

To give unto them beauty for ashes, the oil of joy for mourning....
—ISAIAH 61:3

I was twelve the winter Mother decided to make soap. We'd just visited a mountain homestead where the farmer's wife was leaching wood ashes, which she would boil with rendered lard to produce her family's soap. Mother was inspired. Soon, back home, a package arrived at our door: a soap-making kit. Proudly, Mother showed us the hopper that would hold the ashes over which water would be poured and the crock for holding the resulting lye.

And, of course, I was involved. It was my job to collect the fireplace ashes Mother needed for her soap. Week after week, scoop in hand, I shoveled ashes into leaky brown bags and stored them in the basement. Inevitably, I was called back to vacuum the fine ash silt that settled on the living room furniture. When I finally escaped, I'd run upstairs to bathe (with store-bought soap) to get the dust out of my hair and ears.

When spring came, Mother spent an entire day pouring water through the ashes we fed into the hopper. She boiled the resulting foaming liquid with perfumed oil instead of lard, but everything else she did just as the mountain woman had done, adding salt to the mixture and pressing it into molds to create bars of what—much to my surprise—was really and truly a fragrant and effective brown soap.

Ashes—like sins, I thought, remembering that long ago event—*are dirty and ugly, coating everything around them in their gray pall. But in the right hands, those dusty, dead ashes could be transformed into something cleansing and health-giving.*

Soon today I'll join others while our pastor places ashes on our foreheads, a symbol of penitence. And as he does, I'll be putting my sins in God's hands, asking Him to make of them something He can use.

Father, may this season of Lent be a time of true transformation.
—JOHN SHERRILL

Point your kids in the right direction—when they're old they won't be lost.
—PROVERBS 22:6 MSG

I was five; my mother's birthday was the next day, so I decided I'd buy her a present. I put the thirty-five cents I'd saved into my pocket, slipped out of the house, and walked the dozen or so blocks to the five-and-ten-cent store. "I want to buy a present for my mother," I told the lady behind the counter.

"How much money do you have?"

I showed her my thirty-five cents.

Nodding seriously, she said, "I see." She showed me some things, but I only shook my head. Then she picked up a little blue glass jar with white bumps all over it and a powder puff inside. Wow! How could that lady have known that Mother had broken a jar just like this one!

"That's it!" Then fear. "What does it cost?"

"Uh...thirty-five cents. Would you like me to wrap it? Wrapping is free."

I carried the little brown sack with the gift-wrapped jar in it all the way home. I was so excited that it didn't seem far at all.

The next day while her friends were having birthday cake and coffee, I gave Mother my present. She was really surprised! Then she asked, "Where did you get this, Keith?"

"I walked to the store to buy it," I said proudly.

"You what?" Suddenly she looked frightened. "Don't ever do that again!"

I cried, and she picked me up. Hugging me, she said, "I love the present, but you shouldn't walk downtown alone." Then she wept and held me until I could wiggle free. As I was running out, I heard one of her friends say, "How in the world did you teach him to do that?" Mother just shook her head. But I knew how. All my life I'd seen my mother giving presents to everyone she knew, and I wanted to be sure she'd get one herself.

Lord, thank You for a mother who lived the virtues she wanted to see in me.
—KEITH MILLER

I have set before thee an open door, and no man can shut it.
—REVELATION 3:8

*M*y mother died eight years ago at the age of ninety-two. Some days I miss her more than others, but truth be told, the thing I really have a hard time with is the fact that I can't go home again. I've ridden by the old house three times; I no longer belong there. Still, some part of me can't accept that.

While shopping for a greeting card, I was drawn to the section marked *Mothers*. My heart thumped wildly, tears filled my eyes, and I blinked rapidly. Unexpectedly, a smile brightened my face, for I was suddenly home again, about to run up the three steps to the open door and be welcomed by my mother, probably wearing her red apron. We'd hug at the door and she'd light up like a Christmas tree because I was home.

I picked up a card hesitantly. The bungalow house was amazingly like Mother's, but the thing that stole my heart was the open front door and the amber glow from inside the house—the unmistakable love that spilled through it and the curtained windows. The front porch beckoned me. Twilight approached; lightning bugs would be out. Pink camellias bloomed near the porch. The lawn was Easter-basket-grass green.

Carefully, I read the words on the front of the card: "For me, home will always be an open door." Almost reverently, I opened it. "And you'll be standing in it with a welcoming smile. Happy Birthday, Mom."

The card's been sitting on my desk for several years now. Whenever I feel the need, I go home again through that open door, if only for a few precious seconds.

Father, bless Your holy name for doors You keep open forever.
—MARION BOND WEST

FEBRUARY 19

May your unfailing love come to me, O Lord, your salvation
according to your promise...for I trust in your word.
—PSALM 119:41–42 NIV

When I was a boy getting ready for school each morning, I often found my mother sitting at the kitchen table, reading her Bible. After seeing my father off to work in a Pennsylvania coal mine, she turned to the Good Book before making breakfast for her three children. I can still visualize her bowing her head over her well-worn King James Bible, eyes closed, chin resting on a half-clenched hand, probably praying for each of us.

It took twenty years from the time I left home before I gave my heart to Jesus, but when I did, the first thing I wanted to do was read the Bible. In nearly four decades since that eye-opening moment I've read God's Word from cover to cover almost every year, in more than a dozen different translations. My favorite is the New International Version, maybe because I spent a year working for the International Bible Society during the time it was producing the NIV Study Bible, and I was able to contribute some thoughts for its footnotes.

And today, as I finish yet another reading of Psalm 119, I can't help but remember one of the reasons I feel so drawn to the Good Book.

Thanks, Mom.

Father, thank You for the light You give me in Your Word.
—HAROLD HOSTETLER

I bowed down heavily, as one that mourneth for his mother.
—PSALM 35:14

I was nine, and had more baseball cards than Cooperstown.

I wanted to organize them (I know—it's hard to believe I ever wanted to organize anything), and I asked my mom for help.

I realize now what I was asking then. I was asking a woman who woke up at 5:00 a.m., made our lunches, sent us out the door, took two buses to work (as a teacher in the Pittsburgh public schools), came home, took my sister to night classes, came home for a second time, corrected papers, put us to bed, and went to sleep herself around midnight. I was asking this woman, who didn't know Richie Allen from Charlie Rich, to sort through a couple of hundred baseball cards.

And she did. Of course she did. She could be nothing but kind; it was as immutable as her eye color. It was her nature—five-foot-two, Irish American, and kind.

My mother taught us the value of kindness, no matter how small the act. And when she died, when my family foundered in grief, we found out something else. We found other people who must have had the same kind of parents, people who performed those small acts of kindness when we needed them most, who reminded us of all the friends we have, the continuity of life, the Light Perpetual upon my mother's face, now and forever.

I still think about my mom. I miss the way she would laugh (quietly, behind her hand, but often); I remember her voice on the phone (always asking about us, never talking about herself); I remember that she could make sense of baseball cards and wayward socks and student papers and lives.

I remember it all. But I have no regrets. How blessed we were to have her.

Dear God, thank You for my mother. Hold her always in Your loving hands.
—MARK COLLINS

Train a child in the way he should go, and when he is old he will not turn from it.
—Proverbs 22:6 niv

*M*y daughter Katherine is very bright, but she's not very fond of homework. Often she'd tell me she had none, only to remember it the next morning. I felt she should do her schoolwork on her own, and this frustrated me. So I encouraged her to be more responsible and reminded her what would happen if she wasn't.

One morning Katherine had "forgotten" three assignments, and there wasn't time for her to complete them without being late for school. "You'll have to tell your teacher that you didn't do them," I said.

On the way to school, Katherine burst into tears. "My teacher will be mad at me, and it's all your fault!"

I couldn't believe that she was blaming me—I'd told her for weeks that this would happen—and then I thought of how often I blame God for what I do to myself. I needed to answer my daughter in the same way the Lord answers me.

"I love you, Katherine," I told her as we reached the school, "but I can't make your choices for you. You did this. You have to face the consequences. Tell your teacher the truth and apologize."

My daughter flounced out of the car, hesitated, and then ran back and hugged me. "I'm sorry, Mom," she said.

> *Lord, You are my Father and my teacher.*
> *May Your patience and love always inspire me.*
> —Rebecca Kelly

Children's children are a crown to the aged.
—PROVERBS 17:6 NIV

I came home early one evening and noticed the flashing light on my phone, indicating that I had a message. I pushed the button and immediately heard the sobbing voice of my six-year-old granddaughter Gabriella, who was about to lose her first tooth.

"Oma," she sputtered, "I have a very loose tooth"—deep, shaky breath—"and I'm scared." Another shaky breath. "Bye." The next message clicked on, and her daddy's calm voice said, "Mission accomplished."

I laughed out loud as I replayed the messages. I didn't push erase because I wanted to save this audio-memory and the other memories it triggered:

I was about Gabi's age, sitting on a kitchen stool, very late at night, crying and holding my mouth. My mother was beside me, encouraging me. I'd been in bed in the lower bunk, whimpering and fiddling with my loose tooth, when my know-it-all older sister leaned over the top bunk and told me, "It'll come out in the middle of the night and you'll swallow it and die." That did it. I got out of bed to face the ordeal of having my first tooth pulled, so I wouldn't die.

Gabi's daddy, our son, also age six, was fearfully and tearfully peering into the bathroom mirror with his daddy behind him calmly tying a long piece of dental floss around his wobbly tooth and gently showing him how to pull both ends of the dental floss to pop out the tooth.

These memories made me smile and thank God for the gift of the generations and the opportunity it gives us to see and remember the precious milestones that mark the stages of growing up.

Lord, thank You for the many ways
that children remind me of myself—and of You.
—CAROL KUYKENDALL

Even when I am old and gray, do not forsake me, O God.
—PSALM 71:18 NIV

We were moving my mother from her Connecticut house of forty years into a retirement community nearby. She hadn't balked at selling and giving away and cleaning out. In fact, she seemed fairly cheerful in accepting that in her eighties she couldn't keep up the house and yard anymore.

"I don't mind this move," she told me. "It's the next one I dread. That will be the one to the nursing home, I'm afraid."

Mom was wrong. Her next move, after recuperation from colon cancer at ninety-one, was to private care in Virginia a few miles north of me. Then she moved, at ninety-two, to a fine assisted-care facility in Pennsylvania. But that was too far away, so at age ninety-three, we moved her to another assisted-care place near us. She had now had three "next" moves, none of them to a nursing home.

In the meantime, however, Mom took out her dusty faith and began to reassess it. She decided really to believe that God loved her, personally; that the Bible's teachings on eternal life were accurate and that Jesus really was the Savior; that in trusting Him she would find the ultimate confidence for her "next" move. With joy, I watched my mother come to a peace about death and dying—the peace that passes understanding, the peace Jesus alone gives.

Mom has not made her ultimate "next" move yet, but now she faces it as a woman of faith, with anticipation and without fear.

Lord of all life, thank You that no one is ever too old
to come to You in new or increasing faith.
—ROBERTA ROGERS

Again, the kingdom of heaven is like unto a merchant man, seeking goodly pearls.
—MATTHEW 13:45

*M*y grandson Daniel is two, with round cheeks and a smile that nearly runs out of room and a welcoming heart. When I come to visit, he is waiting at the door with shining eyes and that amazing smile. When he wakes in the morning, he comes looking for me with that same irrepressible delight. Wherever Daniel appears, he makes me feel as if I'm the sunrise on his horizon.

David, Daniel's younger brother, just turned one. Although we don't really know him yet, he has my grandmother's dimple in his chin. She and I giggled a lot. I have high hopes for David. Another grandson, Joshua, almost four, I call "moonchild." He and I both like the moon. One wintry evening when I was visiting him in Alaska, I carried him outdoors in bare feet and pajamas to admire its brightness. Later that night the moon glow through his bedroom window cast its luminous purity across his sleeping face.

These encounters with my grandchildren have become perfect pearls, strung together in love. For me, they're the "pearly gates" swinging wide on heavenly joys right here, right now!

> *Jesus, jewel of God, lead me to my true pearls.*
> —CAROL KNAPP

"For where your treasure is, there your heart will be also."
—LUKE 12:34 NIV

*T*had lunch recently with my friend Sandy O'Donnell. Sandy told me that she'd recently sent her college-age daughter Shannon her old Bible that she had used as a child. Sandy's eyes twinkled as she confessed, "I put three crisp twenty-dollar bills between the pages of Shannon's old Bible. She doesn't know they're there, and I'm wondering how long it will take her to find them."

Treasures buried in God's Word. I loved it.

I was already a young mother before I discovered the treasures in the Bible. After attending my first Bible study, I came away feeling like the richest woman in the world. That feeling continues to this day. Every time I read the Bible, I find new treasures on each page.

I travel a lot, and I'm often in hotel rooms. So I've started a new habit: Inspired by Sandy, I reach for the Gideon Bible, open it, and place a twenty-dollar bill inside. I want whoever finds it to realize that there are other treasures waiting there to be discovered.

Lord, thank You for the treasures of Your Word, precious beyond price.
—DEBBIE MACOMBER

Charity [love] beareth all things, believeth all things,
hopeth all things, endureth all things.
—1 CORINTHIANS 13:7

The telephone woke me. The time: 3:00 a.m. The caller was the son of one of my dearest friends. Even before I was fully awake, his sobbing voice was telling me that his mother had just died. Her death was no great surprise to me because she had been suffering from a terminal illness, and I had spent two hours at her bedside the afternoon before.

"I feel terrible," Bill said. "Just before Mother died, she tried to tell me something. She kept repeating, 'Monica, Monica.' I don't know anyone named Monica. Do you?"

"Yes, I think perhaps I do. Let me come over this afternoon and we'll discuss it."

The name Monica was familiar. Yesterday afternoon Bill's mother had said to me, "For a long time you have known that my boy has lived a wild and irresponsible life. I have prayed and prayed that he would become a Christian. I've tried to be patient like Monica, the mother of St. Augustine. I hope someday my prayers, too, will be answered."

Before seeing Bill I looked up the story of Monica in a reference book: "Monica, his mother, having patiently and persistently prayed for seventeen years for her son's conversion, gave him Romans 13:13–14, and thereby in the garden Augustine was converted." I turned to the book of Romans and found this: "Let us walk honestly, as in the day; not in rioting and drunkenness, not in chambering and wantonness, not in strife and envying. But put ye on the Lord Jesus Christ, and make not provision for the flesh, to fulfill the lusts thereof."

Later that day I told Bill the story of Monica and her son. That was several years ago. My heart overflows with joy when I say that, today, Bill is one of the most respected men in town. The patience and prayers of my dear friend were rewarded at last!

Lord, thank You for never giving up on us.
—VELMA SEAWELL DAVIES

February 27

*Like arrows in the hands of a warrior are sons born
in one's youth. Blessed is the man whose quiver is full of them.*
—Psalm 127:4–5 NIV

*M*y husband Wayne and I were blessed with four children in a five-year span. By the time Dale, our youngest, was born, I hadn't slept through the night in three long years. The house was in constant chaos, and in those pre-disposable-diaper days, the washing machine was going day and night. My hands were more than full with the demands of our growing family. Thankfully, I was blessed with wonderful parents who visited us often. Soon after Dale's arrival, my mother came to help.

Early one morning, when our newborn woke for his feeding, his older sisters and brother came looking for attention. Jody sat on one knee and Jenny on the other, and Ted shared space with his infant brother on my lap. All too soon, the older three started squabbling and whining.

My mother woke up and joined us in the living room. "Oh, Debbie," she said with a smile, "these are the happiest days of your life."

Aghast, I looked at her and said, "Mom, you mean it gets worse?"

Now, in retrospect, I can see how very blessed I was. Mom had the perspective to see it then; thank God, I can see it now.

> *Lord, give all parents the patience, the prayer and the sense
> of humor they need to raise their children in Your grace.*
> —Debbie Macomber

FEBRUARY 28

Behold the Lamb of God, which taketh away the sins of the world.
—JOHN 1:29

*W*hen our daughter, Julie, was about four she overheard her daddy and me discussing blood transfusions. She quickly questioned me about the procedure. I was busy cleaning up the kitchen and didn't give her very good answers. Finally, trying to reassure her, I said, "You don't have to give any, so don't worry about it."

She persisted, "But I need to know what I'd do if someone needed it."

I forgot all about our discussion. Days later Julie came to see me, looking very serious, and said matter-of-factly, "I made up my mind, Mama. If you ever need blood, I'm going to give you mine. You can count on it."

"Thanks, Julie," I smiled politely.

It was nearly a month later when I learned from Julie that she thought she would be required to give me all her blood and would die in order that I might live. Her face brightened as I explained that people only give a pint. I even showed her a pint jar. She went put to play with a new spring in her step and I sat trying to comprehend that my four-year-old daughter had been willing to give me all her blood, should I need it.

And while I sat there I thought about how willingly and lovingly Jesus had given all His blood because nothing but His blood could wash away the sins of the world.

Jesus, sometimes I don't like to think about Your blood sacrifice. Forgive me.
Thank You that Your blood has washed away my sins.
—MARION BOND WEST.

FEBRUARY 29

Their soul shall be as a watered garden;
and they shall not sorrow any more at all.
—JEREMIAH 31:12

*M*y cousin Pam and I had coffee together this morning, and we both ended up crying. She asked about my eye, and I told her I could see only the big *E* on the eye chart, though it had been three weeks since my surgery. Pam's eyes started to water in empathy. Then I asked about her niece Shelley, who has stage-four cancer and is worried about her six-year-old daughter. "I'd gladly give up my life if Shelley could have hers," Pam said, "and if Skylar could have her mother." That was when I had to get out my tissues. We looked across the table at each other and realized we were crying in grief for the other. That was when we started laughing.

We both knew these were not laughing matters, but we'd held in our feelings for too long. We just needed someone to cry with and someone to laugh with too. Then Pam said, "I've been through so many painful times in my life, but right now I feel as though I'm in a state of grace." *How could that be,* I wondered, *with all she has to bear?* "Isn't it miraculous?" Pam continued. "When life gets hard, the spirit grows strong. Again and again I realize that the Holy Spirit has eyes that can see through all kinds of darkness!"

I always feel better after spending time with my cousin.

> *Thank You, Loving God, for good friends who pass on the state*
> *of grace You've given them. May I be graced with the ability to see*
> *with the eyes of the spirit and with ways to pass on that vision.*
> —MARILYN MORGAN KING

March

MARCH 1

Trust in him at all times; ye people, pour out your heart before him.
—PSALM 62:8

"I saw a robin!" My mother's voice on the phone had the singsong quality of smug victory. She might as well have added, "*Na-na-na-na-na!*" She likes to win this game.

Mom and I have an annual competition to see who can spot the year's first robin. It started the year I left home, and it's been going on for more than two decades. Here in Connecticut, the first robin is a big deal. It means that the winter will, indeed, end, even when we're convinced it's going to go on forever. Mom and I are not winter lovers by any stretch of the imagination. For both of us, it's always been a long, gray crawl from Christmas to Easter. So the first robin is an important signpost, and even more so this year.

My grandmother has been ill for months, and my mother's older sister died shortly after Christmas. Our lives have been touched by melancholy, and the road ahead looks bumpy and gray as mortality looms large in our lives. To make matters worse, it's also been the coldest winter in a decade. It's hard even to imagine Easter. Then Mom's call came. I couldn't remember the last time she sounded so excited.

This year's sighting was the earliest yet. Three days later, I saw a dozen robins gathered together in some undergrowth by the road. A dozen! It was nine degrees out. Mom may have had the victory, but we both won this year.

God's lesser creatures know what we advanced folk sometimes forget: Easter and spring always come. Sometimes, we just have to wait awhile.

> *Lord Jesus, let me never forget that You are risen*
> *and present in all circumstances and in all seasons.*
> —MARCI ALBORGHETTI

Do everything without complaining or arguing.
—Philippians 2:14 niv

*Y*esterday I asked my daughters Caeli and Corinna to hang up their jackets.

"Sure," said three-year-old Caeli, who hung her jacket on its hook.

"Ugh!" said five-year-old Corinna, throwing herself onto the couch. "It's the same every day! Why do I have to hang it up every time I come home?"

Later that same day, I sat reading to the girls while they colored: Caeli drawing circles with whatever colors were in front of her and Corinna complaining that she didn't have the colors for a true full rainbow. Eventually, I put the children's storybook down to continue my Bible study. The girls enjoy being read to regardless of the story, so I began reading aloud from chapter two of Paul's letter to the Philippians: "Do everything without complaining or arguing."

Suddenly Corinna stopped coloring, looked up, and asked, "Are you sure that's in the Bible?"

Laughing, I repeated the verse, assuring her that I wasn't making it up. She decided that if it was really in the Bible, she needed to learn it. So we wrote the verse on a piece of paper and started memorizing it. Not only did Corinna recite the verse at dinner, but she also called her grandparents to recite it for them.

Corinna's behavior hasn't changed overnight, but she's moving along the right path. Now she understands that these are God's rules, not just Mommy's. When she complains, we repeat the verse and try to think of the positive aspects of the situation. What a great daily reminder for me too!

> *Heavenly Father, help me to have such faith that just hearing one of Your commandments will cause me to stop, listen, and learn.*
> —Wendy Willard

That their hearts might be comforted, being knit together in love....
—COLOSSIANS 2:2

*M*y mother knew how to do Aran knitting, the unbelievably complicated combination of stitches that creates diamonds, knots, and twists of yarn. Imagine twenty-four rows, each with different instructions and no margin of error—even one wrong stitch destroys the whole sequence. I've been knitting sweaters for more than twelve years, but I've never even attempted the advanced Aran pattern. My good friend Ellen wrote this wonderful set of instructions, but I knew they were much too hard for me.

But somehow there was a connection in my heart between this craft and my mother, apparently effortlessly creating sweater after spectacular Aran sweater for every member of the family. How did she learn it? Why did she knit so faithfully for us all? There were no soft words of love from this difficult lady, but did we realize we were all wearing outward and visible signs of her inward and spiritual affection?

Then one peaceful day I found myself on a porch, looking out toward the Blue Ridge Mountains of Virginia, with a sheet of instructions on my lap. I'd decided to attempt an Aran sweater. Four times I started, and four times I looked at the lopsided lines of stitches full of strange holes, unraveled the whole thing and started over. Finally, on the fifth attempt I managed a respectable dark green sweater complete with diamonds and cables.

As I held it in my hands, I felt I had finally, after many false starts, knitted a bond with my mother that I never achieved in her lifetime. Did she see my struggles and feel my woolen outreach? I think so.

> *Lord, with the work of my fingers may I weave together*
> *memories of the past and hope for the future.*
> —BRIGITTE WEEKS

MARCH 4

All these people were still living by faith when they died.
—HEBREWS 11:13 NIV

Several years ago, I met a lady named Joan who was just returning from the funeral of her son. Early in her marriage she gave birth to two handicapped children. Her husband couldn't deal with the situation; he divorced her, and she was left alone with the children. After struggling heroically for several years, and after much prayer, she placed the more severely handicapped child in a facility that could better handle and care for him. She maintained close contact with the school and visited her son as often as she could. At age nineteen, he died.

"Why don't I feel sad?" Joan asked me.

Then she answered her own question. "Dolphus, I gave my children to the Lord years ago, and I did everything that I could do to care for them. I made the best decision that I could, and trusted the Lord for His will to be done."

Joan didn't know why God gave her two handicapped children. She wanted God to heal her son on this earth. When this didn't happen, she kept on living by faith that God would take care of him. And when he died, the eyes of faith showed her God's mercy at work.

There are times when, despite earnest prayer, God doesn't give me what I want. That's when, like Joan, I need to live by faith.

> *Lord, when You give me a cross, also give me a strong back,*
> *a praying spirit, and a trusting heart.*
> —DOLPHUS WEARY

*"Thus says the Lord, the God of Israel, 'Write all the words
which I have spoken to you in a book.'"*
—JEREMIAH 30:2 NASB

*T*he warm embrace of books wraps itself around you the moment you step into my living room—floor-to-ceiling shelves of books. The somber and bright colors of their spines sport an extraordinary range of titles and reflect the influence they have had in giving texture to my life. The lower shelves are reserved for children: Dr. Seuss, fairy tales, Rudyard Kipling's *Jungle Book* and all of Winnie-the-Pooh.

Dusting the main surfaces of the living room is done with a few quick flicks. Dusting the bookshelves is a never-ending job because of all the pauses of flipping through pages and sitting on the stepladder to reread cherished passages. It took me hours and several cups of tea to dust Anne Morrow Lindbergh's *Gift from the Sea*!

Several special books have a place of honor on my library table. This morning as I dusted, I peered into *Cornerstones of Christianity*, published in 1914. It's been in the Angus family for generations and came to us when Grandma died. "I remember sitting on Mother's knee while she read its Bible stories to me," my husband said. He turned to page three and ran his fingers along the words:

Book of books
Inspired by God
Beautiful in Expression
Light of Life
Enduring Eternally.

*Light of our life, Book of all books...the cornerstone that strengthens
and sustains us now and forevermore. Hallelujah, Lord!*
—FAY ANGUS

MARCH 6

And what I say unto you I say unto all, Watch.
—MARK 13:37

"Oh, look," my mother said, "I think I see a deer up in the woods."

My stepfather Herb and I looked in the direction she was pointing. The three of us were on a driving tour of Arizona after a memorable visit to the Grand Canyon. On this day, we were braving the steep roads and hairpin turns of the White Mountains.

"Oh, Herb, over there, isn't that some kind of hawk?" my mother said. "Beyond those trees, could that be a coyote?"

"Gosh, Bebe," I finally said to my mother, who usually spent extended driving time listening to tapes or reading out loud from the newspaper, "where did this new interest in the great outdoors come from?"

"Well, surely you saw that sign when we started up the mountain," she answered, still peering out the window. "You know: WATCH FOR WILD ANIMALS."

I caught Herb's eye in the rearview mirror from my place in the backseat and giggled.

"I'm sure that was a coyote," my mother was saying.

Of course, the sign was meant as a warning for drivers, but my mother had turned it into an opportunity. I thought about some of the ways I could do the same.

I might respond to YIELD by resisting the urge to score a point in every conversation and listening more thoughtfully to the views of others. I could turn DRIVE CAREFULLY into a challenge to care for each fellow traveler I came across. SLOW could remind me to take time to enjoy the scenery as I pass through the seasons, and STOP might prompt me to put a halt to negative thoughts and useless worries.

Maybe Mother was the only one among us who saw where the sign was really pointing. I didn't know if I would ever pass through the White Mountains again, so I set my gaze on the deep woods that rimmed the road, watching for wild animals too.

> *Father, as I pass through this world of wonder,*
> *let me watch for the signs that point me to You.*
> —PAM KIDD

As a mother comforts her child, so will I comfort you.
—ISAIAH 66:13 NIV

Today is my brother's birthday. Bill is forty-six. For forty-two years he shared his birthday with our mother. All eight of her children miss her, but today my brother misses her most of all.

I don't know what it's like to have a birthday for two. I suppose, as a child, sharing a birthday (like sharing anything) was not so great. I imagine it was very special for him as an adult. Today, as it was last year, his birthday is all his own.

When Bill and I were kids, my older sister and I took him to the park to climb trees. Bill wasn't much of a climber, but Sue and I often perched him on a low limb and watched while he crawled far out to the end, until the limb's delicate outermost branches bent to the ground or broke. Sue and I were alarmed when he fell, but Bill was fearless. Regardless of the outcome of his balancing acts, he was always ready to try a new tree and go out on its limbs.

Bill grew up, and like his mother, he was never afraid to go out on a limb for God. They were passionate about their beliefs, and they didn't care if they alarmed other people. And they knew that God would keep them safe if the limb bent or broke.

He is still out there. I'm inching my way up the trunk. It's boring, but safe. I don't like to alarm people with my beliefs, or even make them uncomfortable. I'm getting braver, but I don't know about going out on a limb. My brother swears that it is safe out there with God.

It must be. Mom always wanted him out there, and she'd always meet him halfway.

> *Dear God, help me to have the courage to trust You*
> *the way my mother trusted You.*
> —TIM WILLIAMS

"Remember the Lord in a distant land, and think on Jerusalem."
—JEREMIAH 51:50 NIV

*M*y mother moved into an assisted-living home after Alzheimer's made it impossible for her to live alone. She'd only been there a week when I got a call from the supervisor. "I hate to tell you this, but your mom's been swiping things from other people's rooms. Socks, candy bars, T-shirts. Nothing big, except that one lady's cross is missing."

My mom? Stealing? This was the most honest person I knew, who once drove twenty miles back to a store where the clerk had given her too much change— less than a dollar and considerably less than it cost in gas to return the overage.

The next time I visited, I gently chided her for the pilfering. "You've got to cut that out, Mom," I said, sitting with her in the lunchroom. "Did you take that cross?"

She shook her head, her curly gray hair bouncing.

"Sure about that?" I pressed.

Mom turned away, then reached into her purse and pulled out the small silver cross. She set it down on the table gingerly and stared at it. "I wasn't trying to steal" was all the explanation she gave.

Later I turned over the cross to the supervisor, apologizing. "Don't, don't," she said. "Your mom's a charmer. She's just trying to hang on to the things that mean the most to her."

The next time I came out I brought Mom a small silver cross. She stopped stealing after that.

Eventually we had to move Mom to a facility where she could receive more care and where, of course, she charmed everyone. She even led prayers on Friday morning. She had forgotten almost everything else, yet the prayers came to her lips as if she had freshly committed them to memory. And when she died, the saddest people of all were the people she prayed with on Friday mornings with that little silver cross I gave her clutched in her hand.

> *Lord, Mom is with You now. Teach me never*
> *to forget You, just as You never forgot her.*
> —EDWARD GRINNAN

MARCH 9

And they came, bringing to him a paralytic carried by four men.
—MARK 2:3 RSV

*I*t's a scary thing to have your son phone, offhandedly chat awhile, then finally give the real reason for his call. "Mom, I have some health problems that will involve some serious surgery. But don't worry."

Of course I worried. What if something happens to John? Now, my children may be married and away from home, but they're still my kids. And in situations like this, I turn to God even more than usual.

That's when I recalled the story in Mark of the sick man carried to Jesus by four friends. Why four? I wondered. The Gospel doesn't say, but it seems logical that if the man was too sick to make it on his own, he'd need a stretcher and four carriers, one for each corner.

If it worked in biblical times, it should work now, too, I reasoned. So with motherly concern, I looked for four friends of my own—friends who truly believe in prayer—who would agree to carry John on a "prayer stretcher." I think it helps to pray specifically—not just a vague, "Lord, take care of John." So I said, "Mary, will you take the left front corner, please? Sue, right front. Bonnie, left rear. Kathie, right rear." My position? I reasoned that every team needs cheerleaders. I'd be one, encouraging each prayer and giving them updates on John's condition.

For two months, the four stretcher-bearers continued their faithful vigil. When surgery day came, John's wife Marie said, "Neither of us is afraid. We both sense John is being carried on a bed of prayer."

And how does the story in Mark end? When Jesus saw the faith of the four friends, He said to the paralytic, "Get up, take your mat and go home" (Mark 2:11, NIV).

And within a short time, that's just what John did.

Father, You've told us that anything is possible if we have faith. Please show me how to have that faith—the faith that moves mountains!
—ISABEL WOLSELEY

MARCH 10

"So do not worry, saying, 'What shall we eat?' or 'What shall we drink?'
or 'What shall we wear?' For the pagans run after all these things,
and your heavenly Father knows that you need them."
—MATTHEW 6:31–32 NIV

*L*ike other single parents, I've had many years of worrying about feeding my children, clothing them, and providing shelter. I worried that I'd fail. I worried that I'd die and my children would become orphans. Surrounded by endless cares, it was easy to feel alone.

When my daughter Lanea was about nine, I decided to transfer her to a private school. We lived in Richmond, Virginia, but I worked twenty miles south of there. My son Chase was in daycare where I worked, but I worried about Lanea in Richmond. Though it put a strain on our budget, the new school was much closer to where I worked.

Lanea has fond memories of musicals and school celebrations. But she still groans about her memory verses. Braids and beads jiggling, she would sigh as she obediently recited the lines: "Do not store up for yourselves treasures on earth, where moth and rust destroy, and where thieves break in and steal. But store up for yourselves treasures in heaven" (Matthew 6:19–20, NIV).

The words were a duty to her, but they were encouragement to me. "So do not worry, saying, 'What shall we eat?' or 'What shall we drink?' or 'What shall we wear?'" She would look around the room as she shifted foot to foot and continued, "...your heavenly Father knows that you need them" (Matthew 6:31–32, NIV).

What Lanea thought were tears of pride sliding down my face were really tears of joy and relief. She didn't know that I was worrying and that I felt alone. But her drills reminded me that God knew and that He cared. When I worry today, the memory of Lanea's voice reminds me that He still does.

God, today and every day You are with me and You care for me.
Help me to hear Your reassurance, even in the voice of a child.
—SHARON FOSTER

*The world is a looking glass and gives back
to every man the reflection of his own face.*
—WILLIAM MAKEPEACE THACKERAY

*W*ell, how was your morning?" my husband asked as we sat down for lunch one day.

"Oh, I don't know. John got up on the wrong side of the bed, and Karen left for work grumbling. Even Paul wasn't his usual sunny self this morning."

"Sounds like you're not in a very good mood today," Rex observed sympathetically.

"Me! *I'm* all right. It's just that the kids are so moody. Maybe it's the weather."

Later it dawned on me that Rex really had spotted the trouble. If the children were grouchy, it was because they were mirroring me. Looking back, I remembered that I *had* felt kind of "down" when I woke up. I was tired of the rain and dreading the ironing that was waiting for me. I realized, then, how just one person's sour mood can infect a whole family.

Since then, I've been taking a little time, each morning, to assess my mood and turn over to God any "clouds" that are hovering over me, before I get the family up. It has helped. You really can affect the emotional climate of your household, or the place where you work, by keeping a controlling finger on your own mood thermostat. Try it today and see.

Let my face mirror Your love, Lord, all through this day.
—MARILYN MORGAN HELLEBERG

MARCH 12

Like most couples, Wayne and I have not had the perfect marriage. At one point we separated for nearly eighteen months before deciding that just wasn't the solution. Once we reunited, though, it wasn't smooth sailing. Old resentments surfaced, and I struggled with letting go of the pain from the past. One weekend I felt I needed to get away, and visiting my parents was the perfect excuse.

When I arrived, my mother insisted on picking up a bucket of her favorite chicken for dinner. For some reason she decided to drive. I climbed in the car with her, and she said, "Look behind me. Is anyone coming?"

I twisted around and checked. "You're clear."

"Great." She revved up the engine, and we shot out of the driveway and onto the street.

"Mom," I asked, suddenly suspicious, "can't you look behind you?"

"Good grief, no. I've had a crick in my neck for nearly twenty years." She proceeded to show me the elaborate way she twisted the rearview mirror to check for traffic behind her. I couldn't keep from smiling and joked with her about it.

The next day, as I was heading home, it struck me that God was speaking to me through my mother. She looked forward, not back. God seemed to be asking me to do the same: Concentrate on the present, look with faith toward the future, and release the pain of the past.

Lord, I'm grateful for the miracles You've worked in my marriage, for the husband You gave me, and for all the years we've shared together—the good with the bad. May we both look to You as we step toward the future.

—DEBBIE MACOMBER

The Lord hear thee in the day of trouble;
the name of the God of Jacob defend thee.
—PSALM 20:1

*W*hen our son was twelve and had been sick since age ten and a half, he had a third relapse of hepatitis. From the first attack he had been troubled with nausea, weakness, and liver cramps. Now he faced weeks in bed and months of reduced activity.

"I guess I'm not ever going to get well," he cried.

Emotionally I went to pieces and was no support for him at all. Something had to change.

One day in the market I greeted another nurse, a Christian woman with whom I had worked briefly. When she asked about my son I guess the despair I felt showed.

"Just take one day at a time. That's all you can do," she said.

Her concern warmed me, but the advice seemed trite. Still, what else could I do?

I began to ask God each day to give us strength to make it through that day. I tried to help our son center his interests and thoughts only on that one day, not to look ahead to a future that might be bleak. That kind of future we couldn't contemplate without despair, but today ended at sundown and that we could manage. Some days, of course, were easier than others, but always my prayer was answered.

A year later we knew that he was well. Two years later he was named "Most Valuable Player" of his soccer and track teams. He's in high school now. The other day he said, "You know, I was thinking about when I had hepatitis and my stomach began to knot up and I thought, 'How did I ever make it through that?'"

"God led you through," I said with a full heart. "One day at a time."

Lord, when the future is not bright remind us that
with You we can always manage one day at a time.
—DEE ANN PALMER

Then said Jesus, Father, forgive them; for they know not what they do.
—LUKE 23:34

I recently heard a woman stand up in court and say this to the man who had murdered her daughter: "I forgive you. I refuse to let you haunt my heart any longer, and I choose to let you go into God's hands.

"You took my daughter. Not a moment will go by for the rest of my life without me yearning to touch my sweet child and hear her voice and her laugh and her thoughts and dreams. Not a second. You stole her from me, from her father and her brother, from the hundreds of people who loved her, and the thousands more who would have loved her.

"But I forgive you, because I will not let you steal my life also. I pray that God will forgive you. I pray for your healing. I pray for your wife, for your parents, for your sister. I pray for those who can never forgive you.

"It has taken me four long years to say these words, but I will not have you in my mind or my heart one minute longer. I hand you to God. You are God's child, and in Him is forgiveness and peace beyond my understanding. I commend you to Him. My sweet baby girl will stay with me in my heart until I die and see her again, and I *will* see her again, I know that beyond the shadow of a doubt, but I will never see or think of you again, for I give you to God. Amen."

There was not a whisper or a rustle for what seemed like years after she sat down.

O God, O Father, forgive us, help us, hold us in Your hands, soothe and salve that mother, keep that young woman in Your love, heal that twisted man. And please, never ever let me forget the way a woman forgave a man the unforgivable.
—BRIAN DOYLE

Little children...ye have known the Father.
—1 JOHN 2:13

"Keri, where are you?"

I wandered about the house in search of our three-year-old daughter. "I'm in here, in the kitchen, under the table," she answered.

"What are you doing under the table?"

"Oh, me and God...we're just talking."

How is it that we adults manage to make something as simple as talking to God so infinitely complicated?

Many roadblocks separate me from the God Keri visited with so naturally under the kitchen table. First, there's my dark side: Sometimes I feel inferior to other people and, in retaliation, I say mean things about them. At other times, I'm afraid that God really isn't out there or, if He is, He doesn't have time to listen to me. Then there's my lazy side: I put off the effort that's required to build a solid relationship with God.

I'm sure you have your own list of obstacles that keep you one step removed from a free and open dialogue with God. And yet, because of them, we can discover the single most important thing there is to know about the practice of prayer—Dr. William R. Parker and Elaine St. Johns call it "the Key to the Kingdom"—honesty. For me, it sounds like this:

God, You know the person I want to become. But when I find myself around Mae, with her money and her important job and her perfectly decorated house, well...I say mean things about Mae. I'm sorry I do that, God.

This month will be honesty month. Take at least ten minutes every day to talk honestly with God. Tell Him who you are and who you want to be. Don't be afraid to tell Him the whole truth. You are His beloved child. He already knows every single thing there is to know about you. But like a good Father, He's hoping to hear it straight from you!

Father, I want to come to You as pure and honest as a child.
—PAM KIDD

"Which of you, if his son asks for bread, will give him a stone?"
—MATTHEW 7:9 NIV

I tasted hope today. It had a rich, luscious flavor, soothing as the rolling hills around me. It came in the shape of gnarled apple trees and grass. Andrew and I were visiting a possible new school for our son John. This one was utterly unlike his current school. There was no asphalt basketball court, no chain-link fence, no yellow-painted cinderblock to lend false cheeriness to an otherwise dismal environment. It wasn't the nightmare alternative we had visited the week before, filled with posters warning against guns and domestic violence. ("Things have gotten better," the social worker there told us. "We don't accept so many gang members anymore.") Nor was it the sunny but overly sanitized school an hour's drive away, where every door was locked, even the bathroom.

Here there was a pond and a swimming pool. The class size was eight students per teacher. The grounds were gorgeous. The admissions officer asked insightful questions. She had read John's paperwork, understood his needs and thought this school could help him. My heart cried out, *Yes! Yes! Accept him!*

They did.

After the nightmare years of choosing among bad options, we finally had a good alternative. The city will pay for the school. A school bus will take John door to door. At last our son will be in an environment that is truly therapeutic. It may not solve all his problems, but there is tremendous joy in being able to give your child bread instead of a stone.

Father, thank You for being patient with me
even when I'm not so patient with You.
—JULIA ATTAWAY

We give thanks to God always for you all.
—1 THESSALONIANS 1:2

The phone rang on a Sunday afternoon, and I was surprised to hear from the mother of one of my daughter's classmates. She was calling to thank me for driving her children home from school a few days earlier when she had been called out of town for work. I told her it was no trouble at all. "Maybe," she said, "but you really helped me out. I wanted to let you know." Her call made me realize how good it felt to be appreciated. When I thanked her for thinking of me, she told me about her new habit.

"I spend a few minutes every Sunday afternoon calling or writing a note to thank someone who's made my life a little better that week. Just to let them know I appreciate them."

What a great idea, I thought. *I can do that.* I started by writing a note to my sister-in-law for the bouquet of home-grown roses that she'd brought by my house the day before. It quickly turned into a note of gratitude for the many thoughtful things she's done for me over the years, some I'm sure I'd forgotten to thank her for.

I've learned that I never run out of people to appreciate, like the neighbor who loaned my daughter a bike or the librarian who enthusiastically runs our mother-daughter book club. Forbes magazine founder B. C. Forbes said, "A word of appreciation often can accomplish what nothing else can accomplish." And what's that? The realization that my life is constantly blessed by the kindness of others and, I hope, their realization of how valuable they are to me.

Lord God, as the Creator of all good things,
You deserve my first and greatest thanks.
—GINA BRIDGEMAN

MARCH 18

I stood in the middle of the busy department store, locked in my own sorrow. My daughter had just been hospitalized for an overdose of drugs and alcohol. No matter how hard I prayed, she kept going downhill. Now her life hung in the balance. As I gazed ahead, I spied Armando Llanos and quickly turned away. I hadn't seen Armando or his wife Eva for some time, and he didn't know about my trauma.

But I didn't get away from Armando fast enough. "Shari, how are you?" he called in his heavily accented English as I tried to duck into another aisle. A native of Colombia, he'd lived a rough life. A dramatic conversion had turned him around, and now he talked about Jesus wherever he went. As he approached, I couldn't stop my tears from welling up, so I told him about my daughter.

"We need to pray, sister," he said softly, putting a hand on my shoulder. Then, to my embarrassment, he began to pray aloud right there in the bath and bedding department.

Armando's prayer seemed inappropriate and out of place, and I was embarrassed as I felt the stares of people rushing by. Yet, somewhere in the middle of the prayer, a warm rush of love filled me. "Jesus is going to heal your daughter," Armando said when he finished, his face glowing. "But it may take some time, like it did with me."

Jesus did heal my daughter. And it did take some time—several more years, in fact. But Armando's prayer had two immediate results: It pulled me out of my depression, and it taught me that our Lord isn't ashamed of being called on anywhere, even in a department store.

Jesus, help me to keep my pride from getting in the way of my prayer.
—SHARI SMYTH

MARCH 19

*Giving thanks always for all things unto God
and the Father in the name of our Lord Jesus Christ.*
—EPHESIANS 5:20

One cold night I stopped by my twin sons' room to check on them before going to bed. They both appeared to be asleep. However, Jon murmured, "Cold, Mama." Checking in their closet, I couldn't find a blanket, so I slipped off my bathrobe and covered Jon with it. In the moonlight that came in through the window, I carefully tucked it under his feet and chin. He was so still and quiet, I was sure he was asleep.

The boys were nearly eleven and I didn't often tuck them in at night. I went on down the dark hall to my bed and climbed in wearily. It had been a long, hard day. I knew I'd be asleep within minutes.

"Mama," came the call from the boys' room. I sighed, hoping Jon didn't need anything else.

"Yes?"

In a tone, soft for Jon, he said, "It was nice when you took off your robe and gave it to me and even tucked me in. Thanks."

The unexpected thanks from my son touched my heart and caused me to smile in the darkness. My boys seldom expressed gratitude. I was always after them to say thank you.

"You're welcome," I answered. " 'Night. Sweet dreams," I added, happily.

And then I didn't go right to sleep. Instead, I thought about how Jon's thanking me for such a little thing had pleased me. Prompted by his gratitude, I began to thank my Father for many little things I'd neglected to say thanks for through the day.

Father, God, thank You, thank You, thank You.
—MARION BOND WEST

The wisdom from above is first pure, then peaceable,
gentle, reasonable, full of mercy and good fruits.
—James 3:17 NASB

ore than fifteen years ago, I went through an emotionally draining period. I spent a good deal of time alone in my basement office, struggling to come to grips with things. Then one day the postman rang the doorbell to deliver a small parcel. I recognized our daughter's handwriting on the label and wondered what had prompted her to send me a gift. Inside, nestled in some crumpled tissue paper, was a pewter pear.

As I lifted the pear's lid, a gentle breeze blew through the open window, scattering the contents of the pear across the kitchen floor. Scrambling to retrieve the snippets of colored paper, I noticed our daughter had printed out a different Bible promise on each one. There must have been several dozen all told. I could just imagine her in her pajamas, sitting cross-legged on her bed with her Bible in her lap, painstakingly printing out each promise she found. I phoned her that evening to thank her.

"That's your prayer pear, Mom. I found it in a secondhand shop and decided to fill it with some encouraging verses. And you know what? I think I benefited just as much as you will."

Thank You, Lord, that the fruit of Your Spirit blesses the one
who manifests it just as much as the one who is refreshed by it.
—Alma Barkman

March 21

And gladly would he learn and gladly teach.
—Chaucer

*M*y teenage son asked me to come out into the frigid winter night to see Jupiter through his telescope. Bill had become very interested in astronomy. Here in Alaska, stars are not visible in summer but are brilliant in the deep nights of winter. The only chance he had of seeing anything was when it was clear and very cold.

I was not anxious to get all my down-gear on to go out and look at a blob in the sky. The spotting scope wasn't strong enough to see much. But he was so excited I couldn't turn him down.

Outside the night air was so cold I could hardly breathe. Bill lined the telescope up for me. I looked through and there was the blob of light I could see with the naked eye, only bigger.

"Adjust it, Mom," he said impatiently, and as I turned the dial suddenly it came into complete focus. Floating around Jupiter were three tiny bright moons. I was amazed and excited. I'd never seen the planets like that before.

Isn't it amazing how often, when you put your own inclinations aside and do something to please somebody else, unexpected dividends flow into your life?

Father, don't let inertia rob me of the wonders that are waiting.
—Susan M. Blake

MARCH 22

Underneath are the everlasting arms.
—DEUTERONOMY 33:27

After my father died, when I was very young, I had only one fear—that something might happen to my mother. Most of the time I was able to cope with it, but occasionally something would happen that would set loose my fears.

Many of my mother's clothes came from her sister in New York. They were gently used, but quietly elegant and perfect for her job at the local bank. Whenever a carefully wrapped box arrived from her sister, I adored watching Mother try on the clothes. But one day a package arrived without my knowing about it.

I was in the living room when Mother walked in, modeling some of her new clothes. Mother beamed. "Do you like this cape, Mannie?" she asked.

I gazed in silent horror. I had no idea what a cape was; I had never seen one before. The scary red and gray thing with fringes hung from my mother's shoulders. Why is she still smiling? Where are her arms and hands? Tears rolled down my face onto my green overalls.

"What's wrong, Mannie?" Mother asked.

"Where are your arms, Mama?" I wailed.

She knelt down on the floor beside me, and out from under the cape came my mother's wonderful arms—hands and all—as she embraced me in a long, tight hug. Then she threw the cape on the floor and somehow made me laugh.

Later in life, when fear stalked me once again, I discovered another set of faithful arms. All these years later, they continue to comfort me.

> *Father, the old hymn is true! "Leaning, leaning,*
> *safe and secure from all alarms, leaning, leaning,*
> *leaning on the everlasting arms" (Elisha A. Hoffman, 1887).*
> —MARION BOND WEST

MARCH 23

She looketh well to the ways of her household....
Her children arise up, and call her blessed.
—PROVERBS 31:27–28

*L*ast spring our newspaper printed an unusual photograph of a downtown traffic light. There, right inside one of the three cuplike openings, was a tiny robin's nest.

This traffic light hung over one of the busiest intersections in the city. It was certainly not a quiet spot. Horns blared, brakes screeched, and trucks emitted sooty diesel smoke and fumes.

Yet there inside the nest, built right against the bright red light that flashed off and on, day and night, three little fledglings slept and fed peacefully. In the midst of all the noise and clamor, Mother Robin had established a niche of serenity for her family.

My mother did something similar for me. Early in their married life my parents did not have a great deal of security, and there were ups and downs. But had my mother waited for ideal conditions in which to raise a family, I would not be here today. And yet I have carried the fruit of her transforming love and devotion within me all my life. It has sustained me in times of sorrow and blessed me in times of joy. My mother's quiet strength and steadfast faith are a priceless legacy to me.

> *Father, I thank You for my mother and for her courage in being mine.*
> —ISABEL CHAMP

March 24

Fill my cup, Lord; I lift it up, Lord.
RICHARD BLANCHARD, HYMN

I was a wreck! My son had driven a grocery cart through the cake-mix display at the supermarket, my daughter had bathed eight stuffed animals in a tub of water, and the dog had turned over three newly potted geraniums on the rug. I could go on, but I won't depress you. I was having one of my dry-cup days.

I get them. Maybe you do too. They are the days that leave me empty as a dry cup. You know the ones—ringing phones, children's quarrels, spilled grape juice, overdue library books, and a frantic tangle of errands and demands. All together these little frustrations can wear a hole in my day through which peace and perspective drain away.

You know what I did? I dropped everything and carried my dry cup to an armchair in the bedroom. Hidden away from the distractions, I closed my eyes and held up my cup to God for a refill. I didn't think of the forty boxes of cake mix crashing down, or the water-logged animals, or the carpet full of potting soil. I thought about God. I imagined Him pouring His love and peace and strength down upon me. There, in those few silent moments, He filled my cup. Filled it up. And I returned to the little human things of life, my cup brimming with peace.

On the dry-cup days, Lord, help me to seek a quiet corner for a refill.
—SUE MONK KIDD

Now I lay me down to sleep,
I pray the Lord my soul to keep.
If I should die before I wake,
I pray the Lord my soul to take.
A CHILD'S PRAYER

This was the little prayer that I taught my son Chris when he was four. He always said it before my goodnight kiss.

One morning I woke up to a sunshine-filled bedroom, and I couldn't help but wonder, *Why isn't there a prayer for waking up?* Then and there I composed this one:

As I waken from my sleep,
This brand new day of Yours I greet.
Safe You've kept me through the night
I'll serve you now with all my might.

I taught Chris this new prayer of mine, and when our next son came along, I taught it to him too. Now it's a family tradition, a way for all of us to greet the day in the same prayerful way that we end it.

I want to be close to You, Lord, night and day.
—KAREN LANGFORD BROWN

MARCH 26

When I look at thy heavens, the work of thy fingers....
—PSALM 8:3 RSV

*W*hen we first took Rome, my little grandson, to church, he was six weeks old. He was sound asleep in his "chariot"—the name I've given the carrier used by parents these days. Rather than disturb him, my daughter Heather set him (still in his chariot) in the aisle and let me sit next to him. I reached down and wiggled my finger into his tiny fist, and we sat through that first service holding hands. My grandson was unaware of me, but because he was holding on to my finger, whenever he had tummy rumbles and squirmed in pain he instinctively squeezed more tightly to me until the discomfort passed.

I wondered how often I had done the same. Long ago God had tucked His finger into my own hand and, because of that, I had instinctively squeezed more tightly to Him.

What a wonderful picture, I thought, so happy with Rome's wee hand curled around my finger. While I've certainly appreciated the security God's finger has given me over the years, I'd never before understood the idea that the ebb and flow of my own frail humanity might actually give God pleasure.

> *Dear God, with Your finger You wrote the commandments,*
> *You cast out demons, and You created the stars.*
> *You've tucked that same finger into the curl of my hand.*
> —BRENDA WILBEE

The Lord was my support. He brought me out into a spacious place.
—PSALM 18:18–19 NIV

*I*t seemed to be taking a while for my son to take his first steps. A fast crawler, Solomon had turned into a leaner, walking in endless circles around the coffee table, holding my hand, and keeping a pinky on the table. It was obvious that he could carry his own weight; the only thing holding him back was uncertainty about his footing. He still needed someone to lean on.

We were at my mom's for brunch one cold morning when Solomon leaned on a chair and picked up his boots. A small snow boot in each hand, he stood up, and in a moment took his first solo step toward me. "One, two, three," a roomful of my relatives whispered along with me as Solomon made it across the living room rug. In eight steps, he reached me and put his boot in my lap, unaware that he had let go of the chair. For the next few days, Solomon walked—but only with his hands full and outstretched, as if the things he held gave him grounding.

Solomon had found his balance, but I know he still had Someone to lean on, holding those boots, leading him step by step.

> *Lord, thank You for being there to lean on*
> *when I launch out into the unknown.*
> —SABRA CIANCANELLI

Wherefore be ye not unwise, but understanding what the will of the Lord is.
—EPHESIANS 5:17

*M*other always seemed to be able to bring out the best in me, and, looking back, I can now appreciate what a difficult task this sometimes was. For instance, there was my brand new job with the local newspaper. I loved the work, I loved my own little corner near the City Desk, I loved typing my own news stories, and then one day I hit a snag. In tears I went home and told Mother I was quitting. A competitive paper had scooped us on a fast-breaking story, and my superior blamed me, the cub reporter, when I had had nothing to do with it.

"All right," Mother said rather casually, "leave if you like. But why not wait a while? Right now, if you quit, they won't care. But if you hang on and make yourself really valuable, then they'll be sorry to lose you."

This "make 'em sorry" idea appealed to me mightily and I returned grimly to my job. But after a few weeks I got so caught up in the work that, when I was blamed for missing another story, I was too busy chasing the next one to fret.

One day a few months later I was thrilled to become a member of the Women's Press Club of Georgia. Going home that day, I finally realized what Mother had been up to. It wasn't that she thought that "showing them" was such a good idea. But she knew I'd be making a mistake to quit. So, instead of arguing, she had employed a little stratagem in order to keep a stubborn daughter on the right path.

> *Thank You, Heavenly Father, for the many ways our parents guided us, and help us who are parents now to be loving and wise in the lessons we try to teach our young.*
> —MAY SHERIDAN GOLD

MARCH 29

I am bringing all my energies to bear on this one thing:
Forgetting the past and looking forward to what lies ahead.
—PHILIPPIANS 3:13 TLB

*T*he game was on the line when my grandson David, eleven, came to bat in the top of the ninth inning. There were two outs and a runner on second base, and his team was behind by one run. I held my breath as David fouled off the first pitch, swung at and missed the second, took a ball low, and fouled off the third ball. Then he drilled a high fastball past the diving first baseman, batting in the tying run. He stole second and ended up scoring to give his team a 13–12 victory. I don't know who was more excited, David or his cheering grandma!

But the next game was different. David batted 0 for 2, and had trouble getting the ball over the plate when he pitched. He was pulled from the game in the fifth inning, and his team was knocked out of the tournament.

Still, my young grandson is able to keep baseball in perspective: The main thing for him is doing his best and having fun. He accepts his successes and failures, his wins and losses, for what they are—an inevitable part of the game. He did the same thing after the loss as after the win: He practiced batting to improve his skills. That's a pretty good example for living life, wouldn't you say?

Lord Jesus, thank You for loving me just as much
when I strike out as when I hit home runs.
—PENNEY SCHWAB

MARCH 30

This is the assurance we have in approaching God:
that if we ask anything according to his will, he hears us.
—1 JOHN 5:14 NIV

How I love this computer/Internet/cell phone age! I know there are abuses, but most of the pluses outweigh them.

For example, here I am in Virginia furiously typing and through the speakers of this same computer I can hear our son Peter, live, directing air traffic from a control tower more than five hundred miles away. If I want, I can "Google Earth" the airport and zoom in until I can see a satellite shot of the control tower where he works. Or I can fly over the skylighted roof of our son Tom and his wife Susan's house in Georgia. Or follow, as I did, our son John on a week's trip in the mountains and by the sea in Croatia. I can find the grass landing strip in our son Dave and his wife Matti's backyard in Kentucky, and fly up Fort Valley inside our own Massanutten Mountain. What fun!

As the mother of four sons, I bless e-mail daily because I know from their college years that receiving "snail mail" letters from them is a pipe dream.

Then there's the Webcam. Bill and I bought two; one perches on a speaker by our computer and the other sits on a desk in Georgia. And our grandsons Jack and Luke look at the grainy square on their computer screen and see us, live, waving, laughing, playing peekaboo with them. And they respond, "Grandpa! Grandma!"

The cell phone—well, that goes without saying. How did I ever survive a trip to the grocery store without one?

All this communication and technology have enhanced my faith in how God can be close to and personal with me; He's had this expertise all along.

> *Lord, You know where I am. You listen and see and know*
> *all about me, live. And You rejoice to hear from me as much*
> *as I do when I hear from children and grandchildren.*
> —ROBERTA ROGERS

MARCH 31

He that is not with me is against me.
—LUKE 11:23

*S*itting in the bleachers at the Little League ball field on a chilly Saturday, I overheard two mothers talking about a teacher I knew and respected. They were complaining that the teacher wasn't doing right by their children. *The teacher's only trying to do what's best,* I thought. This world would be a whole lot better place if people realized they were on the same side and pulled together for a change.

Then a question came into my mind: And you, Karen, what are you doing to support the Little League team today?

Well, I'm here, I thought. Then I looked down at my hands. I hadn't been clapping; I was still wearing my gloves. It's easy to get trapped in your own concerns without even knowing it, the inner voice seemed to say. Pulling together takes effort because first you have to pull away from yourself.

I looked back out at the baseball diamond and decided perhaps it was time I stopped just occupying my spot on the bench and started occupying a place on the team. I began to call out something encouraging after each play. As I yelled, "Way to hang in there!" when our boys finally stopped a runner at third base after dropping the ball at first and second, even the mothers who had been raking the teacher over the coals smiled.

> *Lord, help me to do something today,*
> *no matter how small, to be part of my community.*
> —KAREN BARBER

April

Blessed are they that mourn: for they shall be comforted.
—MATTHEW 5:4

I had prayed for this to be just another day, but on the first anniversary of my mother's death I awoke to a wet and windy Saturday in the Berkshire Hills, the kind of raw early April morning that makes spring seem hopelessly far off. I'd wanted to hike a favorite stretch of the Appalachian Trail, but the weather sabotaged my plans and I found myself wandering aimlessly through one of the musty secondhand bookstores for which this part of Massachusetts is known.

I needed another book like I needed a hole in my head, as Mom would have put it. I missed Mom saying things like that, missed them more than I ever imagined I would. I thought her long decline from Alzheimer's had prepared me for her death, but sometimes my feelings about losing her were unexpectedly poignant, like today.

As my eyes roamed the shelves, a title on a worn red spine leapt out at me: *The Southpaw's Secret.*

It was a boys' book, part of the relatively short-lived Mel Martin mystery series by John R. Cooper that I'd been crazy about when I was a kid. Mel Martin was a high-school baseball star, and a crafty sleuth to boot. The books had already gone out of print by the time I read the two volumes I inherited from my older brother, but I was hooked. I don't know how many hours Mom spent helping me hunt down the other Mel Martin books.

Mom was a great sleuth herself, especially when it came to finding things for me: the Beatles' first album, for instance, which sold out the Monday after their historic appearance on The Ed Sullivan Show. Mom was able to unearth a copy in a tiny electronics store in Walled Lake, Michigan, about thirty miles from our house. Mom spent half her life finding obscure stuff I had to have.

Except *The Southpaw's Secret,* the one Mel Martin book she never was able to track down. And now it had found me. After all these years.

You are there, Lord, to help us find what we need.
—EDWARD GRINNAN

We glory in tribulations also: knowing that tribulation worketh patience.
—ROMANS 5:3

*M*y son Ross was on the mound for his Little League team, pitching for only the second time in his nine-year-old life. He walked two, and his confidence was shaken. Then he threw one wild pitch and hit the batter on the foot. Now he was really rattled. He gave up a couple of hits and runs, and the bases were still loaded. Suddenly, he pulled himself together, striking out two and catching a pop-up to end the inning. After the game I told him how proud I was of his tenacity and wondered how he got through that tough spot. He shrugged his shoulders and said, "I don't know, Mom. I just kept throwing the ball."

I've been thinking a lot recently about that beautifully simple philosophy. I'm not a quitter, but I have my limits. A friend and I have been trying for more than a year to work with a local business on an idea we think will help both the company and the community, but a lot of difficulties have blocked our way. I'm trying to use the ideas and the inspiration God has given me to make the project work, but I'm starting to doubt myself and am ready to give up. Then I hear Ross's innocent words. They're akin to Paul's encouragement of Timothy: Forge ahead, strengthened by God's power. Only then will I know, as Paul did, that "I have fought the good fight...[and] finished the race" (2 Timothy 4:7, RSV).

Win or lose, Paul's aim was to finish the task God set before him. I need to do the same. In my trials I'm learning that while God doesn't promise victory, He does offer a guarantee: If I "just keep throwing the ball," God will be beside me every step of the way.

Give me courage and strength, Lord, to follow through and finish the job.
—GINA BRIDGEMAN

April 3

Not that I complain of want; for I have learned,
in whatever state I am, to be content.
—Philippians 4:11 RSV

*W*hen our family lived in New Zealand, I wasn't sure what I missed most: my clothes dryer, dishwasher, or central heating. After rushing outside to rescue a load of clothes from a rainstorm—and burning a pot of pasta in the process—I decided it was the dryer I really missed.

The next morning I battled a black mood while running a load of laundry and listening to my preschooler's favorite music tape for the umpteenth time. When the washing machine spun to a stop, I scooped the wet clothes into a wicker basket and called, "Elizabeth, want to come outside with me?"

"No, I want to build with my blocks."

"Okay. I'll be back in a few minutes." I left her banging her blocks to the "Hokey Pokey" and headed for the yard. *Ah, silence.* As I pinned the clothes on the line, I heard the soothing sound of a little brook gurgling nearby and the chirping of birds. Stretching a sheet across two lines, I glimpsed the azure sky dotted with cotton-ball clouds and felt the warmth of the sun, which had not yet penetrated the house. "Thank You, Lord," I whispered.

Then I laughed. What I had considered a burden—going outside to hang up the laundry—turned out to be a blessing, forcing me outdoors to soak in nature's sounds and sights. And when I stepped inside, I brought the sunshine with me. I sat down on the floor to build a tower with my daughter, and we sang a chorus of "The Wheels on the Bus" along with her tape.

Is there a burden in your life that could be a blessing? For me it was a day without a dryer.

Lord, help me accept the trials in my life and see Your goodness.
—Mary Brown

APRIL 4

I sought the Lord, and he heard me, and delivered me from all my fears.
—PSALM 34:4

*M*y daughters Lindsay and Kendall gave me an unusual present on my fifty-something birthday—a gift certificate to get my ears pierced. For years I've resisted getting them pierced, even though my daughters and most of my friends have pierced ears. "I don't like the thought of getting two more holes in my head," I rationalized. "Besides, I've got plenty of clip-on earrings." But I rarely confessed the real reason: I was afraid of the pain.

"Mom, let's just do it," Lindsay told me as we sat at the kitchen counter.

"Yeah, Mom, pierced ears are cool," Kendall added. She knew she was hitting a vulnerable spot. I dread the thought of growing hopelessly uncool and stodgy as I get older, and I count on my daughters to tell me what's cool.

"I don't know...." I hesitated.

Just then my son Derek walked in. "Maybe you're right, Mom. At your age, why bother?" His comment sealed my resolve.

"Get the car keys and let's go," I said with finality.

Soon I found myself sitting in the middle of a busy mall where shoppers could stop and watch a nervous, middle-aged lady get her ears pierced. First the technician carefully marked an X on each ear lobe, then picked up the piercing gun and with a quick *pop, pop,* she was done. She gave me a handheld mirror, and I could hardly believe myself. I had pierced ears!

"Wow," I said, grinning. "Let's go celebrate!"

> *Father, I know pierced ears don't have a thing to do*
> *with my "cool quotient" in Your eyes, but thank You for daughters*
> *who care enough to help me not to stay stuck in my fears.*
> —CAROL KUYKENDALL

APRIL 5

And they were in the way going up to Jerusalem; and Jesus went
before them...and as they followed, they were afraid.
—MARK 10:32

They had reason to be afraid, these disciples following their stubborn leader into the stronghold of His enemies. To me this reluctant trip represents the journeys in my own life that I don't want to take. One of them was to the nursing home in Sudbury, Massachusetts, where my elderly mother was dying. I'd made the five-hour drive from New York many times, but this one, I knew, would be the last. Our son had brought two-year-old Lindsay up from Florida, so I could show Mother her great-granddaughter. "Before she dies" were words we didn't say.

In Mother's room Lindsay sat very quietly on my lap. I'd worried that the sights and smells of a nursing home might be frightening for her or that Mother's beautifully wrinkled face might seem forbidding. After perhaps half an hour, Lindsay began to squirm. "She's sat about as long as a two-year-old can," I apologized to Mother.

I set Lindsay down and took her hand to lead her to the door. She pulled free and ran straight to where her great-grandmother sat bent in her wheelchair. Reaching up a tiny hand, she stroked Mother's cheek. Again and again, that gentle stroking. Mother's eyes opened, blue as the little girl's, and the two smiled at each other.

Watching, it seemed to me that Jesus was showing me Mother as He saw her—not an old and ailing woman, but a wide-eyed young girl at the beginning of life. This vision of Mother has stayed with me through all the years since: Jesus' gift delivered by a child on the journey I didn't want to take.

"Jesus went before them." As He goes before each of us down every fearsome road.

Help me follow Your steps, Lord Jesus, into each and every day of my life.
—ELIZABETH SHERRILL

April 6

And Jesus, crying out with a loud voice, said, "Father, into Your hands
I commit My Spirit." And having said this, He breathed His last.

—Luke 23:46 NASB

The inevitable finally happened: Jesus was arrested on the night of Passover, interrogated, brutally tortured, and then condemned to the most shameful of deaths—crucifixion. Hanging on the cross in shock and pain, He gradually slipped into a coma. On the edge of the chasm between life and death, He felt rejection and despair and, according to Mark's gospel, shrieked, "My God, My God, Why have You forsaken Me?" (15:34, NASB).

Theologian William Barclay wonders if perhaps, in His final moments, as His vision blurred and His lungs could no longer breathe, Jesus gazed at His mother, standing at the foot of the cross, and remembered the bedtime prayer, echoing Psalm 31:5, that she, like every Jewish mother, taught her child to pray: "Into Your hands I commit my spirit."

Sometimes when confronted with the monstrous evil and destruction in our world, it's hard for me to believe that I haven't been abandoned. It's difficult to believe that love will conquer evil and that goodness will prevail. But in these very moments, I must whisper with childlike faith, "Father, into Your hands I commit my spirit."

Dear Father, please teach me, Your child, to pray
in the words Jesus uttered on the cross.

—Scott Walker

Therefore if any man be in Christ, he is a new creature:
old things are passed away; behold, all things are become new.
—2 CORINTHIANS 5:17

The Easter I was five, we were in the middle of the Great Depression. There was no money for new dresses for my sisters and me. But Mama dyed some old organdy curtains a lovely shade of mint green. Using a pattern cut from old newspapers, she cut the dresses out. Then she sewed them by hand, making French seams, and added wide ruffled collars. They were the most beautiful dresses I had ever seen.

Easter morning Mama dressed us in our finery, then brushed our hair into long curls and warned us to behave while she got dressed for church. My sisters sat quietly while I fidgeted in a big, scratchy chair. I had a bad habit of chewing on my collars, and soon my beautiful new dress was surely ruined. Ashamed of what I had done, I started to cry. Mama took one look, went to the sewing room and returned with another collar, complete with tiny snaps. She snapped off the chewed-up collar, and snapped on the new one.

"See, honey," she comforted me, "Mama made some extra ones for you—just in case."

I was so relieved to know that she knew my bad habit, anticipated it, and forgave me, that I never chewed a collar again.

God knows my sins. He foresaw my shortcomings long before I was born. He still loved me so very much that He sent Jesus to save me and the Holy Spirit to comfort me.

Lord, I thank You for anticipating my weaknesses and redeeming them.
—PAT SULLIVAN

For the gift bestowed upon us by the means of many persons thanks may be given.
—2 CORINTHIANS 1:11

*T*t was a wonderful Easter. Morning worship at our son Patrick's church in Texas featured an excellent choir and inspiring sermon. Our daughter-in-law Patricia prepared a veritable feast for dinner. Our traditional family egg hunt—held indoors because of spring snowflakes—ended with only two children in tears, and they were soon comforted.

Then my husband Don said, "We need to head home, so we can stop in Amarillo and get Penney's Easter surprise." I looked at Don, then at my smiling children and grandchildren. My heart dropped to my toes. Without thinking I blurted out, "Not a dog! It better not be a dog! The last thing I want or need is something else to take care of."

Shock, hurt, and dismay registered on every face. I tried to backtrack but, of course, I couldn't undo the damage. Finally Don said, "Will you at least look at her?"

I agreed, and Patrick found an old cat carrier for us, "just in case." You can guess what happened: I met a fat, wiggly ball of fur and promptly fell in love with Tarby, a golden chow.

Is she something else to care for? Oh yes. She has to be fed, watered, groomed, walked, and trained. Is she worth it? Absolutely. Her wagging tail and yips of "hello" never fail to lift my spirits. She's always ready to walk along with me or sit silently beside me. If I go away, whether for an hour or a week, she joyously welcomes me home.

The gift I didn't want turned out to be the next-to-best Easter surprise ever.

Gracious God, thank You for giving all of us the most precious Easter gift of all in the resurrection of Your only Son, Jesus the Christ.
—PENNEY SCHWAB

God has surely listened and heard my voice in prayer.
—PSALM 66:19 NIV

I've been noticing young mothers with their children lately. Maybe it's because my own children are now in their thirties and forties, and I like to remember what they were like when they were little.

On Easter morning I enjoyed seeing all the children dressed up for church in new pastel colors. The little girls wore hats and the small boys sported new suits. The young fellow who sat in front of us each Sunday wore a solid white suit with short pants. His hair was combed perfectly, and I couldn't help but steal glances at him sitting attentively next to his mother. When we stood to sing, he climbed up on the seat so he could see better. That's when I saw he was wearing very old, but obviously beloved cowboy boots with his new white suit. Had his mother forgotten to have him change shoes? He sang loudly and clapped along with the lively music about a risen Savior. He and his mother exchanged looks of pure love.

Sadly, I knew I would never have allowed one of my sons to wear those boots with a brand-new suit on such a special Sunday. We would have fought all morning, but I would never have relented. My unhappy child would have worn matching shoes to church, probably asking himself what a loving God had against cowboy boots.

As the pastor prayed, I peeked at the little boy. His head was bowed and his hands folded underneath his chin. He didn't move an inch. He may have been only four, but he had obviously come to worship with a happy heart.

Dear Lord, help my inside and outside to match
when I come to worship You. Amen.
—MARION BOND WEST

*And I John saw the holy city, new Jerusalem, coming down from God
out of heaven, prepared as a bride adorned for her husband.*
—REVELATION 21:2

*I*t's such a big church, mom," said my daughter Charlotte as we looked around St. Bartholomew's, the beautiful and spacious city church where we worship. "We'll need so many flowers—that'll be really expensive."

Weddings are like that. It's hard to keep one's mind on the holy and profound nature of the event when florists, dressmakers, and caterers keep tripping across the stage in the most distracting way. And then there's money. Of course, it's not supposed to be important in approaching this sacrament, but there aren't many families who aren't concerned about the amazing expense of a simple wedding.

Charlotte is both sensible and loving. "St. Bart's is beautiful, Mom. We don't need lots of flowers," she decided briskly. "Just an arrangement on the altar. The church will do the rest by itself." And I certainly wasn't going to argue.

The big day was in April, and as we stepped out of the car in front of the church, I suddenly noticed that the cherry trees along New York's Park Avenue had flowered almost overnight. They were all covered with a glorious mass of white blossoms.

As we entered the church through the big bronze doors, I gasped. This was the Saturday after Easter; for Easter, the church had been filled with flowers, including spectacular white hydrangeas high above the nave. I had assumed that their day of glory was past and they would have been swept neatly away. But now I saw that the hydrangeas were live plants, not bouquets, and they brought the springtime into the whole church.

All I could think, as my husband and I walked carefully and sedately down the aisle with our daughter, was that God had sent His own florist to the city streets and to the church—especially for Charlotte.

Lord, help me to appreciate Your divine generosity.
—BRIGITTE WEEKS

April 11

Thanks be to God for his indescribable gift!
—2 Corinthians 9:15 niv

I shouldn't have been snooping around in Mother's bedroom, but I suspected there were some things in there that I might be interested in. I'd noticed Mrs. Melton at church calling Mother aside to the trunk of her car and saying something about "clothes for Roberta." Mrs. Melton's daughter Paula was a few years ahead of me in school and had lovely clothes. I thought she might have given us something that I could wear to a concert at my junior high school that Friday night.

I wasn't disappointed. In a shopping bag were all sorts of designer clothes, the likes of which I'd only dreamed about. And just my size too! The outfit that really stole my heart was a royal blue wool tweed jumper with a dropped waist and a pleat in the center. A Peter Pan-collared blouse went with it, complete with kitten scatter pins. These were no ordinary hand-me-downs.

I confessed my snooping to Mother. "You can't wear those, honey," Mother said. "I know people mean well when they give us things, but it's embarrassing. Someday you'll understand."

"No one will know, Mother," I begged. "Paula doesn't even go to my school. Please."

But Mother was firm in her decision.

I've heard that when we get to heaven, there are going to be all kinds of unopened gifts with our names on them—the presents God provided for us while we were on earth that, for one reason or another, we never enjoyed. I've decided that in this new year, I don't want to miss one more of them. As a second thank-you to Mrs. Melton, I'm going to savor every present God places in my path this year.

Thank You, Lord Jesus, for all the indescribable gifts You have for me.
—Roberta Messner

April 12

Love...always perseveres.
—1 Corinthians 13:6–7 niv

*E*verything I'd read about labor and delivery promised ninety seconds of contractions maximum, with three to four minutes of relief in between. *I can handle that*, I thought. But the books lied, or else I missed the chapter about the labor-inducing drug that sent an army of torturers into my body every other minute for twenty hours! I was in shock from the intensity of the pain, and by the time I gave birth I was completely exhausted.

Perhaps I was still in a delivery-room fog, but the tiny baby now wrapped like a burrito and surrounded by family didn't quite feel like mine. "Do you feel like a parent yet," I asked my husband, hoping I wasn't the only one. Apparently I was.

Hours later, alone with the sleeping infant parked near my bed, everything still felt surreal. The baby was quiet and still like a doll, and had been asleep for hours. I needed sleep, too, but my body still hurt. I couldn't get comfortable, and every movement—no matter how small—was torture. Finally I drifted off, but just as my dream began, the little burrito woke me up. His loud, urgent cry penetrated deep inside me to a place I'd never known. It made me sit up, gritting through the pain as I inched toward my son. I picked him up and cradled him close to my body, and to our mutual relief the crying stopped. And during that peaceful moment, as I fed my little boy, I finally felt like a mother.

Thank You, Lord, for the love that even in pain can find a gift of joy.
—Karen Valentin

April 13

But remember the Lord your God, for it is he who gives you
the ability to produce wealth, and so confirms his covenant,
which he swore to your forefathers, as it is today.
—Deuteronomy 8:18 niv

*W*hen I picked up my six-year-old daughter from school, she was jumping around like a pogo stick. "Hey, kiddo," I said. "What's up with you?"

"Mommy, look!" Katherine showed me two quarters. "Nicholas paid me."

Boy? Money? My rather gullible daughter? All my systems went to red alert. "Paid you to do what?"

"Make paint for him."

"What did you use to make the paint?" I was suspicious, but then I still can't get the glue Katherine made from Play-Doh, wax, and something else off one of the porch chairs.

"Just rocks and dirt." My daughter did a little hopping dance around me. "And he liked it so much that he paid me."

I recalled the first time I had made money. I was five, and I pulled up half my mother's flower garden and went around the neighborhood, selling the flowers (dirt, roots, and all) from my little red wagon for a penny each. I had made about thirty cents before Mom caught up with me. Replanting flowers, by the way, is a lot harder than selling them.

"Good work, honey. So what are you going to buy with your quarters?" I could stop on the way home and let her get a treat for herself.

"I'm giving them to God at church," Katherine said. At my surprised look, she added, "The rocks and dirt are His, Mommy."

Heavenly Father, never let me forget that You are
the source of all bounties and blessings.
—Rebecca Kelly

The sheep follow him; for they know his voice.
—JOHN 10:4

*S*omeone gave my youngest son an orphan baby lamb. Since he works and goes to school, too, the chore of feeding Cuddles became mine. One night when the lamb was about three weeks old, my husband, Rex, and I were going out for the evening. I was rushing about trying to do my work and get ready to go. The lamb was crying for her bottle from her pen.

"We'll be late!" Rex warned.

"But I'm not ready, and Cuddles is starving. I have to take her a bottle."

"Give me the bottle. I'll do that," he said impatiently. He strode to the pen, hurriedly thrusting out the bottle of warm milk. "Here, lambie; here, lambie," he rumbled. But his was not the right voice. The small sheep stopped in her mad dash to reach the bottle. She shook her head in anger and suspicion, stamped small impatient feet. When Rex held the bottle closer to tempt her, she retreated just as far as she could. She ate only when I came and called her with the right voice.

Jesus is my Master. I long to respond as faithfully to His voice. Other voices speak to us, some of them well-intentioned, but only His leads us to eternal life.

Thank You so much, Father, that You keep calling until I hear You.
—LUCILLE CAMPBELL

APRIL 15

And let us not be weary in well doing: for in due season we shall reap, if we faint not.
—GALATIANS 6:9

I had arrived in Baltimore for a visit, and a friend and co-worker I hadn't seen in years picked me up at the airport. Once my student, she is now a teacher. She asked me how things were with me and my children.

"Lanea is working, finishing her degree program. She's very happy and independent. Chase will be a senior next year! Can you believe it?" I told her some stories about my two wonderful offspring. "How about you?"

"We're fine...if he survives," she laughingly said of her only son.

"Don't kill him. He's a good kid." We laughed together.

"Yeah," she said. "That's the funny thing. He is."

"You'll make it."

"You just don't understand." She shook her head as she switched lanes.

"Sure, I do. He's not doing his homework, and you think he might fail. And even worse," I tell her, "sometimes he does his homework but still doesn't turn it in, right?"

"How do you know that?"

"It's not just you. I try to tell other moms that it's not personal. I've been through it."

"Not *you*?"

"Yep."

"Not Chase?"

"Yep. Take a deep breath, be firm, but keep loving him. He'll grow out of it. Reassure him that he'll make it. Remind him of the good things he does, what a good person he is. I think it's adolescence or something. It's just a season. It's not the end of the world. Good things will come."

"Yeah," she said with a laugh, "if we make it through this fall."

Lord, thank You for allowing me to practice patience and unconditional love. Help me to see beyond the moment and put things in perspective, and give me hope for the great things to come.
—SHARON FOSTER

APRIL 16

Jesus saith unto her...I ascend to my Father,
and your Father; and to my God, and your God.
—JOHN 20:17

*M*y daughter and I were talking long-distance. The birth of her second child was imminent, and she had invited her father to be with her, though he would have to wait in the hospital's visitors lounge.

"It was so comforting last time knowing Dad was nearby," she said. "I guess I'm just a daddy's girl."

I felt a twinge. I'd also been at the hospital last time. Now I was in Southern California caring for my aged aunt, and I would miss this birth. Still, I wanted so much to ask, "Aren't you my girl too?"

All day long I couldn't push her "Daddy's girl" remark from my mind. I knew parenting wasn't a competition, but her words hurt. I lay in bed that night feeling lonely and left out. "Father," I prayed, "where do I fit in?"

His answer came quietly to my heart, *You're a daddy's girl too. You're My girl.*

Peace filled me. Here was the essential relationship for me and my family: We were each a child of God. Everyone had a place. Everyone belonged.

I drifted to sleep, thankful for the bond between my daughter and her dad, secure in my place as her mother, and safe in the arms of God.

> *How blessed I am, my God, to reap the richness of the mystery*
> *of both father and mother love, held within Your heart for me.*
> —CAROL KNAPP

APRIL 17

A time to mourn, and a time to dance.
—ECCLESIASTES 3:4

was napping when the phone rang. "I've got bad news," said my brother. "When I stopped to see Mother, I found her on the floor. She'd apparently fallen and hit her head on a table corner. She's dead."

Mother was seventy-six, in reasonable health, and still living comfortably alone. My brother, a doctor, made a point of stopping to check on her every day at noon. On this day she was suddenly gone. No chance for a last hug, an expression of appreciation or a regretful good-bye. I missed her most painfully whenever something good happened. My first thought was, *Oh, Mother will be so pleased!* But I couldn't tell her. She was gone, leaving a huge space in my life.

So I have learned something about mourning, and my bigger question is, "How does a grieving person move from mourning to dancing?"

The Voice within replies:

> *I feel your pain and grief, my child,*
> *for death has walked before Me too.*
> *It takes away your loved ones*
> *to where you cannot follow.*
> *But you can choose to dwell*
> *in loving moments lived,*
> *or cling to sorrow and live a broken life.*
> *You can choose to cling to your loss*
> *or you can learn to dance again.*

O Holy One, comfort all who grieve today. Hold them close till they can once again make the choice for life. Then let the dance begin!
—MARILYN MORGAN KING

My times are in thy hand.
—PSALM 31:15

*A*lthough I dearly loved my mother-in-law, I dreaded the times when she traveled to visit us. She took the arrival time printed on an airline ticket as a guarantee and fretted if a flight was even a few minutes late.

When she planned to visit us in Uganda in the early 1960s, John and I wrote to warn her that East Africa was often in turmoil and flights were erratic. As the day of her arrival approached, we made the eighteen hour drive to Nairobi, Kenya, and were parked by the landing field at her plane's scheduled arrival time.

Of course, we brought along food and lots of bottled water and games and schoolbooks to keep the children occupied. To our delight, instead of the ten- or twelve-hour wait we were prepared for, Mother Sherrill's plane touched down only four-and-a-half hours later. As the steps were rolled up to the aircraft, we stood at the barrier to watch the passengers deplane.

The door opened and Mother burst onto the gangway; she must have been literally pressing against the door. Our welcome was drowned out in a volley of tearful apologies. It took a good part of the drive back to Uganda to convince her that no, we hadn't been worried; no, the late arrival hadn't spoiled our plans.

And as I tried to reassure Mother, I seemed to hear a silent voice speaking to me too. Living in developing countries had taught John and me that trip schedules were not in our control. But what about my schedule for the spiritual journey? What about the timetable I set up for prayers to be answered? What about my impatience over someone's slowness to see the truth I saw? Like Mother pushing on an airplane door, didn't I often strain at delays as though the timing of spiritual growth—mine and others'—was in my hands?

Lord of the journey, help me to rest in Your perfect time.
—ELIZABETH SHERRILL

"Because you are precious in my eyes, and honored, and I love you."
—ISAIAH 43:4 RSV

*T*t was time to say good-bye to my little granddaughter Hannah. Our far-flung family had gathered for a rare reunion. Now Hannah was continuing on to visit her other set of grandparents. As she waited in her car seat in the rented van, I leaned in and said, "You have lots of fun with Grandma Patti."

Hannah was quiet for a moment. I could tell she was thinking hard about something; perhaps she was visualizing the special things she and her other grandmother would do. Then she looked at me intently, and in her no-frills four-year-old style she said, "But I will still love you." Hannah's heart held a space for me no matter who else was there.

I've thought about Hannah's words a lot since then. They remind me of the way God loves me. He has billions of people to attend to, but He still loves me. He sees all my failures and mistakes, but He still loves me. He knows my every thought and doubt, but He still loves me. And I have the sure sign of His love for me in the shape of the cross on which His Son died.

Lord, in all the times and places of my life, Your love never leaves me.
—CAROL KNAPP

"All your children shall be taught by the Lord,
And great shall be the peace of your children."
—ISAIAH 54:13 NKJV

*M*y daughter was about to make another trip abroad with just her backpack. I was worried. How was she going to buy food, find safe places to sleep, travel on reliable modes of transportation? All this costs money, much more than she had.

"Mom, you're just going to have to let go of me," she said impatiently.

But how could I let her go so far away? Wasn't that the same as abandoning my duty as a parent?

About this time, a friend gave me a poem by an unknown author to help me understand what letting go really means:

To let go does not mean to stop caring; it means I can't do it for someone else.
To let go is not to be in the middle, arranging all the outcomes,
    but to allow other persons to affect their own destinies.
To let go is not to fix but to be supportive.
To let go is not to be protective; it's to permit another to face reality.
To let go is to fear less and to love more.

When you love someone deeply, letting go is incredibly hard. But I realized I must let go, for I do not own what I love. Now, when I look at my daughter happily settled in Australia with the man she loves, doing work she's passionate about, I know that God has done much more than I could have imagined. And it happened because I got out of the way and let Him do it.

Father, thank You for Your promise that "all your children shall be taught by the Lord, and great shall be the peace of your children" (Isaiah 54:13, NKJV).
—HELEN GRACE LESCHEID

For we know that if the earthly tent which is our house is torn down, we have a building from God, a house not made with hands, eternal in the heavens.

—2 CORINTHIANS 5:1 NASB

*M*y mother adored my little log cabin, and it was a special place of refuge for her when her cancer became terminal. When the hospital discharged her, Mother came to live her last days with me. Those rock-solid log walls became the backdrop for a hospital bed, suction machine, and oxygen tanks, as friends gathered around with home-cooked meals and comforting words.

Some months before, I'd designed a sign and hung it in the front yard by the arbor. It featured an angel and the words, ON THE WAY TO SOMEWHERE ELSE, communicating the conviction Mother and I shared, that life is a journey where divine opportunities are often disguised as detours.

The afternoon of Mother's death, as the mortuary staff carried her tired and tattered earthly body through the screened-in porch she so loved, we children followed behind. When we came up the cobblestone path leading back to the house, I saw the words as if for the very first time: ON THE WAY TO SOMEWHERE ELSE.

With the Lord rebuilding my home and heart, my once-frightening detour had become the setting for Mother's ultimate journey: to her eternal home in the heavens not made with hands.

Dear Lord, help me always to make my heart Your home.
—ROBERTA MESSNER

I will always be ready to remind you of these things,
even though you already know them.
—2 PETER 1:12 NASB

I've always been a compulsive photographer. Four-year-old Solomon has eleven large albums dedicated to him. Henry, our six-month-old, is quickly getting used to my constant picture-taking that accompanies every one of his milestones: smiles, sitting up, reaching for a toy, a funny face while eating bananas.

Solomon's first sentence, "No cheese, Mama," had nothing to do with food. It was a protest against my incessant camera-pointing and my instruction to "Say cheese!"

Our bookcases have been taken over by photo albums. My office desk has stacks of pictures from last year's Easter egg hunt, the Fourth of July parade, and our summer vacation on Cape Cod, and now my computer files are overflowing with still more photos.

"You guys are such proud parents," a friend of mine remarked at the legion of photos I had taken commemorating Solomon's graduation from preschool.

"It's not that," I said.

"What then?" she asked.

I shrugged.

Later that night as I washed Henry's baby spoon, I realized what my picture taking is really about. Each photo is my attempt to keep them young, so that years from now, when they're grown, I'll still have my little boys.

Lord, it's good to watch them grow, but let me
never forget the way they are today.
—SABRA CIANCANELLI

The small change of human happiness lies in the unexpected, friendly word.
—ANONYMOUS

*I*n the midst of my kitchen chores I was surprised to have the front door swing open. Julie, our oldest child, came in. She'd been married three months. I was still trying to get used to her living elsewhere. Sometimes I even unconsciously set her place at the table.

Julie handed me a small bunch of daffodils and said, "Guess what!" as she opened the refrigerator and bent to see what was inside. As I put the flowers in water, I answered happily, "What?"

She began telling me some small details of her new life as she made herself a sandwich. She'd learned to make pineapple-upside-down cake, from scratch, and in college she was now giving injections in the medical course she was taking. We sat at the kitchen table, and I watched her eat, hanging on to her every word.

It was a short visit. Julie had to go to work. I thanked her for the flowers and for stopping by; then walked to the door with her and waved as she drove out of the driveway.

Back in the kitchen I sat and looked at the flowers. My daughter's visit was as bright and dear as the early spring daffodils. Suddenly, I picked up the phone and dialed my own mother's number. She lived a hundred miles away. When she answered, I said, "Guess what!"

"What?" she answered expectantly. Like Julie I didn't have any big news, just little details of the day, tidbits about the children. But I'd come to understand in the last hour how precious small talk can be. Just before I hung up, my mother said, "You made my day."

> *Father, thank You for my mother and my children*
> *and the circle of love we're inside.*
> —MARION BOND WEST

But in fact God has arranged the parts in the body,
every one of them, just as he wanted them to be.
—1 CORINTHIANS 12:18 NIV

I read recently that by the time you reach age seventy-five, you might easily have slept the equivalent of twenty-five years of your life. I think I've already spent at least that much time watching. Last week I watched my son Ross play trombone in a jazz band, my daughter Maria dance in a recital, and my husband Paul's barbershop quartet in concert. Soon, I'll begin the springtime rite of sitting on hard metal bleachers watching countless hours of high-school baseball.

I was telling my mom that maybe I should be doing more and watching less when she laid the truth on me in her reliably sensible way. "We all can't be stars," she said. "Somebody has to watch, or it would take all the fun out of performing." Then I remembered how our daughter rushed up to us after last year's school musical. "Did you see my dance?" she wanted to know. The fact that Mom and Dad had seen her seemed as important as the dance itself.

My mom also pointed out that there's more to my role than simply watching: Somebody has to drive to rehearsals, get the piano tuned, and volunteer to bring the post-game snack. None of that may be glamorous, but I've learned that the performance—or whatever form that "starring role" takes—couldn't happen without the supporting players. We watchers play an important role in the lives of others, who need to know that someone is cheering especially for them.

Lord, whether watcher or doer, help me find my place in Your great creation,
knowing that it's the exact place You have planned for me.
—GINA BRIDGEMAN

Feed me with the food that is needful for me.
—PROVERBS 30:8 RSV

*T*took Maggie to the dentist yesterday. At six years old, she's had more dental bills than the rest of my children combined. While three-year-old Stephen and I waited for the drilling to be done, I read him a book in which rather saccharine animals preached oral hygiene. Brush twice a day. Floss. Drink tap water. Don't eat sweets. Don't eat sticky snacks like dried fruit or granola bars.

Wait a minute—raisins are dried fruit. Can't my kids eat raisins? The thought gave me a headache. We've already done away with candy and most sweets. I take into account low fat, good vs. bad cholesterol, a balance between Omega-3 and Omega-6 oils, and limited use of processed foods. I eliminated the foods to which my children are allergic (fortunately, only nuts and shellfish). Then I have to factor in what we can afford to eat, and the likes and dislikes of seven individuals. Oh, and don't forget how much time I have available to prepare the food. That goes into the equation too. It's impossible even if raisins aren't a forbidden fruit.

But after mentally banging my head against the wall, I settled down to itemize what was left for my shopping list: a variety of meat, poultry, fresh vegetables, fruit, and two eggs a day; dried beans, honey, molasses; whole-grain bread; milk, yogurt, and cheese; sweets and carbs in moderation. Good stuff, food my great-grandmother ate, with ingredients whose names she'd recognize. I cook it with less fat and better equipment, but maybe feeding a family isn't any harder today than it used to be.

Lord, help me to be thankful for the simple gifts You give.
—JULIA ATTAWAY

I tell you, now is the time of God's favor, now is the day of salvation.
—2 CORINTHIANS 6:2 NIV

few weeks ago, our oldest son Sam told us that he'd been thinking about taking a year off from college, perhaps in a program abroad. I was glad he was looking for new challenges, but I felt a pang of sadness at the thought that he might be so far away.

Today, I sat on a plane next to Sam's brother Ned, traveling home from a cross-country trip to visit several universities as he decides where he'll spend his next four years. It's been a wonderful trip for my husband Matt and me as we watched Ned experiencing the world opening up before him and imagining his future in exciting new ways. Yet today, as we sat side by side in companionable silence, I felt sad knowing he wouldn't be beside me much in the coming year.

Before long, the in-flight movie commenced and together we watched the story of a man, his wife and family, and their mischievous Labrador retriever. It reminded me so much of our own family and Nellie, our delightful and very poorly trained black Lab! But when a scene opened with a veterinarian in it and the dog lying on a table, I found tears streaming down my face. Our Nellie is ten years old, and I immediately thought about the fact that we may not have too many more years with her.

Then I looked over at Ned; I was sharing a wonderful moment in his life. My husband was by my side, holding my hand. I would get to see Sam again next weekend. And when I walked through the door of our house tonight, Nellie would come bounding to greet me, with a big doggy grin and a wag that made her whole body wiggle.

Dear God, please help me to live in the here and now, to experience this moment and all the love I feel in it to its fullest, and bring that love to all I do today.
—ANNE ADRIANCE

That My joy might remain in you, and that your joy might be full.
—JOHN 15:11

*S*itting in front of a shopping center waiting for a friend the other day I was feeling impatient and fretful because she was late. The passing parade wasn't helping much. Whining children tugged impatiently at their mothers' coats. Some were even screaming. The mothers wore grim expressions. Their expressions seemed to match my mood.

Then a mother and her child came out of the store, and I shall never forget them. Never. She was the happiest-looking mother I'd ever seen. And her son was wondrously contented. They weren't aware of other people at all.

The young mother was in a wheelchair and held the little boy on her lap. She managed the chair herself. They appeared to be alone. She rolled them out of the store and, once on the sidewalk, she did a little fancy spin. Round and round they went as the little boy laughed out loud. She did too. I could almost hear the child think, *Look at my mama. Isn't she something!* Then they disappeared into the crowd. When my friend came I was still smiling, and I uttered a silent prayer:

Father, teach me again that joy never depends on circumstances.
—MARION BOND WEST

Adam called his wife's name Eve; because she was the mother of all living.
—GENESIS 3:20

What to get my wife Carol for Mother's Day? There was a book she wanted and a CD. The boys had made cards...but it'd be nice to show her how much I appreciate all that she does: the cooking, the carpooling, the shopping, supervising the homework, arranging the doctors' appointments and music lessons.

"Take the day off," I said. "Enjoy yourself."

"Really?"

"Sure. We'll be fine."

That Sunday Timothy and I did the week's grocery shopping and got dinner ready, and I supervised his homework. In the late afternoon I took him to his soccer game and brought him home. But just as we pulled into the driveway, he frowned. "Dad, I think I left my sweatshirt back at the field."

"Are you sure?"

He nodded gravely.

An hour later we returned home after searching the field in the waning light. "Where have you been?" Carol asked.

"A little detour," I said. How to explain that the dirty sweatshirt on her son's back was part of her present? "I guess I found out how complicated your days really are," I said. "Happy Mother's Day!"

> *God, help me remember how much work it takes to be a mother.*
> —RICK HAMLIN

The Lord hath appeared of old unto me, saying,
Yea, I have loved thee with an everlasting love.
—JEREMIAH 31:3

*R*ecently, I ran across a pile of my mother's hankies I'd stashed away after her death nearly ten years ago, and a flood of memories suddenly surfaced.

The nine-inch square of voile with lavender daisies in one corner reminded me I used to tuck it in the pocket of my best dress—with its four points peeking out "just so"—when I had a date. Beneath it was a smaller, mostly blue hankie featuring Peter Rabbit. Mom knotted my nickel in one of its corners so I wouldn't lose it on the way to Sunday school.

The most colorful hankie announced its presence in the pile because red poinsettias and green leaves marched clear around its border. Back then I carried it only at Christmastime. Near the bottom of the stack was one with edging Mom had tatted, along with an embroidered "Isabel" in red in the center.

I recalled, too, how Mom's handkerchiefs always smelled like lily of the valley; how she'd dampen a hankie's corner to clean a spot from my face; how she'd wrap one around a cut finger and the hurt immediately felt better.

Well, I'm preserving Mom's prettiest handkerchiefs—on which the scent magically lingers—by using them on pillow tops, framing them to hang on walls, using them as doilies beneath a pretty dish. This way, they serve as reminders of the days when I took them to church and Mom kept me amused during long sermons by making "twin babies in a cradle": folding the hankie into a triangle, rolling the two opposite ends toward the middle for the "babies," pulling the other two points back against themselves for the "cradle," gently swinging the hankie to make the cradle rock. Can't do that with a tissue, you know.

Thank You, Heavenly Father, for reminders that
You still love Your kids—no matter what our ages.
—ISABEL WOLSELEY

What time I am afraid, I will trust in Thee.
—PSALM 56:3

When our son John was two years old, he fell off the deck of our house. His fear of heights since that incident has been almost a phobia, so when his Boy Scout troop was planning a ski trip, John had mixed emotions. He really wanted to go, but he was also afraid he'd "chicken out" when it came time to get on the chair lift or start down the slopes. My friend Linda suggested I teach John to hold onto the thought of God's constant protection, and she offered a specific way to do this. "I taught this to my daughter," said Linda, "when she gave up her security blanket. So I call it a security prayer."

At the end of his nightly prayers, John was to say over and over in his mind as he was falling asleep, "The love of God protects me." By the date of the ski trip, the truth of those words was firmly implanted in John's heart. He repeated the security prayer in his mind as he learned to ski, and came home elated because he had conquered his fear, with God's help.

I'm fearful sometimes, too, aren't you? Maybe you and I could increase our awareness of God's constant protection by using Linda's security prayer. I'm going to try it. How about you?

The love of God protects me. Yes!
—MARILYN MORGAN HELLEBERG

May

But if any widow has children or grandchildren, let them first learn to show piety at home and to repay their parents; for this is good and acceptable before God.
—1 TIMOTHY 5:4 NKJV

ven though it was one of those gorgeous days in Florida, I was feeling lonely and left out because it was my son Michael's thirty-seventh birthday, and he was a thousand miles away in Cincinnati, Ohio. I missed all four of my children and their families, scattered in California, Wisconsin, and Ohio. I was feeling envious of my snowbird friends who only come to Florida for the winter and then head back north to be near their kids and grandkids.

I'd already left two messages on Michael's home phone and two on his cell phone. *Where is he?* I'd sung "Happy Birthday" off-key—twice—and wanted to talk to my son! Finally, late that night, I checked my messages and there was a long, over-the-top-happy message from Michael. "Mom, it's been a great day! We all went to church. Then Amy and the kids took me out to brunch and then home, where I opened gifts. Thanks for the shirts and the tie—they're terrific! Then I got to play golf with a good friend all afternoon on a perfect, gorgeous day. Right now I'm relaxing in my hammock, Amy's baking my birthday cake, the pizza's on its way, and later I'm going to go play basketball. Mom, sometimes I feel like an old man, but my wonderful wife and kids made this such an extra-special day for me that I can't complain. I even loved your singing. Call me! I love you!"

I couldn't have topped that day for my son, no matter what I did. I didn't get to hug him in person, but that phone call sure made me feel like I'd been hugged.

Lord, help me to treasure every phone call, e-mail, letter, and visit with my kids and to be grateful they're all on their own making their own happiness.
—PATRICIA LORENZ

MAY 2

I'd just stuck a nickel in the slot of the pay phone when an operator came on the line and said, "That will be another five cents, please."

"But I already put in a nickel," I protested.

"The cost is now ten cents," was her answer.

Well, I didn't have another nickel, so I had to be consoled with having my original five-cent piece plink into the metal cup below. At least it was returned.

In our area, the increase came in 1951, when television was still such a brand-new medium we gawkers stopped and stared at the test patterns on TV sets on display in appliance-store windows. I remember the date because I'd just learned I'd been accepted to a school that trained hopefuls for on-camera work, and I couldn't wait to get home to call a friend with my exciting news.

A dime remained the price of a telephone call until 1985. I recall that date because my son had just bought his ten-year-old daughter a pair of "penny loafers," the kind with a slot in its top side, just the right size for inserting a coin. "Here's a dime for each of your new shoes," I said. "Always keep them there so you'll be able to phone someone if you need to."

"Grandma, don't you know it takes a quarter to call anybody?" No, I didn't. I resisted the impulse to reminisce about what I used to be able to buy for a dime and that there were live operators "when I was your age." She might realize I was older than she'd already thought. Certainly I wasn't about to tell her I could even remember a song titled "Hello Central, Give Me Heaven." I'd have to try explaining what Central was.

*How grateful I am, heavenly Father, that it costs nothing to talk to You.
What's more, Your line is never busy—and You're never too busy to listen.*
—ISABEL WOLSELEY

All thy children shall be taught of the Lord;
and great shall be the peace of thy children.
—Isaiah 54:13

*M*y son Chase stands over six feet tall. Looking at him, his beautiful ebony skin contrasting with the pale colors of his blue-and-white choir robe, my heart aches with pride at the man he has become. He's much younger than the other choir members and the only African American.

My daughter Lanea and I are visiting the church Chase attends each Sunday. He sings, and they pay him a small honorarium. It's an answer to prayer. "Please, Lord, find Chase a church home while he's away," I prayed as he packed his things to leave for school. "And he needs a little pocket change. And, oh, by the way, does he know the Lord's Prayer by heart?"

My son hugged me and smiled down at me. "I know the Lord's Prayer, Mom. Relax."

Before he was conceived, his father prayed for a son who'd look just like him, and Chase came into being, a gift from God. After his father died, I worried and prayed that Chase would not become a statistic. An African American, father deceased, no male role models in the home, being raised by a single mom—it all added up to disaster. So I prayed. When pneumonia threatened his childhood, I prayed. When a snowboarding accident and peer pressure threatened his teens, I prayed.

Chase has survived, flourished, and is now enrolled in the North Carolina School for the Arts in Winston-Salem, where he's studying opera. As I listen to the choir, I can hear his powerful sometimes tenor, sometimes baritone voice rising above the others. He's singing the Lord's Prayer. And I know that all my prayers have been answered.

Thank You, Lord, for being a father to the fatherless and a husband to widows.
—Sharon Foster

MAY 4

O Lord, thou hast searched me, and known me.
—PSALM 139:1 NRSV

O n the morning thirty years ago when my son was put into my arms, I waited until the nurse was out of the room and then, my eye still on the door, I pulled loose the deftly bound blanket and began to examine the tiny person it had hidden.

He seemed perfect to me, even the crooked little toes, so like his father's large ones. I marveled, as any new mother might, that this wonderful child had grown for these past nine months inside my body.

And I wasn't the only one. Everyone thought he was beautiful. Why, the first words the nurse had said in the delivery room were, "Look at those eyelashes! Wouldn't you know? Wasted on a boy."

Someday I thought, stroking his silky cheek, *someday, he's going to have to shave.* I laughed aloud at the thought.

The psalmist remembers that same wonder over the creation of a person when he says in Psalm 139:13–14: "For it was you who formed my inward parts; you knit me together in my mother's womb. I praise you, for I am fearfully and wonderfully made."

As I read the Psalm this morning, I see the Parent of us all bending in love over me. And I see that the marvel we share in God's creation is nothing new. Yet it is new for every parent at every birth. God not only made me, God loves me, searching me with the eyes of a love-struck mother marveling over her newborn child.

> *Let me know, O God, Your tender searching love*
> *that awakens in me the desire for You.*
> —KATHERINE PATERSON

MAY 5

Therefore shall a man leave his father and his mother,
and shall cleave unto his wife: and they shall be one flesh.
—GENESIS 2:24

As I began helping my daughter Kendall plan her wedding, I needed plenty of advice, so I attached myself to friends who had already been through this experience.

"Beware of the tensions that can flare up in a mother-daughter relationship at this hectic time, filled with so many decisions," one warned me.

"You'll get along better if you just let her make most of the decisions," said another. "In fact, it's probably best if you simply have no opinion."

Kendall and I did just fine with cake flavors and flower colors and musical selections. But I was surprised by the passion I felt about one choice. It had to do with the lighting of the unity candle, a part of the ceremony that symbolizes the couple's two lives becoming one. Usually, the mothers come forward before the wedding party enters and light two separate candles, representing the bride and groom. Then, following the vows, the bride and groom take the two candles and together light the single unity candle. Now here's the choice: Do they blow out their individual candles, or leave them burning? "You don't snuff out who you are in your new union," I told Kendall. "You continue to grow as individuals, even when you're married."

"Mom, I appreciate your opinion. David and I will talk about it," Kendall calmly answered, which was her tactful way of letting me know this would be their decision.

Later I told one of my mentor-friends about our little conflict.

"Often the tensions have nothing to do with the decision at hand, but with other emotions we're feeling," she said.

Her remark helped me recognize the real fears behind my feelings. It wasn't so much about snuffing out their individuality in marriage, but about snuffing out their connections to their families. It was about learning to let go—about leaving and cleaving.

Lord, help me to bring my fears to You, and trust
Your provisions, for You have ordained this "letting go."
—CAROL KUYKENDALL

MAY 6

Whether we live therefore, or die, we are the Lord's.
—ROMANS 14:8

I am walking in the woods, spring violets peeking through the dead leaves, when suddenly I recall a childhood memory. I am ten years old. Mother, an apron tied over her work dress, is talking to me. "I think we could grow some violets here," she says, pointing to a shady spot. I stare at the bare patch of ground near the corner of our farmhouse.

"We could dig them in the woods." Already she is moving toward the tractor shed for the shovel.

Soon Mother and I are headed through the gate toward the back pasture and the woods that border it. I am not sure how much help my small hands will be, but I like being with Mother, being a part of whatever she suggests we do together. We easily find a patch of violets, and Mother begins to dig. Carefully I wrap the plants in the newspaper we've brought and nest them into a small basket.

"I think that will be enough, don't you?" I nod.

The month of May is a difficult one for me. Next Sunday is Mother's Day; a week later, it's Mother's birthday; and the end of the month brings Memorial Day. Those first few Mays after Mother's death, I could scarcely comprehend how one small set of squares on the calendar could hold so much sadness.

My grief has mellowed over the years. The hurt is more like a tender spot than it is a gaping wound. Life has gone on. The violets Mother and I dug and replanted that spring took hold and bloomed every year until we sold that farm and moved to another. I like to think they might be blooming still.

You are Lord of life and death. I place myself—
and my loved ones—in Your eternal care.
—MARY LOU CARNEY

[God] is able to do exceeding abundantly above all that we ask or think.
—EPHESIANS 3:20

*P*lease pray that I can find the right place for my mother," my friend Denise asked when she had to move her mother from the house in Brooklyn where she'd lived for thirty-six years to an assisted-living facility.

"The problem," she told me, "is Muffy."

Muffy was a Brittany spaniel. "Mom's had so many losses—Dad, my brother, most of her friends. Muffy is her lifeline!"

And that created a dilemma. Some of the places Denise visited had a no-pets rule. At others, the problem was the health-care aides her mother would need. They were allergic, or fearful, or from cultures where animals were never brought indoors.

At last Denise located an attractive retirement community where, she was assured, the dog would be welcomed by all concerned. Over a strenuous weekend, Denise got her mother and belongings moved to her new home, only to have the aides refuse to enter the apartment with the dog there. Denise was frantic, taking weeks off from work to provide her mother's daily care.

What about those prayers? I wondered. Why had faith and effort resulted in such a wrong choice?

But as it turned out, they hadn't.

Bringing Muffy back from his morning walk one day, Denise noticed a man helping his wife from a car into a wheelchair beside a pile of suitcases. Seeing the dog, their faces lit up. "A Brittany spaniel!" the man exulted. "We haven't seen one since ours died last year. Looked just like this one!"

"Does he live here?" the wife asked hopefully. "Would you bring him to visit us now and again?"

It even "happened" that the apartment they were moving into was directly across the hall from Denise's mother—and the man handled his wife's care himself. Muffy lives with them now, and Denise's mother visits him and her new friends every day.

> *Father, I'd forgotten that Your answers to prayer*
> *always encompass more than just the needs I know of.*
> —ELIZABETH SHERRILL

"Today I am reminded of my shortcomings."
—GENESIS 41:9 NIV

My son Ross was preparing for the SAT, searching the house for pencils to take to the college entrance exam. "We must make a lot of mistakes around here," he said, laughing, "because all I can find are pencils with no erasers."

He had a point. I make my share of mistakes and not just when I'm writing. Just last week, angry about a friend's criticism, I spoke too harshly to her. Now the friendship is in trouble. I regretted my words and wondered why I couldn't control my tongue. What does God do with mistake-makers? I asked myself.

Turning to the Bible for some sort of answer, I was surprised to see that God puts His mistake-makers to work. For instance, the disciple Peter was devastated by his denying Jesus. But not only did he find forgiveness, he went on to be used by God to bring thousands to Christ. In another passage, the apostle Paul says he wants to do what is good but somehow can't seem to do it. Still, God used him to bring the Gospel to the entire Gentile world.

Maybe I needn't feel so bad about my house full of eraserless pencils. At least they show that we try to correct our mistakes. I needed to do that with my friend: apologize for being so quick-tempered. Maybe my mistake wouldn't mean the end of our friendship.

> *Mistakes are never the end of the line with You, God.*
> *Thank You for Your forgiveness, the ultimate eraser.*
> —GINA BRIDGEMAN

MAY 9

A time to laugh....
—ECCLESIASTES 3:4

I was babysitting three of my grandchildren, and it was time to bathe two-year-old Thomas. I got him and all his toys into the tub, and began to wash him, sitting at an angle on the edge so I could continue talking with Jamie and Katie, his sisters. Then, before I could catch myself, I lost my balance, slipped backward, and fell into the tub—fully clothed.

My granddaughters laughed hysterically. Thomas, observing them for a few seconds, threw his head back and joined in the laughter. As I sat in the warm water with my arms and legs extended, I felt this tremendous laugh making its way out. I leaned against the pink tiles and let it come. The four of us were joined together by our laughter, which lasted for perhaps three minutes and was exhausting and satisfying and unforgettable.

Of course, I wouldn't have laughed in my young motherhood days. I would have resented anything that made me look less than perfect, and would have been in a nasty mood for the rest of the evening, probably not speaking. And we would never have mentioned the incident again.

I'm glad I have finally learned—through experience, age, and God's grace—that there's a time to laugh, even at myself and my humanness.

Father, help me to see the lighter side of things.
—MARION BOND WEST

MAY 10

Your love has given me great joy and encouragement,
because you...have refreshed the hearts of the saints.
—PHILEMON 7 NIV

I don't wear a lot of makeup. But today I'm going to have brunch with my daughter and talk about her wedding next year. So, as I stood before the mirror, I reached out for a lipstick and began to put it on. As the light brown color rolled smoothly on, I realized with a sudden flash—a mix of joy and pain—where that lipstick had come from.

Months before, as I was convalescing from a long illness, a friend had encouraged me to stop hiding and to stop feeling that I couldn't manage the routine of daily life. Her idea? "Come out to lunch," she said. "We'll go to the little restaurant across the street."

Across the street seemed to me like crossing the Red Sea. But I did as I was told, put on an outfit that had hung untouched in my closet for months, and crossed the street. My friend was already there, sitting at a comfortable table by the window looking out over the busy street, where people were going calmly about their daily lives. After we had ordered our lunch, she handed me a small gift bag. "Here," she said, "you need this."

Surprised, I looked into the bag. And there was a lipstick. Not a garish or brightly colored lipstick, but the one I am wearing today as I go with delight and eagerness to meet my daughter. After that lunch with my friend, I carefully put on the lipstick and began to look forward.

Thank You, Lord, for the support of friends
and the grace-filled touch of a lipstick.
—BRIGITTE WEEKS

But thou art a God ready to pardon, gracious and merciful.
—NEHEMIAH 9:17

*M*other's Day was a bit of a downer for my mom when I was growing up because our pastor's annual sermon was based on the thirty-first chapter of Proverbs. Always. In fact, I had it memorized by the time I was ten.

This particular chapter describes the attributes of the perfect woman. But Mom took its words so literally, she'd pull out a lace-trimmed handkerchief— the one with "Mother" in the middle of embroidered daisies—and dab her eyes while she pondered how short she'd fallen of the biblical ideal.

One year her tears started with the reading of "She openeth her mouth with wisdom; and in her tongue is the law of kindness." She remembered that mere hours before, she'd admonished me, "Why aren't you dressed for church? If I told you once, I told you a dozen times. Now get ready!"

I remembered that too. And after being scolded, I was in no mood to try being one of the perfect kids also depicted in that chapter: "Her children arise up, and call her blessed."

More tears and an hour later, Pastor told the congregation, "When we turn to page one twenty-six for our closing hymn, 'Faith of Our Fathers,' substitute the word mothers for fathers because it truly is through the faith of their mothers that little ones learn the straight and narrow way." Mom's tears intensified, and then I felt guilty at being the cause of them.

Fortunately, Pastor concluded the service with an encouraging benediction: "Lord, we can't undo our mistakes or begin our lives over, but You are a forgiving God, and You give us another brand-new day to try again."

That made me feel better. Mom, too—because I heard her, and others around us, whisper a relieved and thankful "Amen."

Lord, today and every day, help me to put my mistakes behind me and try again.
—ISABEL WOLSELEY

MAY 12

There is more pleasure in loving than in being loved.
—THOMAS FULLER

I sat looking out the church window. It was Mother's Day and I hadn't heard from my son. *He's forgotten,* I thought, shifting uneasily in my seat. Of course my son and his wife have a very busy life. They are preoccupied. Still... Disappointment settled around me like fog as I listened to the minister's sermon.

"Mother's Day is a time of love," he declared. "Don't let the day pass without saying 'I love you'—children to your mothers, and mothers to your children."

Mothers to your children. I sat up straighter. Why not? Why shouldn't I be the one to call? I picked up the telephone the moment I got home.

"Gary," I cried eagerly, "I'm coming over to take you both out for a Mother's Day supper. I want to celebrate the wonderful children God gave me."

"Hey, Mom, I'm glad you called," he answered. "We've been trying to reach you. We've already made reservations!" My depression was gone. That day turned out to be one of the happiest days I've ever had.

> *Lord, help me remember that I can never feel sorry*
> *for myself when I am busy loving.*
> —DORIS HAASE

Behold, thy mother.
—MARK 3:32

*W*hen I was a little girl, the Saturday before Mother's Day always included a trip to the florist. There we would pick up white cardboard boxes. Inside were carnations—a white one for Grandma and red ones for my mother, my sister, and me. "This is to honor your mother," Grandma would say as she pinned the bright flower to my dress before we left for church on Sunday. "Red says that your mama is alive. White means she's already gone on to heaven." She touched her own pale flower tenderly.

It was Anna M. Jarvis of Philadelphia who—almost a hundred years ago—began a letter-writing campaign to a variety of influential people, which eventually resulted in establishing Mother's Day as a national holiday. It was Anna, too, who championed the wearing of carnations. Her own dear mother had loved white carnations, and Anna thought that the flower represented the purity of motherly love. Later, red carnations were added for those whose mothers were living.

I don't see red and white corsages on Mother's Day anymore. But this year I think I'll go back to that tradition—with a bit of a change. I'll wear a white and red carnation. White to show that my mother "has gone on to heaven," but red to show that she's very much alive there!

Unlike even the fairest flower, Lord, a mother's love
never dies. Thank You, thank You, thank You!
—MARY LOU CARNEY

He that hath a bountiful eye shall be blessed.
—PROVERBS 22:9

*I*t was Mother's Day, and though it had been nine years since my mother's death, it seemed like only yesterday that I'd said good-bye. I drove to a local restaurant for what I hoped would be a quick breakfast away from all the holiday hoopla. I was disappointed to find the place filled with mothers and their children.

While I waited for an open booth, I filled my mug at the self-serve coffee station. As I sipped my coffee, a small woman and a little boy entered the restaurant. "Money, Mama," the boy begged, his eye on the jukebox. "No money for music, Jules," the woman said. "Settle down. Mama worked all night, and she's tired."

Tired didn't begin to describe her—try worn out by life. One thing was certain: No one was taking her out for Mother's Day. The woman collapsed into the chair next to me in the waiting area. "Coffee!" she said.

An idea hit me: Ask her how she takes her coffee and serve it to her with a smile. I was arguing with the inner voice as I stirred two sweeteners and a creamer into the dark liquid. What good could this possibly do? This woman's problems go way beyond a cup of coffee.

As I served her the coffee, I gave her knuckles a little squeeze. Her face stretched into a weary smile. "I wanted some coffee all night long," she said. "Never did get around to it though."

Later, as I left the restaurant, I caught sight of the woman and her son. She was still smiling. The boy sat perched on the edge of the booth. His long slender arms reached across the table until his hands found hers.

Help me to reach out to strangers, Lord, with a happy heart.
—ROBERTA MESSNER

MAY 15

The blessing of the Lord makes rich, and he adds no sorrow with it.
—PROVERBS 10:22 RSV

lizabeth's voice sounded troubled on the other end of the line. "Mom," she said, close to tears, "I got the things you asked for, but now I can't find the money!" I'd sent her off to the shop around the corner to pick up a few groceries, and she was calling on my cell phone.

After asking a few questions, it became clear that the twenty-five dollars I'd given her had fallen out of her pocket. I made my voice sound unflustered. "Put the groceries back, honey, then walk through the store and back home the way you came. Maybe you'll see the money on the ground."

While I waited for Elizabeth, I reflected on the day many years ago when a friend and I went into New York City to go to the planetarium. Glowing with newfound independence, I reached into my jeans when I got home to give my mom the twenty dollars that was left over. It was gone.

In that moment I knew I was far from grown up; I felt irresponsible, unreliable, and foolish. My mother must have sensed that, for although money was tight she said nary an angry word. Her silence was a balm and a blessing. Now was my chance to be wise like her.

"I'm never going to the store again!" wailed Elizabeth as she walked in the door. I sat her down and told her my story. Then I gave her another twenty-five dollars and sent her back out for the groceries.

Lord, make me a good steward of the blessings my mother gave me.
—JULIA ATTAWAY

MAY 16

*When we love each other God lives in us
and his love within us grows ever stronger.*
—1 JOHN 4:12 TLB

*M*om, Canyon and I have decided to get married...in three days!"
It was my oldest daughter Jeanne, an artist living in New York
City. She and Canyon had known each other for years, and our entire family
rated him a ten on the scale of great catches. But getting married in three days?

"We were going to elope, but decided we wanted some of our friends there.
We want you to come."

I began to stammer, thinking of my role as mother of the bride.

Jeanne interrupted, "We're getting married at City Hall. Then we're going
to Riverside Park to have our own religious ceremony. We'll have a late lunch
at an outdoor cafe, then take the Circle Line harbor lights cruise around lower
Manhattan. All you have to do is get on a plane and join us."

The morning of the wedding, Canyon asked me to make a chuppah, a Jewish
wedding canopy. Just give me an umbrella, a hot glue gun, lots of ribbon, and
I'm in heaven! It was a grand chuppah.

I watched Jeanne get dressed in a lovely blue dress from the fifties that she
had bought at a resale shop for fifteen dollars. An hour later, Jeanne, Canyon
and I took the subway to City Hall where we giggled at the magistrate's forty-
five-second civil ceremony. Later, in the park, Canyon and Jeanne exchanged
rings again and read prayers in what seemed much more like a wedding than
the courthouse event. It was a day of perfect weather and lighthearted wonder.

Best of all, it was a commitment before God and the state. A wedding, pure
and simple, blessed with spontaneity, the laughter of friends, the deep love of
husband and wife, and the awe and joy of one very proud mother, who learned
that weddings come in all sizes, shapes, and styles, and if you just let it happen,
the day will be graced with blessings.

Lord, help me to accept that my ways may not be others' ways.
—PATRICIA LORENZ

MAY 17

"Before they call, I will answer; and while they are still speaking, I will hear."
—ISAIAH 65:24 NASB

As I tumbled the wet laundry into the automatic dryer, my thoughts went back to a windy spring day more than forty years ago. Awkwardly pregnant with our second son, I nevertheless toted a heavy wicker basket full of wet clothes out to the wash line. *Squeak, squawk, squeak,* the pulley protested each time I pinned another garment to the line. The noise attracted the attention of a telephone repairman high up on a pole across the back lane, and we exchanged a neighborly wave.

I continued to hang out the wash. Next to a row of embroidered tea towels and snowy pillowcases, five white shirts were soon billowing in the breeze. If there was anything my husband Leo liked better than putting on a fresh white shirt every morning, it was getting into his old work clothes after school to garden—the soil underneath the clothesline was soft and black.

Later after hearing the clothes snapping in the wind on the line outside, there was an ominous silence. Looking out the window, I groaned, "Oh no!"

The clothesline had broken, and most of my snowy white wash had fallen onto the garden plot.

I wearily pulled on my rubber boots, picked up the clothesbasket, and trudged back outside. Coming around the corner, I was startled to meet the telephone repairman face to face.

"Saw the whole thing happen, ma'am, so I came down the pole to give you a hand. Free service and lifetime guarantee!" he grinned, pulling a pair of pliers from his leather tool belt. With a few deft twists, he quickly mended the broken clothesline.

Forty years later, as I stand here folding a pile of laundry, I think about that kindly repairman so unselfishly giving of himself to help a stranger in her plight. It reminds me of another "Free service and lifetime guarantee"—God's profound promise. He anticipates our needs and comes unbidden to help us splice the breaks and put the broken ends of life together.

Thank You, Lord, for sending kind people to help me when I have been in need.
—ALMA BARKMAN

MAY 18

Jerusalem remembers all her precious things that were from the days of old.
—LAMENTATIONS 1:7 NASB

*D*espite my best intentions, our house is always a little messy. Cracker crumbs speckle the living room rug, toothpaste fingerprints smear the bathroom mirror, and toy cars hide under the couches. Evidence that we have a toddler and an infant is everywhere.

I was complaining to my mom about housework, telling her that my laundry is an ever-growing mountain no matter how hard I try to keep up, when Solomon rubbed his fingers on the windows I'd just cleaned. I shook my head and sighed. "It's no use," I said.

"Listen," my mom said, "before you know it, all of this will be a memory. So try to enjoy it."

"Enjoy fingerprints?" I asked, rolling my eyes as I picked up a puzzle piece that had strayed outside its box.

"Someday," Mom said, "you'll look at your clean house and miss these days."

I'll admit I still grumble when I pass my cloudy windows. But now, before I get out the glass cleaner, I try to find the blessing in it all. When my house is clean and my windows are crystal clear, I will hold on to the memory of that little handprint.

Lord, the next time I reach for the vacuum cleaner,
remind me that someday this mess will be a memory.
—SABRA CIANCANELLI

MAY 19

Count it all joy, my brethren, when you meet various trials.
—JAMES 1:2 RSV

*M*any years ago my husband Larry's mother Enid came to visit us in Ohio for a much-needed vacation. Larry and I had made numerous plans for entertaining her—trips to museums, galleries, shopping centers, points of interest such as Serpent Mound, an ancient Indian earthworks. Instead, we spent the week confined to our home during torrential rains that dropped fifteen inches during seven days, a record for that area. Rivers overflowed; roads all around us closed due to flooding. At one point we couldn't even get out of our own driveway.

At the end of the visit, as we traveled toward the airport via numerous detours around still-flooded highways, I apologized to Enid for her disastrous vacation.

She smiled. "I came determined to have a good time no matter what happened, and so I have. If it had to rain, then I'm glad it was so memorable."

I've been helped many times since then by the memory of her positive attitude. Such as one year, when the pump on our well quit up at our cabin in the mountains when we had twelve guests under our roof. I started to panic, but Larry said, "Relax. We can carry drinking water from the lodge, and we can flush the toilet with water from the river."

"Okay, Enid," I whispered to the air, "looks like we're going to have a memorable weekend."

The pump didn't change, but my attitude did. And guess what? We had a good time.

Lord, please help me count as joy any challenge today that comes my way. Amen.
—MADGE HARRAH

All discipline for the moment seems not to be joyful,
but sorrowful; yet to those who have been trained by it,
afterwards it yields the peaceful fruit of righteousness.
—HEBREWS 12:11 NASB

*W*hen God's answer to an urgent but selfish prayer turned out to be an unmistakable no, I begged Him to tell me why. All I seemed to hear was: Remember the peach tree? But no memory surfaced until spring arrived and the Georgia fruit trees began to blossom.

I'd been about nine, and I had talked back to my mother. Mostly, I was a goody-two-shoes and I wasn't used to being punished. But when I saw Mother's face, I took off running.

She ran right after me. I sprinted out the back door and down the seventeen wooden steps. She was right on my heels. I fled through the backyard and ducked into a tiny hole in the hedge that separated our yard from our neighbor's. To my horror, she squeezed through the hole and the chase continued. I ran right through the middle of the leisurely Sunday-afternoon croquet game in the Fowlers' backyard. As I hopped over the wooden balls, the game stopped like a freeze-frame in a movie.

Mother was just inches behind me when I saw the old peach tree that I often climbed with my friends. I scrambled up it and jumped several feet through the air to the hot tin roof of a garage, feeling safe at last. But there came Mother right up the tree, climbing almost effortlessly. I stared in terror as she sailed through the air like Peter Pan and stood facing me, only slightly out of breath. Our neighbors watched silently and attentively.

"Would you like me to give you your discipline up here or back at home?" Mother asked. I climbed meekly down the peach tree, and we walked home together as the croquet game started up again.

My Abba, thank You for the times You have
pursued me relentlessly and corrected me. Amen.
—MARION BOND WEST

MAY 21

"Honor...your mother."
—EXODUS 20:12 NIV

$\mathcal{I}$ watched the miles click by on the odometer. The 250-mile trip to Mother's seemed to get longer every time I drove it. But I knew why. It was because it wasn't Mother I would find at the end of this long drive; it was her grave.

If only I lived closer, I thought as I turned off the expressway. With my sister living in Florida and many of Mother's friends aged or deceased, I knew the chances of anyone visiting Mother's grave were slim. How I longed for her to have fresh flowers and an occasional friendly voice!

I parked my car and walked toward the grave, carrying a bouquet of daisies. *What's that?* I thought. I got closer and stopped, amazed—and then amused. A huge, perfect ear of corn rested on top of Mother's headstone.

I laughed aloud. Mother's love of fresh sweet corn was legendary. She gave it to her friends; she made it for her friends; she ate it and called her friends to regale them with how good it had been. Someone had been here. Perhaps many someones.

I remembered my friend telling me about leaving stones on her relatives' graves, a sign of both remembrance and respect. Reverently, I placed my bouquet next to the corn. And awhile later, when I turned the car around for the long drive home, I felt a little better about Mother's final resting place. And about the friends who visited her there.

> *When my loved ones are out of my care, Lord,*
> *I'll remember that they're never out of Yours!*
> —MARY LOU CARNEY

He shall make amends for the harm.
—LEVITICUS 5:16

Cooking has never been a pleasure for me, and it was especially stressful when my four children were small. I sometimes dream that we're all young again and that I'm in the kitchen, happy and content.

Recently, Jeremy, one of my twin sons, came to live with my husband Gene and me for a short time. Jeremy had made some stunning changes in his life, which had been marked by addictive behavior fueled by refusing to take medication for his bipolar disorder. Now we were seeing an amazing new young man emerge.

One spring Saturday afternoon as Jeremy trimmed our hedges, I made supper for a friend who'd had surgery. Pot roast, asparagus casserole, and banana pudding were on the menu. As I layered a large bowl with vanilla wafers, Jeremy came through the back door, hot and tired. He leaned on the kitchen counter, poured himself a glass of iced tea, and smiled. "Wow, Mom," he said, "banana pudding—my all-time favorite!"

"It's not for us," I answered without looking up. "I'm making it for a friend at church."

There was silence, and our eyes met. I had to look way up at him now, but the years unexpectedly rolled back and I saw myself staring down at a small redheaded boy and saying, "No!" to cookies or punch or whatever he asked for. As Jeremy went into the living room, an inaudible voice suggested, *It's never too late, Marion.* I made a miniature banana pudding in a custard dish, and a burst of joy filled my heart and, it seemed, the entire kitchen.

In the living room I presented the pudding to Jeremy. "For me?" he asked. "For me? Thanks, Mom!"

Show me more ways, Lord, to make those I love happy.
—MARION BOND WEST

So I commend the enjoyment of life, because
nothing is better for a man under the sun.
—ECCLESIASTES 8:15 NIV

I rushed home from work to babysit Indy and Noah, my two grandsons. I hadn't seen them much lately. I was juggling my job, school, housework, and gardening. There was no time for anything else.

I was still in my business suit and heels when they arrived. Four-year-old Indy grabbed my hand, ready to run to the pond to feed the ducks.

"Grandma," he said excitedly, "go get your play clothes on!"

"Oh, Indy," I laughed, "I don't have any play clothes."

He looked at me wide-eyed. "What do you wear when you play?"

It was the third time that week the issue of play had come up. When a delivery man hustled to my door with a package, I joked that he was as busy as I was. He smiled and said that the key to life is to remember to find time to play too. I responded with a blank stare.

It came up again two days later at a seminar. When asked to create a personal schedule that included time for me to do something just for fun, I came up empty-handed.

The following Saturday afternoon when the boys came over, I wore my newly labeled play clothes—jogging pants, tie-dyed T-shirt and tennis shoes. I took their little hands in mine and we ran to the backyard, not to weed the garden, not to rake the leaves and not to do homework at the patio table, but simply to play. Now that's an accomplishment!

Father, Indy, Noah, and I are lying here on the grass and watching
the sun set across the pond. We just wanted to say thanks
for a really fun day and a beautiful pink sky tonight.
—MELODY BONNETTE

MAY 24

Whatsoever a man soweth, that shall he also reap.
—GALATIANS 6:7

*M*y mother heard this legend years ago when she lived in the Azores. There was a woman who baked bread for a rich family. Always she made enough bread for her employers and her own family. She also baked a "charity loaf" as an offering to God for the safe return of her oldest son, who'd gone overseas to seek his fortune.

The charity loaf was collected daily by a crazy old hunchback. Instead of showing his gratitude with a petition to God for the safe return of the woman's son, the hunchback had an irritating way of taking the bread and then cackling out an odd couplet:

The evil you do stays with you,
The good you do comes back to you.

After months of having her daily charity so rewarded, the woman could stand it no longer and did a terrible thing. She put a fatal dose of poison in the loaf she was baking for the hunchback. "Today will be the last I will ever have to listen to that wretched hunchback," she vowed. Suddenly she shivered. Realizing what she was about to do, she flung the poisoned bread into the fire. When the hunchback came, she gave him one of her family's loaves, not even resenting the inevitable couplet.

That night the woman heard a tapping at her door. Her son was home again, tattered, penniless, and nearly dead from hunger. "It's a miracle I'm here," he said to his overjoyed mother. "A mile away I started to faint. I hadn't eaten for three days and didn't have the strength to move another inch. But a little hunchback came along eating some bread. When I asked him for a crust, he gave me the whole loaf. It was like giving me life again! Mother, why are you looking so pale?"

Take from me all temptation to do evil, Lord, lest it poison someone I love.
—MANUEL ALMADA

The Lord is your keeper.
—PSALM 121:5 NKJV

*B*ringing in the groceries from the car, my husband stopped me at the door. "You have to see this," Tony said, leading me to our clothesline. "Be careful. Don't touch."

I followed him to the old tote bag that we keep pinned to the line to hold clothespins. Inside was a neatly wound bundle of sticks.

"I was hanging out clothes," Tony said, "and put my hand in. There's a nest inside the tote with little eggs. Can you believe it?"

Later that day when I took the clothes off the line, I stood on tiptoe and looked inside the tote. A startled wren flew out. It landed in a nearby oak and watched as I walked toward the house. While I folded the clothes, I worried that I'd frightened the bird and that she would abandon her eggs. Later, washing the dishes, I looked out the window at the clothesline, hoping to see a sign of the bird, but the tote was still.

That night, rain poured onto our tin roof and woke me up. I thought of the mother bird and her nest. "Please keep the bird and her eggs safe," I prayed. The next morning and every time after, when I felt the need to go check on the birds, I prayed instead. Days later, as we barbecued, I saw the mother bird fly into the tote. A symphony of chirps erupted. As hard as it was not to peek, I held off going near.

For almost two weeks the mother bird flew to and from the tote, and each time she arrived, the bag came to life with music. When enough time had passed and there was no sign of the mother bird, I cautiously stood on tiptoe and looked. An empty nest never looked so good!

Dear Lord, help me to remember that sometimes as much as I want to help, my efforts are best spent putting my trust in You.
—SABRA CIANCANELLI

Beloved, let us love one another: for love is of God.
—1 JOHN 4:7

Conversations with my six-year-old granddaughter Olivia resemble the old game of Twenty Questions. This one took place while we waited for my hamburger and her chicken strips at a local café.

Olivia: "Who are your children?"

Me: "Your mom Rebecca and your uncles Patrick and Michael. You know that."

Olivia: "Are Emilee and Aaron your children?"

Me: "No."

Olivia: "Is Katie your child?"

Me: "No. Katie is your mom's birth mother, and Emilee and Aaron are her children. You know that too."

Olivia: "Well, my mom is adopted, you know!"

Me: "Yes, I know."

Olivia: "How did you decide who got her?"

Me (thinking quickly): "I got her because I was older."

Olivia: "Who loved my mom more, you or Katie?"

Me: "We both loved her the same."

Our food arrived. Olivia stopped talking to dip her fries in ketchup. I spent the momentary silence thinking about love. Despite what I'd told Olivia, surely I loved Rebecca more than Katie did! After all, Katie wasn't part of her life for twenty-three years.

But love is a two-way street. In order for Rebecca to be a beloved part of our family, Katie had made the heart-wrenching decision to place her for adoption. I'd told Olivia the truth after all: Katie and I loved Rebecca the same, and that love had given us the added joy of knowing and loving each other. Love multiplied, because none of us can ever outlove our generous, giving, amazing God.

Loving Lord, thank You that we're all beloved parts of Your precious family!
—PENNEY SCHWAB

MAY 27

Blessed are they that mourn: for they shall be comforted.
—MATTHEW 5:4

The sight and sound of weeping used to embarrass me. And then, one memorable day in May, I learned how helpful—how beautiful—tears can be.

I'd always gone to the cemetery alone. It seemed right to be by myself at my son's grave. Mark had been thirteen when he died after a year's struggle with a rare form of cancer of the blood, and during all my graveside visits since then, I'd prayed to God, asking Him to comfort me in my loss. Memorial Day came. Because holidays had always been a family time for us, this year my husband suggested that we take all of our children along when we visited Mark's grave. In preparation for this, our older daughters prepared a basket of fresh flowers, and eleven-year-old LeAnn worked on a macramé design she called "the Eye of God." Purple had been Mark's favorite color, so big brother Mitch selected a purple floral arrangement in the shape of a cross. My husband and I carried a lovely purple wreath.

At the grave we carefully placed our tokens of affection. Suddenly five-year-old Heidi wandered away from us, then returned a few minutes later holding two fistfuls of white clover she had picked. I'd forgotten that she was the only one who had not brought a gift. Kneeling down, she tenderly positioned the small flowers on her brother's grave. Tears streamed down her cheeks. Soon all of us were weeping together.

Mark's death had left us feeling separated from him, separated in a way from one another. Now in our grief we were bound together in unity as we realized that Mark was still with us and that we still had each other in a closer and stronger way.

"The gift of tears," I once read, "is the best gift of God to suffering man." That Memorial Day I discovered the healing truth in those words.

Lord, thank You for the comfort of tears.
—JO LINDQUIST

MAY 28

"Cease striving and know that I am God."
—PSALM 46:10 NASB

I hadn't yet turned sixteen when I learned to drive. I'd sat through driver's ed in school, but now I was getting some hands-on experience. My mother sat in the passenger's seat of our station wagon, and I eased it out of our driveway and into the street.

"What on earth are you doing?" my mother said.

"I'm driving, Mom." My eyes were hawklike, focused straight ahead. My neck and shoulder muscles were knotted. My sweaty hands gripped the wheel tightly at the two and ten o'clock positions, just the way I'd learned in driver's ed. *A good driver keeps her hands on the wheel at two and ten at all times and keeps her eyes on the road.* I'd memorized the rules for safe driving and gotten an A.

"Julie, what are you looking at?"

"The nose of the car. I'm steering the car between the two lines. It's hard!"

"Nobody drives like that! Look way out down the road."

"How will I stay between the lines if I quit focusing on the car?"

"Trust me, you drive by looking ahead. Focus as far down the road as you can see."

I shifted my glance to the horizon. Until recently, I approached life the same way: I wanted to be in control with my hard-steering technique. But now I'm learning to let go, focus far down the road, and look only toward God.

Father, for today, I'm trusting You.
—JULIE GARMON

Share each other's troubles and problems, and so obey our Lord's command
—GALATIANS 6:2 TLB

*Y*ears ago when I was a single parent of four, I had a number of unhappy, stressed-out, overworked days and weeks. But luckily I learned a wonderful truth from a friend. "Take time for yourself," she encouraged. "Go to a movie, have your nails done, take a class, go to the library and read magazines. Be good to yourself and then you'll be able to be good to your family, your boss, and all the people who depend on you."

So I learned that we humans were not created to spend every waking moment in the service of others. We are not meant to just be someone's servant, husband, mother, caretaker, or employee twenty-four hours a day, seven days a week. We are meant to belong to ourselves and God and then become absolutely the best person God intended when He breathed life into us. Only then can we be good for others.

Say, isn't it time for a break? How about a cup of tea and a good book? Your family will love the new you. Mine did.

Father, help me remember that my number one responsibility
is to be happy and fulfilled in my own body, mind and soul, so I can
also be the best I can possibly be for the others in my life.
—PATRICIA LORENZ

"When you hear of wars and revolutions, do not be frightened. These things must happen first, but the end will not come right away."
—LUKE 21:9 NIV

*W*hile having my quiet time on the porch early one spring morning, I noticed a man moving along the freshly turned earth beyond the silo just outside our subdivision. His arm swung slowly from side to side. Curious, I reached for the binoculars. He was holding a metal detector, which he swung before him like a scythe.

Our house is built on land filled with the scraps of war. As best we can tell, troops from both North and South camped here during the Civil War. And during World War II, Italian officers were held prisoner at a golf resort a quarter of a mile away. Remembrances of war surround us and lie under our feet. Memorial Day in New Market, Virginia, is every day.

As I watched the relic-seeker with his metal detector, I wondered about the mothers whose sons had fought nearby. Then I thought of our son Peter, who has been to Afghanistan. Did a mother there see the remnants of his tour—a button, a coin? What was left of our son David's months of service in Iraq?

Wars and rumors of wars—Jesus knew they'd come. He knew hatred and greed would erupt and that good people would have to suffer to quench its flames. War is horrible. As the mother of soldiers, I know this well. Yet it is with thankfulness and a bit of pride that I know my husband and sons (and a daughter-in-law) have served our country on the side of justice and freedom.

Lord, as we remember those who have given their lives in war,
we wait in tears and hope for Jesus, the true Peacemaker.
—ROBERTA ROGERS

"If you are wise, your wisdom will reward you."
—PROVERBS 9:12 NIV

*B*efore my daughter Lindsay and her new baby were discharged from the hospital, her doctor came to check her out. Her husband was taking a load of flowers down to the car, so she and I listened together as he reviewed some precautions for Lindsay's first week at home. Then he sat on the edge of her bed and gave her one last piece of advice.

"Let your husband take care of the baby—and let him do it his way," he said. "If you always tell him how to change her or dress her or burp her, he'll simply stop helping. Babies adjust. And in most cases, the difference doesn't really matter."

Lindsay nodded, probably not yet understanding the wisdom of his words. I nodded knowingly. After all, my husband Lynn and I have been married for thirty-seven years.

A few days later I was back home, watching Lynn cut a cantaloupe in half—the wrong way. Everyone knows you cut a cantaloupe the short way, through the fat middle, like a lemon; not the long way, end to end, like a watermelon. I told him so.

He paused, looking at the cantaloupe. "Why does it matter?"

That's when I remembered the doctor's advice. The circumstances change, but the challenge to accept each other's differences remains the same through all the seasons of marriage.

> *Lord, help me to see what doesn't matter,*
> *which will help me know what matters most.*
> —CAROL KUYKENDALL

June

June 1

He that loveth not knoweth not God; for God is love.
—1 John 4:8

I'm always impressed by people who seem to know, right off the top of their head, the perfect Scripture for the moment. I've always had a hard time memorizing Bible verses. Okay, maybe it has something to do with the fact that I don't spend enough time trying. Memorization usually means saying a verse to myself a few times. Sometimes I remember to practice by repeating it the next day, but by day three I've usually forgotten it. So instead of a polished verse that comforts someone, I'm left with a vague idea. I end up mumbling, "You know it says somewhere in the Bible...I could probably find it for you.... Well, basically the idea is...."

Last fall, my son Trace started preschool. After the first day, he came home with a note. "Our memory verse is I John 4:8. Please practice."

I stared at the card. *Are they serious? How can I expect Trace to memorize verses when I can't?*

But I wasn't going to let him be the only child who didn't know his verse, so we got to work. I asked Trace his verse in the car, at home, before bed, and in the bath. I asked him to share it with Daddy and Grandma and with anyone who would listen. I cheered every time he remembered just one word.

Trace didn't memorize his verse by his next preschool class or by the next week. But we didn't give up, and in two weeks he had it down. Amazingly, so did I!

God, please help me to remember that although
perseverance doesn't come easy, it's worth the struggle.
—Amanda Borozinski

*Finally, brethren, farewell. Be perfect, be of good comfort, be of one mind,
live in peace; and the God of love and peace shall be with you.*
—2 CORINTHIANS 13:11

Looking at the clock with one eye, I jumped out of bed. We had only fifteen minutes to get our son to his swimming lesson. "Get up, Solomon!" I yelled. "We're late!" I dashed to the kitchen, started the coffee, and found Solomon's towel. Solomon gulped down a bowl of cereal. He got dressed but couldn't find his sandals. "Let's go," my husband Tony said to him. "Just wear your sneakers."

I was making toast when I heard the car start. My heart dropped; I hadn't said good-bye. I've always felt the need to give my sons a kiss and a hug when we part, and since my sister's sudden death, the need has grown more intense. Running out the door and down the driveway in my pajamas, I waved my arms. Tony stopped the car.

"What did we forget?" he asked.

I ran to Solomon's window and leaned in. "Good-bye, honey. I love you. Have a good lesson."

"I love you too, Mom," Solomon said.

"Is that it, guys?" Tony said. "We're late."

Solomon smiled. "It's never too late to say good-bye. Right, Mom?"

> *Dear Lord, thank You for reminding me that love
> is eternal, and it's never too late to say good-bye.*
> —SABRA CIANCANELLI

JUNE 3

Beloved, I pray that all may go well with you and that you may be in health; I know that it is well with your soul.
—3 JOHN 2 RSV

*W*hen I was a child in a small Missouri village during World War II, I caught a bad case of the mumps. The only doctor in the area was off on a trip and the nearest hospital was over sixty miles away, beyond the reach of our gas-ration stamps. I developed a fever of 105 degrees and a long-lasting headache that threatened to split open my skull. At last I slipped into a lethargy so profound that I could not move, speak, or open my eyes, but I could still hear my mother rocking in a chair near my bed. Her soft murmuring reassured me and eased the pain.

When I finally began to recover after days of illness, I asked my mother, "Who were you talking to while I was sick?"

"God," she replied.

Today we have antibiotics to help combat severe illness, and I believe in accepting the help that doctors can offer. But I know through experience that prayer, too, is a "miracle medicine" that reaches through pain, sickness, and despair to strengthen us with God's healing touch.

What a blessing to have the Great Physician always ready to make a house call! (It helps to have Him around on the good days too!)

Father, today I will reach out to someone who needs
the comfort of Your healing presence.
—MADGE HARRAH

June 4

And whatsoever ye do, do it heartily.
—Colossians 3:23

The grandchildren are coming to visit tonight, and I'm in the kitchen cooking dinner. My mind goes back to a warm summer day in childhood. I was itching to get outside when my mother said to me, "Oscar, I want you to help me prepare dinner."

"But, Mother," I gasped. Not many boys my age cooked or even knew how to. Girls helped their mothers in the kitchen, not boys.

"Learning how to cook might come in handy," she said. "You'll be able to help your wife someday."

I muttered something about never getting married, but indeed I did help her that evening and many more evenings. Mother taught me to boil chicken and to use the broth for cooking baby lima beans. I learned from her how to season meat the day before cooking it and how to prepare string beans, cooked cabbage, pork chops, and gravy. Other things I picked up on my own, like frying bacon for breakfast while making gelatin for lunch, but seventy-four years after my first lesson I'm still at the stove. Indeed, I'm grateful, and my wife Ruby, who hasn't been well recently, seems to be grateful too.

Tonight, for the grandchildren, I plan to serve chicken wings smothered in gravy, fresh-picked string beans, tossed salad, hot rolls, and corn on the cob.

Mother would be pleased.

Jesus, cooking is both creative and a way of serving You each day.
—Oscar Greene

June 5

Let us love one another, for love comes from God.
—1 John 4:7 niv

After years of dreaming about remodeling our house, we finally knocked down the walls between our kitchen, family room, and dining room. But I still have one item on my wish list: a new family table.

I want a user-friendly, sturdy table that people are drawn to, not only to eat, but to read the newspaper or have a cup of coffee or play games. I call it a family table because it's the kind of place where family "happens."

The family table of my childhood was an oblong glass table that my mother inherited from an aunt. My mother insisted it set a proper tone for our family with four rambunctious children. It was the only place where we came together regularly.

Then there was the family table we had when our children were growing up—a heavy wooden trestle table with a bench along one side so we could add people without scouring the house for chairs. Our photo albums show what happened around that table: birthday parties, pumpkin carvings, Valentine's Day dinners, science projects, love.

Now I want a family table with comfortable chairs that beckon both adults and children. I may not get my dream table for a while, so in the meantime I'm taking note of what else beckons and connects people, like our big comfy couch in front of the fireplace, a bunch of stools pulled up to the kitchen counter, and, most of all, the presence of God in the words and attitudes of the people who live in our home.

Father, may Your presence bless our newly remodeled home each day.
—Carol Kuykendall

Hope deferred maketh the heart sick.
—PROVERBS 13:12

*W*hen my friend Alice had to sell her home to pay for a costly stay in a nursing home, I thought my heart would break. My parents had moved across the street from her back in the 1950s. Alice had no children of her own, and through the years she became a doting second mother to me. But now, whenever I passed her home, I despaired of ever visiting her there again. There would be no more moments to remember. "I'm losing everyone I love!" I cried out to God.

When an estate sale was scheduled to generate more money for Alice's health care, she asked me to gather up all the photos around her house. There were boxes of them: antique daguerreotypes of her great-grandparents, black-and-whites in golden Kodak booklets, and color Polaroids of a bus trip to Florida, the only real vacation Alice had ever taken.

I bought some scrapbooks, and that Saturday my dog Spanky and I took them to the nursing home. Alice was propped up in bed connected to her oxygen, surrounded by stacks of photographs, newspaper clippings, colorful pens, and decorative stickers. "Looks like you're about to get this project wrapped up," I observed.

"Oh, no, honey, this won't be done until I'm done," she said with a smile, then motioned for me to hand her the camera that was sitting on top of the bookcase. Just then, Spanky jumped onto Alice's bed, his sharp claws ripping into Alice's memorabilia. Alice pressed her call button: "Code Gold! Another Kodak moment," she said to the voice on the intercom. Quickly, two attendants arrived. Alice handed the camera to one of them, and I pulled Spanky and Alice into a hug for a wonderfully spontaneous picture.

All the time that I'd been fretting about the past and fearing the future, Alice's heart had been full of hope. Even now, she was continuing to make memories.

Dear Lord, help me to be a lifelong learner in Your school of hope.
—ROBERTA MESSNER

And God saw everything that he had made, and behold, it was very good.
—GENESIS 1:31 RSV

*T*talked to my mother today. "Now that I am at the cusp of my tenth decade," she said, and "You'd think your father would change his ways after sixty-five years of my advice," and "I remember going to village baseball games with my dad in the 1930s," and other pithy and wondrous things. Finally we got around to talking about the hip she just broke, which is around number fifteen on what she calls "the old-lady ailment list." She admitted to feeling a little weary of being confined to bed and not being able to walk or cook or drive or use much of "the ancient machine the sweet Lord gave me for a body," she said, trying to laugh.

As usual, she bent the conversation smoothly to my troubles. How does she do that so gracefully? And when I tried to get back to hers, she suddenly started listing all the great things she has "even now that I'm older than dirt." "I have my husband, odd as he is, and five children who have never been arrested, yet, and I have the dearest of friends, and a whopping nine grandchildren, and my brain still works, and I make a mean meatloaf, and every day I hear the voices of people I love. Also there are great birds here in Florida and my tomatoes do surprisingly well in this soil. I just discovered two Neville Shute novels I never read, at least one of my children calls me every day, and the sun is out here when it's raining like the dickens where you are and snowing like the Arctic where we used to live, so what's to complain about? Soon enough heaven, and I'll see everyone ever loved and ever loved me, and can talk baseball again with my dad. But what's the rush? This is a glorious world, the best one ever, don't you think?"

Dear Lord, what she said. Amen.
—BRIAN DOYLE

Though He be not far from every one of us.
—ACTS 17:27

*T*t was 8:00 a.m. when the call came from Colorado Springs. "Your daughter Karen was admitted to Penrose Hospital last night," said the nurse. "I don't really know what the problem is, but Doctor Berman is doing some tests on her now. I'll have him call you as soon as he's finished."

My heart was pounding as I hung up the phone. I felt so helpless! I started to pray, but with Karen 400 miles away, it was hard for me to imagine that my prayers could have much impact. I wanted to be there, hug her, comfort her, pray while touching her. Then, as I opened the door to let the dog out, I caught a glimpse of the sun in the eastern sky. *That very same sun is shining at this moment where Karen is, too,* I thought. Somehow that realization melted the distance, and I was able to pray, believing again.

Karen's problem turned out to be minor, and she was dismissed from the hospital later in the day, but now, when I pray for her, it's easier for me to realize we are in instant contact through God, Who, like the sun, is both here and there at the same time.

> *Lord, You are touching my distant loved one now;*
> *and through You, so am I. Thank You.*
> —MARILYN MORGAN HELLEBERG

JUNE 9

Call understanding your intimate friend.
—PROVERBS 7:4 NASB

*O*n June 9, 1989, I gave birth to Robbie, our third child and first son. More than anything, I'd wanted a little boy. Robbie was born two weeks past due, with a severe birth defect called anencephaly. He lived for twenty minutes. As the doctors discovered the truth during labor, I wanted to say, "Stop everything! There's been a mistake. We'll come back later." Afterward, I glanced out the picture window at the rain. Would I always hate rain? Would I ever laugh again?

After Robbie's birth and twenty-minute life, my husband went home to be with our girls, who were six and eight. My mother-in-law Carolyn offered to stay with me that long night. I didn't think I needed anybody. I didn't have anything to say. I couldn't talk—only cry. Carolyn understood. She plumped my pillow and covered me with a blanket. Without a word, she poured my water and held the straw to my mouth. She didn't ask any questions; she didn't offer Scripture; she didn't even pray. She was just there. I didn't know how much I needed a quiet someone. Maybe that's why I didn't completely reject what she told me a few months later: "God's going to give you another baby."

"I'm not going through that again."

"You're going to have another baby. A boy." I told her it wasn't going to happen. But deep down, I sensed an unexpected, undeniable flicker of hope. On August 6, 1991, our fourth child, Richard Thomas, was born—whole and healthy.

God, thank You for giving me Your quiet compassion
and Your healing promise through Carolyn.
—JULIE GARMON

JUNE 10

I stared in the mirror. Where did all those gray hairs come from? I hadn't noticed them yesterday. My toothbrush flew. Under my breath I mumbled, "Mirror, mirror on the wall, who is the fairest of them all." As I rinsed and dried my face, I glared at my reflection. "Don't answer that." Turning my back, I marched out of the bathroom.

In the kitchen I continued the conversation.

"You're getting old," I said to myself aloud. "No wonder you can't remember anything any more."

"Don't worry, Mom," my teenage son cheerfully said, as he came into the kitchen behind me. "I'll take care of you when you become senile."

"That's comforting," I answered, sarcastically, making a face at him. He grinned and for just a moment I saw my mother's smile shining from his smooth young face. My mother had been gone now for over six years, but I could still hear her voice.

"It doesn't matter how long we live," she reminded me in a soft voice echoing from the past. I could almost see the upward tilt of her chin and the blue sparkle of her eyes.... "The truth is that God intended His children to be forever young in spirit. It's up to us to believe in His intention." Mother's beautiful face had been a living example of eternal youth. White hair and all.

"Amen," I said as the eggs began to fry.

> *Of all the beautiful things You have given us, Lord, I thank You
> most of all for the gift of eternal life. And eternal youth.*
> —DORIS HAASE

JUNE 11

"Rule over the fish of the sea and the birds of the air and over every living creature that moves on the ground."
—GENESIS 1:28 NIV

I watched my three-year-old granddaughter Karis make friends with a ladybug this afternoon on our way home from a walk around the neighborhood. "A ladybug!" she squealed with delight when she spotted the bright red beetle crawling curbside at her feet. She squatted down, resting her chin on her knees, and placed her hand in front of the ladybug, which crawled right onto it, as if that's exactly what the tiny bug wanted to do.

"Oh, cute!" Karis cooed as she brought her hand to her face, so she and the ladybug could see eye to eye. She then stood up and began moving her hands, one in front of the other, so the ladybug could keep crawling forward, getting nowhere. "Are you all right?" she asked her new little friend. "Do you need to find your mommy and daddy?" We slowly walked a few more steps. Then Karis looked up. "The ladybug likes me," she announced with confidence.

I thought about all I read and heard urging us to care for our planet: how to "re" everything. Recycle, reuse, repurpose, save energy, conserve resources, go green. All good stuff, but I confess that I sometimes get too lazy to make the simple sacrifices. But watching Karis tenderly care for one of the smallest of God's creatures gave me plenty of motivation to take better care of all God has given us, so the next generation and all the generations that follow can still make friends with ladybugs.

Father, You have given us the responsibility to care for Your creation.
Thank You for sprinkling our days with motivation.
—CAROL KUYKENDALL

See, I am doing a new thing! Now it springs up; do you not perceive it?
—ISAIAH 43:19

Observing my daughters Julie and Jennifer mothering their children, I sometimes feel guilty about myself as a mother. I didn't teach my girls much about cooking or cleaning, and zero about sewing. I guess our home was sort of—messy. My fondest memories of their childhood are of taking them to the places I loved: libraries, ten-cent stores (particularly the paper doll counter), animal pounds, antique shops.

One Mother's Day I was feeling particularly inadequate, wishing I'd given my daughters more instruction as they were growing up. Then, hesitantly, I opened the card on a gift from my oldest daughter.

Hi, Mom!

Oh, the smell of an antique shop! Memories of sharing a love of something in common. You taught me to love awesome things—books, conversations, old things, unique qualities in others, calico cats. Today in an antique shop, I remembered how you pointed out dusty treasures to me when I was small. Thank you for teaching me to see beauty in hidden places. Otherwise, I guess I might have thought dusting the furniture was important! I can't imagine life without you.

So grateful,
Julie

Her gift was paper dolls from the antique shop—rare ones from the 1940s. Looking around, I noticed that the furniture still needed dusting. Nevertheless, I sat down cross-legged in the living room and tried all of the wonderful, long-ago dresses on my brand-new antique paper dolls. I felt like a child again. And for sure, I felt a whole lot better about myself as a mother.

One of Your finest gifts to us, Father, is our memories. Amen.
—MARION BOND WEST

JUNE 13

Plenty of roses, stars, sunsets, rainbows, brothers and sisters,
aunts and cousins, but only one mother in the whole world.
—KATE DOULAS WIGGIN

It was my friend Elaine's birthday, and I had arranged to take her to lunch. She was on the phone when I opened the door, but she motioned me inside.

"That's right," she continued her telephone conversation. "One dozen roses, and sign the card 'Happy Birthday, Elaine.'"

Was it somebody else's birthday, too? My curiosity won out. "Sending yourself flowers?" I chuckled.

"Nope," she smiled. "They're not for me. They're for my mom. I always send Mom a dozen roses on my birthday, my way of saying, 'Thanks for the greatest birthday gift of all—the gift of life.'"

Thank You, Lord, for my beautiful mother.
—MARY JANE MEYER

JUNE 14

"Whoever welcomes a little child like this in my name welcomes me."
—MATTHEW 18:5 NIV

*O*n a trip to Washington state, my husband Don and I stopped at Fort Columbia. The fort was built in 1904 and served as a coastal defense unit during World Wars I and II. The ocean view was breathtaking! We also prowled around an underground ammunition storage area.

We were going to skip the second bunker, but a teenage girl called from the entrance, "Were you going to look in here? My friend and I want to go in, but it looks scary. We'd feel safer with adults along." So we became tour guides, reassuring the girls about safety and giving a mini-lesson on coast-watching during World War II.

In 2001, I worked on a project sponsored by Kansas Health Foundation that asked children of all ages one question: "What do you need from adults to grow up healthy and safe?" More than three thousand kids responded, most talking about the crucial role parents, teachers, and other adults have played in their lives.

Amy, seventeen, wrote, "I believe it is up to the older, much wiser people to lead me in my search for a safe, healthy life." Joe, twelve, urged parents to get tough: "Kids need to be nagged to do their homework, so they can get better grades." Michael, fourteen, expressed a need shared by almost every young writer: "All of the other things would be nice, but love is better."

My own children are grown, but I can make a positive difference in my grandchildren's lives as well as the lives of other children in my life. I can take time to listen, to understand, and love. After all, two vacationing teenagers showed me that it isn't all that difficult!

Loving God, help me reach out in love to the children who share my world.
—PENNEY SCHWAB

June 15

Grudge not one against another, brethren.
—James 5:9

Rain streaked the windows. It clattered on the roof like horses' hooves and surrounded the house with an impregnable gray curtain. "I hate rain," I mumbled. I'd been cooped up all day with two over-zealous children and one oversized dog. The den looked like a toy-strewn battleground and I felt like a prisoner of war.

I got on all fours and began to pick up the blocks. "I hate blocks," I said, frowning crossly. The children frowned back.

"Can we have a cookie?" asked Bob.

"Cookies make crumbs and I despise crumbs," I grumbled. They pouted at me.

"We don't have nothing to do." Bob said.

"Well, pick up your crayons!" I practically shouted.

His mouth turned down. He started to whimper. Thunder snapped overhead like a giant rubber band. The gloom inside the house deepened. I flipped on TV and heard the familiar music of "Sesame Street." "The dog chewed up my red crayon!" Ann screamed, pointing to the carpet full of red wax.

"I hate the dog," I said.

Then suddenly, a voice on television said, "I hate puppies." I looked up to see if there was an echo in the room. But it was Oscar the Grouch, the outrageous, furry green creature who lives in a trash can, the grumbling crosspatch of Sesame Street. I watched Oscar as he went about the business of hating everything and making everybody miserable, and felt like I was looking in the mirror. I shifted my eyes to the rain-soaked window. There would always be unpleasant circumstances that I simply couldn't change. But I could improve the climate that surrounded them, with a few adjustments to my disposition.

I surprised the kids with a hug. "Want a cookie?" I said.

Lord, keep me from being a grouch—even on the rainy days.
—Sue Monk Kidd

JUNE 16

"Your eye is the lamp of your body."
—LUKE 11:34 NIV

When my son Henry was born, I gazed at him for hours, noticing every detail. We both had dark hair and dark eyes, but Henry looked different. "Now, who does he look like?" my mother asked, peering down at him in his pink-and-blue-striped blanket. "I don't know," I said. "He looks so familiar," she said.

A few weeks later, when my sister was visiting, she looked down into the bassinet and said, "Wow! Those dark eyes—he looks just like you-know-who."

"Who?" I asked.

"Dad," my sister said.

"He doesn't!" I said, almost as a reflex. My father lives abroad; he's been absent most of my life, but as a child I had always hoped we'd be closer when I got older. I suppose I figured that when I had children of my own, I'd understand our relationship. Instead, when I had my first child, Solomon, the love I felt for him confused me more. Curling beside him, reading him stories, I wondered how my father could have willingly opted out of so much of my life.

A few days after my sister's remark, Henry looked at me longingly. Gazing into the depths of his dark eyes, I thought, *What would happen if I extended the same acceptance and unconditional love that I give to this brand-new baby of mine to my father, looking at him with the same loving eyes?*

*Dear Lord, help me to remember that
my relationships are what I make of them.*
—SABRA CIANCANELLI

JUNE 17

"You who travel on the road—sing!"
—JUDGES 5:10 NASB

*M*y husband Leo has a musical background, and he always encouraged our children to sing, especially in the car. At one point, he even composed a little ditty we dubbed "The Manitoba Song," and it became the toddlers' favorite. As they got older, the challenge of singing four-part harmony helped allay the many sibling squabbles that sooner or later erupted in the backseat of the family sedan during long road trips. As teenage voices began to change, yet another dimension was added to our singing.

But it was not to last. As one by one the kids grew up and moved away, six voices were gradually reduced to two—just Leo's and mine. We still sing bits and snatches of old familiar hymns as we crisscross the country to visit our offspring. Scattered across Canada, none of them were home to mark Leo's birthday this year, but they did not forget him. They even drew me into a little family conspiracy, so the minute the package thumped into our mailbox, I knew what was in it.

"A present!" I called to Leo.

"Right on! Another music CD!" he exclaimed as he opened it.

He was rather taken aback to see his own picture on the cover. And that Heintzman keyboard—wasn't that our piano? Through misty eyes, he began to read the label. It featured all four children performing their own renditions of hymns, songs, original compositions, and a funny arrangement of "The Manitoba Song." After forty years, hearing that little tune filter out of a CD made us both cry.

Thank You, Lord, for the growing gift of memories that enrich my life.
—ALMA BARKMAN

June 18

Than the measure of man's mind,
And the heart of the Eternal
Is most wonderfully kind.
FREDERICK W. FABER, HYMN

Our daughter was living at home again after two years of college, and in some ways it was hard on all of us. She was straining for independence, and we seemed to go from one crisis to another, with her dad and I often feeling bewildered. Each day I'd prayed for patience, but it hadn't come.

Then one day I heard our minister say something that hit home. He was discussing difficult family relationships. "Don't pray for more patience," he said, "pray for more love."

That very day I began praying not for my kind of love, but for God's love to flow through me to this child of ours.

I really think things are better now. Why? Because our own love is somehow so limited, so judging, so demanding, so fearful. But when God's love is given, through us, to another, there are no such boundaries.

Jesus, show us how to love with Your love, not just our own.
—MARILYN CONNELL

"You shall be a special treasure to Me."
—Exodus 19:5 NKJV

No one could make Sunday dinner like my mother-in-law Ruth Dale. Her Swiss steak was the richest and juiciest I've ever eaten. My wife Sharon tried to duplicate her recipe in vain. She watched her mother cook it, thinking maybe she was doing something she wasn't aware of, but she wasn't. Sharon even bought her meat at the same store, but it didn't help.

When Sharon's mother died, her secret died with her. We cleaned out her little house, keeping some things and giving the rest to our daughters.

One evening my wife made Swiss steak for supper, complete with whole potatoes and carrots, the way her mother made it. I braced myself for the usual carving challenge, but I was pleasantly surprised.

"Why, this steak is delicious! It's just like your mother's!"

She smiled and pointed at the stove. "It was the pan she used."

I looked at the pan that Sharon had salvaged from her mother's kitchen. It was a heavy-duty aluminum pan, the kind my father used to sell door-to-door when I was a boy. It held the juices perfectly.

I was glad to know that Ruth Dale's secret was not lost, but I was also sad. It was her secret, her special talent. I know, "Imitation is the sincerest form of flattery," but I'm beginning to think that the most flattering thing I can do for someone is not to copy them but to let them be that special, unique person they are.

There was no one quite like Ruth Dale, and there is no one exactly like you or me. Somehow I think that's how God meant it to be.

Help me to be happy, Lord, being me, instead of imitating others.
—Daniel Schantz

He turneth...dry ground into watersprings.
—PSALM 107:35

Sniff! Oh, no! I could hear my mother sniffling, which meant only one thing. Soon she would be crying—over a TV show with a sad ending. I was about fourteen years old, and I rolled my eyes. It was bad enough that my mother cried in private, but it was even more embarrassing that she cried in public—at weddings, at people getting off a plane and hugging ("For heaven's sake, Ma, the flight's only coming in from Toledo!"), and at Hallmark commercials. I'd wanted to ask a girlfriend to stop in and watch TV at our house, but I didn't dare. What if my mother embarrassed me with her emotions?

The whole thing came to a head for me when my mother burst into tears at a stranger's wedding. We didn't even know these people! We'd ducked into City Hall during a rainstorm and had seen a bride, casually dressed in white denim jeans, and groom, in a sport shirt and khakis, rushing out of the marriage license bureau, laughing. They were laughing, and Ma was crying. "Oh, for goodness sake," I said, "you're more emotional about their wedding than they are!"

"They're so young," she said. "You'll understand when you get older."

Three weeks ago I went to the wedding of some twenty-something-year-old friends of mine. To my amazement, as the clergyman began saying, "to love and to cherish," I felt a warm tear trickling down my face. By the time he got to "till death do you part," I was crying openly. And do you know what? It felt good to experience my emotions. I lightly tapped my mother on the shoulder and whispered, "Ma, do you have an extra hankie?"

> *God, just for today, let me not be ashamed*
> *of my heartfelt emotions, but rejoice in them.*
> —LINDA NEUKRUG

JUNE 21

Your love has given me great joy and encouragement.
—PHILEMON 7 NIV

*M*y son walked slowly from the swing with his head down. As he got closer, I couldn't help but notice his wrinkled brow and curled bottom lip.

"What's the matter, Solomon?" I asked. "What happened?"

"They won't let me swing," he whispered, pointing to his older cousins.

"Oh, it's okay. You can sit here with me." I scooted over on the lawn chair and made room for him.

"No!" he said firmly. His eyes filled with tears. "My feelings hurt."

"I'm sorry, honey." I said. "Sit with me. We'll have fun."

"No!" He stomped his boots in the leaves. "Kiss my feelings. Make it better."

I must have looked confused because he pointed to his elbow.

"Here, Mommy!" He thrust his elbow forward. "Kiss here."

Leaning over, I gave him a hug and kissed his elbow through his corduroy jacket.

"Better?" I asked.

His eyes brightened and he was off, running toward the swing set. "Thank you, Mommy!"

Now that I think of it, aside from the elbow part, it makes perfect sense: If a kiss can make a scraped knee feel better, how much more can it do for hurt feelings?

> *Lord, when people around me are hurting,*
> *let me never forget the healing power of love.*
> —SABRA CIANCANELLI

And God blessed the seventh day and made it holy,
because on it he rested from all the work of creating.
—GENESIS 2:3 NIV

*M*y daughter Maria and I decided to take a weekend getaway to Tucson, Arizona, while the guys in the family were away on a Boy Scout backpacking trip. It's a short drive from our home in Phoenix, so I was soon poolside, watching Maria splash in the water. I'd brought some work with me, figuring those two days would be the perfect time to catch up. My bag was stuffed with blank thank-you notes, school forms, and friends' letters to answer.

But once relaxed in my chaise, I put off any work beyond slathering on sun block and reading a magazine. Usually I have trouble doing nothing, but not that Saturday afternoon. The entire day passed, and I didn't do one constructive thing. I started to feel guilty; I had to do more than just relax for a whole weekend. I laid my head back and looked up at the tall, rugged mountains that give this part of the Sonoran Desert its beauty. God created those mountains and everything else, I thought, and then...He rested. God worked hard for six days and then took the time simply to rest.

The Bible seems to say that while work is a gift from God so is time off from it. Relaxation brings rejuvenation and the energy to get back to work. And that's exactly what I did on Monday morning. But Saturday and Sunday were days to do nothing with my daughter, and I enjoyed every minute of it.

Lord, help me keep the balance between work and play that You've created
for my life, so I may stay energized for the work You've given me.
—GINA BRIDGEMAN

I will tell of all your wonders.
—PSALM 9:1 NIV

*M*y daughter Kendall recently took up painting and immediately became smitten with her new hobby. She watched classes on TV and covered canvas after canvas with mountains and rivers and trees and cloudy blue skies. When she came to visit, she sometimes brought her paints. "You've got to try it, Mom!" she urged enthusiastically.

"I can't!" I told her just as emphatically.

"Why not?"

"Because...," I sputtered, searching for the right reason, "because a blank canvas scares me."

A few days later I watched my five-year-old granddaughter sitting at our kitchen counter, a crayon in her hand, gleefully filling blank white pages with stick figures, houses, flowers, and pointy-edged suns. Obviously, blank pages didn't scare her; they represented endless possibilities. When in the process of growing up did I lose that ability to create without fear of the results? When did self-confidence get replaced by self-consciousness? Those are questions I can't answer, but this I know: I don't want to grow so far "up" that I get fearful of trying something new, regardless of the results. So the next time Kendall brought over her box of paints and her easel and several blank canvases, I didn't say, "I can't." Instead, I picked up a brush and began dabbing some color onto a blank canvas.

The result? Well, let's just say Grandma Moses would have nothing to worry about from me. But I'm ready to try another painting, and that feels pretty good.

Lord, help me to see the possibilities in all the blank canvases in my life.
—CAROL KUYKENDALL

I am bringing all my energies to bear on this one thing:
Forgetting the past and looking forward to what lies ahead.
—PHILIPPIANS 3:13 TLB

*B*ecause of illness, my ninety-one-year-old mother had been away from her home in Elberton, Georgia, for five years. She lived for four years with my husband Gene and me, then moved to a nearby assisted-living facility. One day she said, "Marion, you may as well go ahead and sell my house. I'm not going to be able to return."

It all happened in an amazing eight days. A buyer appeared quickly, and Gene and my children and some of my grandchildren helped me to empty Mother's house. After the closing at the lawyer's, I hurried back to Mother. "I did it," I announced, waiting for her questions. *She must have so many,* I thought. Practically everything she owned and loved is gone. She'll want to know how I disposed of each item.

To my surprise, she smiled and said, "Thank you. I knew you could manage."

"Don't you have questions?" I asked.

"No." She looked perfectly content sitting in her electric recliner. "I don't live in the past, Marion. I never look back. I like to look ahead."

"Okay," I said. "But I did bring you something from your house—something I couldn't part with."

"Oh, what?" she asked. She clapped her hands excitedly and her eyes shone.

I ran out to the car and came back with a huge plastic sack. In it were all Mother's hats, going back to the hat she'd worn at her wedding in 1931. While she watched with delight, I stood on her bed and hung the hats on the wall, using my shoe for a hammer. Then I sat back down, and together we silently admired the hats.

Finally, Mother said, "Maybe I'll get to wear some of them again!"

Father, when the time comes, help me to relinquish
the stuff in my life graciously and with thanks.
—MARION BOND WEST

*"But I tell you who hear me: Love your enemies, do good to those who hate you,
bless those who curse you, pray for those who mistreat you."*
—LUKE 6:27–28 NIV

I've been deeply concerned for my friend. Her teenage daughter has moved in with her older boyfriend and his dad. The boyfriend and his dad treat my friend with hostility. To make matters worse, my friend's ex-husband has joined them in their anger at her. Together they've leveled false accusations against my friend and have alienated her daughter from her. Over the past months my friend has poured out her despair to me. Tonight, however, when I phoned her, I heard an amazing change in her voice. "I feel as though a huge weight has been lifted off me," she said.

"What happened?" I asked incredulously.

"Well, when I heard the Gospel reading at church this morning—to love your enemies and to pray for those who persecute you—I knew that somehow I had to do what Jesus said, even though it seemed impossible."

"Considering how you've been treated, it does seem impossible to respond that way."

"I felt that I couldn't but that God could. For the rest of the service, I prayed for them. When I came home, I still felt overwhelmed by my hurt and anger, so I prayed more. Instead of praying for them to change, I simply asked God to do good to them.

"Suddenly, everything inside me changed. I felt a lightness I've never felt before. I know that somehow everything will work out. I'll keep praying for them and trusting God. I finally have peace."

*Thank You, Lord, for helping my friend—and me—
to obey Your Word, even when it seems impossible.*
—MARY BROWN

"Mother is the name for God in the lips and hearts of little children."
—WILLIAM MAKEPEACE THACKERAY

All mothers are special, but some are super special. I suspect that Susanna Wesley, the mother of John and Charles Wesley, fell into the latter category.

Mother of nineteen children, eleven of whom survived infancy, she apparently had a monumental influence on her children, two of whom gained worldwide prominence. We get some insight into the dedication she brought to her maternal role from a practice she instituted for each child. According to John, his mother scheduled one hour a week for each of her children. When that hour came, she put aside everything else and devoted it to that child alone, listening and talking about his or her special concerns. One hour may not seem like a lot, but with eleven children to care for, this wife of a minister no doubt had her hands full, and busy mothers can appreciate her self-discipline.

The most basic unit of society is the family, and how our culture fares depends to a large extent on the strength of the home. Loving parents who give their children a sense of self-worth and make them feel special are engaged in a godly calling. Let us therefore salute mothers, the Susanna Wesleys in history. They are "gems of purest ray serene."

It's also good to recall the positive influences of our own mothers and the sacrifices they made for us. If possible, thank yours personally; if not, thank God.

For the love and guidance of a wonderful Christian mother, I thank You, Lord.
—FRED BAUER

JUNE 27

Thou has put gladness in my heart.
—PSALM 4:7

June was family time in our vacation cabin at Mammoth Lakes in California. For two glorious weeks, we became part of the history of the rustic log cabin built by settlers in 1908. All the furniture, beds included, was made of massive logs. We put our feet up on the iron rail that fronted a huge rock fireplace and sipped hot chocolate to the rhythmic creak of rough-hewn rockers. No phone, no television, just us and the children, and then just us. Now that my husband John was gone, it would be just me.

"It won't be 'just you,'" my son Ian insisted. "Let's all go. You can fish with the kids, Mom, and I'll teach them to tie hooks at the very same table where Dad taught me."

Apprehensive and sad, I went.

Driving up the highway into the Inyo National Forest was like entering a warm embrace. The snow-capped mountains and dancing aspen were still home away from home. As we stepped into the cabin and my son gave me a teary-eyed hug, I once again felt the comfort of John's arms around me.

We pulled out the photo album. The grandchildren giggled over stories—the dog falling through the iced-over lake, a lightning storm that zapped our power, the bear we met on the climb to the top of the falls. We cozied up in the same rockers and hiked the same trails, absorbed in the nostalgia of then. But it was now. Time to move on to new adventures.

Traditions kept. Traditions created. Then and now, both better than good.

For tears and sadness turned to joy and gladness, thank You, Lord.
—FAY ANGUS

For life is the mirror of king and slave... 'tis just what we are and do:
Then give to the world the best you have; and the best will come back to you.
MARY AINGE DE VERE

My y family knows how much I love books.

Last week, my son brought home several boxes of books from a garage sale. All had a woman's name in beautiful penmanship on the inside cover. There were piles of record books from the various clubs she had joined over the years. Her church, and many civic groups were well represented. She was secretary of one, treasurer of another, and president of several others. Here was a college yearbook from 1924. That handsome boy in the graduating class must be her husband; they have the same last name.

I started to feel as though I knew this lady. She played the piano, sang in the church choir, wrote her notes in shorthand, and was an avid gardener. Through a death notice, I learned that her husband had died. After that she seemed to take on even more church work and volunteer jobs. As I dug deeper in her life, I feared what might become of her as she grew older. What would her health be like? Would she be lonely? And then I came across this letter:

Dear Mother,

It won't be long now! We can hardly wait for you to get here. The children are anxious to see you again, and so am I. We found a beautiful apartment for you; all you have to do is look out the window to see the ocean. It's just two blocks away from us, so we can be together often, yet you won't feel tied down. Best news of all, I have met several gardeners, and they're looking forward to meeting you. The church is within walking distance, and you won't believe all the activities in the community.

Welcome to your new life, Mom.

What a relief I felt, reading that letter. But, then, I should have expected it all along. She'd given the world the best she had, and the world was giving it right back.

Lord, bless the stranger we pass but never meet; yet who touches our lives and hearts.
—PAT SULLIVAN

God Almighty...will bless you with blessings of heaven above,
blessings of the deep that couches beneath.
—GENESIS 49:25 RSV

*M*y friend Gary headed straight for the steel guitar hanging on the wall in the music store. I knew he would; it was a ritual each time we went. With a look of absolute love on his face, he would hold the guitar and play the blues in the small display room. Each week his paychecks had to go to matters more important than buying a guitar, especially such an expensive one!

Little did he know that the same kind of guitar was waiting for him in his bedroom. His mother had bought it as a surprise. For days, Gary came home late and woke early, too busy and too tired even to notice it. One day Gary slowed down. He noticed the new, mysterious case sitting in his bedroom and opened it to find the beautiful steel guitar. He was thrilled—and humbled—by the thoughtfulness and generosity of his mother.

"That guitar was sitting there for days!" she said with a laugh. "It just goes to show you that sometimes God has blessings He's just waiting for us to discover, if only we take the time to see them."

Open my eyes, Lord, to Your abundance. Amen.
—KAREN VALENTIN

JUNE 30

"Who has gathered up the wind in the hollow of his hands?"
—PROVERBS 30:4 NIV

I watched the strong winds move across the water on my backyard pond. A storm was approaching and the wind gusts were close to twenty miles an hour.

"It's so easy to see the wind on the water now," I mused. Not so when I was a teenager vacationing in Florida. I spent the summer sunning, water-skiing, and learning how to sail from a tanned blond instructor named Robby. I remember sitting in his small, two-person Sunfish when he said, "You've got to maneuver the boat into the wind. Look for the breeze on the water and tack toward it." He pointed ahead to a darkening rippled area. "The wind on the water looks a bit like fish feeding below the surface."

I squinted into the sun, looking out across the water for some sign that the wind was approaching. I shook my head, frustrated. "I don't see it."

A few minutes later the wind filled our sails. Robby trimmed them and turned toward me. "We can't see the wind, but we can see its effect on the water," he said. "It's a little like noticing God in our life. We can't really see Him, but we can see His effect."

Looking out into my backyard now, I watched my grown children and young grandchildren attempt to fly a kite in the breeze. I watched the wind race across the pond, reach the kite, and lift it high. My grandbabies, their soft, wispy hair blowing in all directions, ran after the kite. My children and their spouses cheered, and Misty, my oldest daughter, video camera in hand, documented it all. I joined along in the cheers, not just for the kite high in the air, but for the ability to see the effect of God's gracious love on my family and me.

> *Powerful Creator, may I always see Your presence in my life.*
> —MELODY BONNETTE

July

July 1

That ye may be blameless and harmless, the sons of God,
without rebuke, in the midst of a crooked and perverse nation, among
whom ye shine as lights in the world; Holding forth the word of life....
—Philippians 2:15–16

*W*hen I was ten, my family moved to a Bible ranch full of darkness. The woman in charge took in welfare cases, young boys and old men whose families were unable or unwilling to take care of them. Many were overworked, some abused, all neglected. Little compassion was wasted on them until Mother got there.

Mum quickly put my two sisters and me to work, playing dominoes with blind Uncle Earl, though we soon found other ways to entertain this quiet gentleman who loved the Dodgers: walks beneath the eucalyptus, smashing a crop of black walnuts and then helping him separate the meat from the shells, proofreading letters to a daughter somewhere. Richie was our age. Mum started paying him a nickel for each word he got right on his spelling. She let us skip our own chores to help with his. She cut his hair and patched his clothes. Joe, developmentally disabled, was a special project. His own mother had died, and Mum took over. She gave him pennies for the birthday bank at church, took him to the cemetery, saved the bread heels just for him.

Mum took them all under her wing: Howard, Jack, Ben.... More importantly, she stood up to the woman in charge. During our first month there, Mum drew a line between us and the darkness—a circle into which no shadow could fall and where we all dwelt safely in her sunbeam of love. We eventually left the ranch, but Mum's love remains—in the lives she forever touched.

Dear God, You, too, draw a line and create a circle of safety and love into which
no shadow can fall, where our hearts and minds can dwell safely in You.
—Brenda Wilbee

July 2

*And suddenly there came a sound from heaven as of a rushing
mighty wind, and it filled all the house where they were sitting.*
—Acts 2:2

*W*e were still living in Alaska, and I was listening to the breeze stir the leaves in the forest of birch trees outside my open bedroom window. At the same time I was meditating on John 3:8 (RSV), where Jesus likens being born of the Spirit to the presence of the wind, saying, "The wind blows where it wills, and you hear the sound of it, but you do not know whence it comes or whither it goes; so it is with every one born of the Spirit."

Suddenly, through the wall on the opposite side of the room, I heard my daughter Kelly begin singing praise choruses she learned on her college campus. As I listened to the sound of the wind—with its intimations of the Spirit of God—and simultaneously heard Kelly's songs of holy adoration, I thought with delight, *Why, this is Holy Spirit surround-sound!* I let it envelop me and carry me to joy-filled heights, buoyed by a sense of God's presence.

Since that experience I find myself deliberately listening for more "Spirit surround-sound." It may be in the wind or waves, in church bells pealing, or in the familiar voice of a loved one. It might come from an unexpected source, such as the swish of a compassionate nurse's uniform in a hospital, or the click of computer keys in a job that the Lord has provided or a prayer of encouragement offered over the phone. It can be any sound that inspires us to glorify God and celebrate the love that Jesus Christ has for us.

Try listening intently today. The music is sure to be there.

Jesus, Your Holy Spirit is waiting to be heard. And my heart is ready to listen.
—Carol Knapp

July 3

"No plan of yours can be thwarted."
—JOB 42:2 NIV

I'm not sure exactly why I decided to take Amtrak to see my family in New York City. A plane would have gotten me there in a few hours rather than the train's two and a half days.

Restless after the first day in my seat, I decided to visit the lounge car where I could stretch my legs. I sat down next to a mother with twin girls who were about four years old. Chattering and lively, the girls pulled at their mother's legs as she read God's Plan for the Single Parent. Touched, I prayed, God, let her find a partner to help her raise these children.

"Can you draw a cat?" one of the girls, Becky, asked me.

My mixture of circles and dots and lines must have passed muster, because her sister scampered over and the next hour was spent with the three of us drawing while their mother read her book. Then the three of us sang a few choruses of "The Wheels on the Train" before I told them that I'd better head back to my seat.

I shrugged off the mother's thanks and nodded toward her book. "I'll pray that God's plan is revealed for you," I said. "I hope you meet Mr. Right," I added with a grin.

She grinned back. "Actually, I'm sure you were part of God's plan for me today. I've been on this train for three days already, and—well, I adore my kids, but I prayed for some peace and some quiet time to read. And there you were."

My jaw dropped. Me? A part of God's plan? But I wasn't important enough, was I? Maybe that's why I'd decided to take the train. Maybe it wasn't my idea at all! I'd keep my eyes open during this long trip for others who might need my help. As part of God's plan, of course.

God, today let me consider how I may be a part of Your plan.
—LINDA NEUKRUG

July 4

Behold, the Lord thy God hath set the land before thee...
fear not, neither be discouraged.
—DEUTERONOMY 1:21

A couple years ago I was visiting two of my children in California, Jeanne and Andrew, and their families. Jeanne's Adeline was three years old and Andrew's Ethan was two and a half. We drove to a little town to watch the fireworks on the Fourth of July and ended up sitting on a brick ledge in front of a grocery store for the best view.

When the booms and flashes began, Ethan started shaking and was soon in tears. I tried to comfort him, but even Grandma's lap couldn't provide shelter from the sensory overload. Then Jeanne put the two little ones together in the front seat of a huge grocery cart shaped like a big toy car. Adeline put her arm around Ethan, and before long they were giggling and staring at the fantastic light show with glee.

Sometimes I'm afraid of things too: noisy politicians, war, rising taxes, hurricanes, health problems. Then I remember: Today is the Fourth of July, Independence Day, the day we officially became a nation under God, indivisible, with liberty and justice for all. We're in this together, and our government, our democracy, under God, is designed to give us a chance to tackle the problems, big and little, that concern all of us. Just like Adeline and Ethan, I find strength in numbers and comfort in the shared goals that we Americans enjoy. God bless America!

Father, keep me thankful for this nation that
protects us while keeping our freedoms intact.
—PATRICIA LORENZ

Nevertheless he left not himself without witness,
in that he did good...filling our hearts with food and gladness.
—ACTS 14:17

’m not a food person. I don’t relish new recipes, and I don’t enjoy cooking and baking. My favorite food as a skinny child was a banana Popsicle. So it’s been next to impossible for me to accept that, for some people, food is synonymous with love.

On a recent hot July day, my son Jon phoned from work, asking in an almost reverent tone, “Have you tasted those tomatoes I gave you, Mom?” I hadn’t. “I’m eating one now,” he explained excitedly. “Mom, they’re incredible. Get one and taste it while we talk, okay?” When I didn’t, his voice gradually took on a ho-hum tone, and the conversation wound down.

Later in the day I was suddenly really sorry I hadn’t sampled the tomatoes, so I called Jon back and invited him to supper the next evening. “What are you having?” he asked cautiously.

“Country fried steak, gravy and mashed potatoes,” I sang out. “Fresh stewed corn, fresh squash, biscuits, cantaloupe, some of those marvelous tomatoes you brought us and...*ta-dah*...fresh peach cobbler!”

“I’ll be there!” he shouted.

Jon *oohed* and *aahed* throughout the meal, speaking in a mellow, tender tone. As I packed up some of the food for him to take home, he looked at me long and hard, then burst into an incredible, impromptu smile that conveyed unmistakably, I love you!

Lord Jesus, whether You were feeding thousands by the
Sea of Galilee or a handful of friends in the upper room,
You always did it gladly. Show me how. Amen.
—MARION BOND WEST

Thou openest thine hand, and satisfiest the desire of every living thing.
—Psalm 145:16

*D*o you sometimes wonder if the prayers of a mother's heart are answered? Recently I've been praying that our twenty-five-year-old daughter Lindsay would know God's love in a special, tangible way. Two nights ago, she called from California; her voice broke as she said, "Mom, my bird flew away." Her bird is a cockatiel that is more than a bird because of the way it responds to Lindsay. Sometimes she lets it fly around her apartment, and when she whistles, the bird echoes the sound and lands on her shoulder.

Lindsay said the bird flew out her patio door that afternoon, flopped around on the roof and then disappeared into the trees. She blamed herself and spent three hours scouring the neighborhood, looking up into tree-tops and whistling. She saw and heard nothing. "When these birds get stressed, they are apt to keep getting farther away, and I know it won't be able to survive long outdoors," she said.

The next morning, Lindsay got up early and looked again before going to work. At noon she decided to drive home and try one more time. As she whistled at the trees around her apartment, a woman appeared and told her she thought she had heard the bird at the swimming pool several blocks away. Off Lindsay went, and as she neared the pool, she began whistling. Way in the distance, she heard a faint echo. Again she whistled. Again the faint echo. She kept following the sound, which got a little louder, until she came to a tall wrought-iron fence, and there on the other side, hopping along the ground, was her bird. Lindsay whistled as she stuck her arm through the wrought-iron fence and the bird jumped on to it, crawling up to her chest where it snuggled down, whistling in response.

"I found my bird!" Lindsay told me gleefully when she called later.

The song in my heart is still singing with praise.

> *Thank You, Lord, for answered prayers.*
> —Carol Kuykendall

JULY 7

*From infancy you have known the holy Scriptures, which are able
to make you wise for salvation through faith in Christ Jesus.*
—2 TIMOTHY 3:15 NIV

I can't think about the Bible for very long without remembering Grandma Fellman. She lived to be ninety-eight and kept her Bible beside her always. A couple of years ago her now elderly daughter, my aunt, sent me that Bible. Its leather cover is worn and tattered, and some of the pages have come loose from the binding and are threatening to fall out. Several people have suggested that I have it restored, but I like it the way it is. Holding it with the spine in my palm, I can feel the impression of Grandma's hand. She held it that way with me on her lap and her arms around me as we read chapter after chapter.

For some people the Bible is just a complicated collection of sixty-six books by thirty-nine authors spanning thousands of years, a historical document needing criticism and correction. Not so for Grandma Fellman. She often told me, "Honey, this book, from beginning to end, is about one thing: the Savior Jesus. The old part is about how we lost touch with God and He made a plan to send Jesus to bring us back. The new part tells Jesus' life story and how He wants us to live. Follow His way and you will never go wrong."

I hope that the next time Grandma sees Jesus, she'll tell Him that lots of us down here are trying to follow His way and she'll ask Him to keep being patient with us.

*Lord Jesus, thank You for the Scriptures that tell us
Your story. Help us to live together in Your way.*
—ERIC FELLMAN

JULY 8

"Blessed are the dead who die in the Lord...they will rest
from their labor, for their deeds will follow them."
—REVELATION 14:13 NIV

I look at the familiar exit sign and feel the lump in my throat grow larger. It has been nine months since I last made this five-hundred-mile round-trip. Nine long months. I pull off the interstate and take the back roads to the small town where she lived. Her house, now owned by strangers, is ill-kept: Trash litters the yard, the shrubs have been pulled up, and one window in the back porch is broken. I push down on the gas, remembering the meticulous way Mother kept everything, and turn toward where I know I'll find her.

The old cemetery where she is buried is small. I park my car between two huge trees and reach into the backseat for the dozen roses I've just bought. Mother's grave is easy to spot, flanked as always by bouquets of purple silk flowers. I stand at the grave. It is a beautiful day...birds, sun, corn swishing in the field next door.

As I brush a few leaves from her grave and place the flowers, I read the stone: AT REST IN HEAVEN. It's easy to imagine my mother in heaven. But at rest? That's harder. She was always working, organizing church dinners, visiting shut-ins, creating missionary lessons, or cooking for just about everyone!

I stoop to kiss her gravestone and, on impulse, pull out one of the roses. I'll take it back with me and place it on my desk at work; not as a reminder of Mother's death, but as a tribute to her life—a life of service, well lived and worthy of emulation.

Help me, Father, to live my life in response to Your voice.
Let me leave a legacy of holy work, done with diligence and joy.
—MARY LOU CARNEY

For with thee is the fountain of life: in thy light shall we see light.
—PSALM 36:9

his is my favorite time of night," my mother said.

"Dark enough so you can see the fireflies, light enough so you can catch them. Do you know what lightning bugs are, Solomon?"

My two-year-old looked confused. "I don't think he does," I said.

Outside, the moon showed through the clouds in a dim yellow haze. Crickets chirped. Stray sparks glistened in the field next door. I held Solomon's hand and pointed to the sparks. "Those are lightning bugs!"

"Look at them all!" Mom said.

The sparks of light twinkled above the tall grass. There must have been a hundred of them.

"Well," Mom said, "what are you waiting for? Go catch them!"

Barefoot, I crept over the dew-covered lawn to the field. Arms outstretched, I reached for flashes, grasping at the air. Years disappeared, and I felt the same excitement I'd felt nearly thirty years earlier. The same yard, the same glorious feeling, being with my mom beneath the stars chasing sparks of light. In the darkness, I followed the flashes and then I had one, a tiny little lightning bug safely caught in my hands.

"Look, your mom's got one!" my mother said.

Solomon cheered. "Yeah! Mama's got a light! Mama's got a light!" Bright yellow twinkled from the creases of my hands.

"That is a firefly, Solomon," my mother said.

"Mommy lights up," he said.

Beneath the stars, we *oohed* and *ahhed* as our hands lit up, catching fireflies until it got too dark to see.

Later that night, as I lay in bed, my eyes tired from the cool night air, I felt as if I'd completed a circle: I'd recaptured a favorite childhood memory and made it stronger and brighter by sharing it with my son.

Dear God, thank You for letting me see Your light through the eyes of my son.
—SABRA CIANCANELLI

JULY 10

A cheerful heart is good medicine, but a crushed spirit dries up the bones.
—PROVERBS 17:22 NIV

*E*ven though major-league baseball isn't my favorite pastime, I jumped at the chance to take my son Andrew to a Milwaukee Brewers game in July 1999. Just four weeks earlier he'd had surgery. He hadn't been out of the house except for short walks and, quite frankly, I was getting impatient with him.

At Milwaukee County Stadium that night, we watched the game, we watched the people, we ate junk food. Then suddenly, just after the seventh-inning stretch, around 9:30 p.m., there was a power failure and the enormous lights that lit up the field suddenly went out. The stadium and field were left in a hazy darkness, and within a few minutes all the players retreated into the dugouts.

Because the score was Milwaukee 10, Kansas City 3, many people got up and left for home. Others blew bubbles, headed for the refreshment stands, or sang songs in groups. I finally pulled a book out of my backpack and started to read under the few dusky lights that were still on in the grandstand.

Twenty minutes later, when I looked up to see that the field was aglow with bright lights once again and the game was ready to resume, I couldn't believe my eyes. I hadn't even noticed when the lights came back on. Andrew said they'd come on very gradually over the entire thirty-minute period.

Gradually, huh? They went from total darkness to bright enough to play ball and I hadn't even noticed?

I started to think about Andrew's healing. He'd gone from major surgery to cheering for the Brewers in four weeks and I hadn't really noticed that he'd been getting a little better each day...gradually. I'd been too concerned about pushing him to exercise harder, sleep less, take fewer pain pills, do a few chores, and call his friends, to notice that he was walking tall, eating normally, and anxious to get out to see his beloved Brewers.

Lord, help me to be patient and loving when my loved ones are healing.
Keep me mindful that it's a gradual process.
—PATRICIA LORENZ

July 11

"The kingdom of heaven is like a king who prepared a wedding banquet for his son."
—Matthew 22:2 niv

"This is not the way I dreamed of spending my Saturday," I mumbled under my breath. My husband Jacob had to work, so here I was doing all the household chores on a beautiful summer weekend. What I should be doing is swimming at the lake, I said to myself, pulling off the yellow gloves I wore to do the dishes. I was feeling pretty sorry for myself and more than a little annoyed as I picked up the bottle of spray bleach and headed into the bathroom. A small voice brought me to an abrupt halt.

"Mommy, what is heaven?"

I looked down at Trace, my four-year-old. He was staring up at me, a serious look in his big gray eyes. I swallowed and knelt down, so I could look into his face.

"Well," I said, trying to think of all the correct biblical answers but drawing a blank, "heaven is..." I looked down at the bleach in my hands. "Heaven is...a big party."

"A party?" He looked confused.

"Yes. A big party, where we get to be with God and all the people we love. Remember how much fun you had at Jeremiah's birthday party? Remember the cake and presents and games?" Trace nodded. "Heaven is like that: a big, wonderful party."

A smile spread across his face. "Awesome, Mommy," he said. Then he hugged me and ran off to play.

> *Lord, when I get caught up in the daily grind, help me*
> *remember the wonderful party You have planned.*
> —Amanda Borozinski

July 12

Through him and for his name's sake, we received grace.
—ROMANS 1:5 NIV

This has been a summer of babies for our family. In July my niece and her husband arrived from Birmingham, Alabama, with their newborn Finn and his fourteen-month-old brother Aiden. While they were here, my first granddaughter was born, Isabelle Grace. Next came my niece Scarlet's baby, Lillian. They, along with my grandsons Drake and Brock, are sure to put the "din" in family dinners for years to come!

My daughter-in-law Stacy has already begun to play baby-friendly versions of hymns for her wee one. "Isabelle's favorite song is 'Amazing Grace,'" she told me recently. "She always gets quiet when it comes on."

When I hold a newborn and look into those eyes, I can't keep from believing in a divine Creator and in His grace—unmerited favor—from the minute we're born. Maybe Isabelle Grace, so fresh from those mysterious realms, knows this in a way we don't...or can't.

Grace. What's so amazing about it? Everything! How blessed I am that my new granddaughter will help me remember that every day.

I praise You, Father, for the miracle of new life
and for life renewed through Your tender and constant care.
—MARY LOU CARNEY

JULY 13

For thus says the Lord God, "Behold, I Myself
will search for My sheep and seek them out."
—EZEKIEL 34:11 NASB

The youth choir rehearsal had almost ended when the lights suddenly went out in the church. There was a lot of commotion as people left the building. At first I thought only our church had lost electrical power, until someone yelled, "The whole city is in the dark." My siblings Sandy and Orland and I quickly walked home. Everything looked different without light.

At home my mother was anxious about us. She grabbed her flashlight and rushed out of the apartment into the dark hallway and down the stairs. She walked down several steps before she slipped and tumbled. She got up and continued down the stairway and into the neighborhood searching for us. We all arrived safely home shortly after, but later that night my mother's left foot began to swell. The next morning she went to the hospital—she had broken her ankle.

When I remember the blackout of 1977 in New York City, it's not the chaos or the darkness that comes to mind, but my mother's love for us. She let nothing get in the way, risking her own safety to search for her children before anyone or anything could harm us.

Dear God, even in my darkest moments, when all
seems dim and bleak, Your love is seeking me out.
—PABLO DIAZ

July 14

And to know the love of Christ, which passeth knowledge,
that ye might be filled with all the fulness of God.
—Ephesians 3:19

*W*hen I was a child, we lived down a dusty dirt road from my paternal grandmother. I loved going to her house to sit with her under the shady pecan trees as she shelled peas or prepared fresh corn from her garden. I was always barefoot, and on scorching summer days I'd hop along on the high spots where the sand was thinner and the heat less intense. Finally, I'd reach the shade of Grandmother's big yard and cool my feet on the green grass.

My grandmother was not a demonstrative person, and at my young age I sometimes wondered whether she really loved me. But then Grandmother would produce a dime from some unseen pocket and my heart would leap. That was my cue to walk to the neighborhood store to buy a soda for both of us. The sand was still unforgiving, but the thought of the cold drink on my parched tongue would have taken me across hot coals. Grandmother may not have smothered me with kisses, but that cold soda on a hot summer day showed that she loved me.

There are times in my life when I feel that God's love is not so evident either, and I wish He would smother me with kisses. But then, just as the heat of the situation seems intolerable, I spot the proverbial dime: It may be a Scripture or a magnificent sunset or a wise word from a friend. Then I know that all I have to do is wait on Him and trust in His love. It never fails. That assurance makes the trip up the hot, dusty road of life worth every bold step.

Father, grant that I may recognize Your love for me,
especially in the small things that often go unnoticed.
—Libbie Adams

Behold, I will extend peace to her like a river.
—ISAIAH 66:12

*M*ama, Ben asked me to marry him," my daughter Keri said. She stood before me, holding out her hand; a diamond sparkled from her third finger. Her words seemed to be coming to me from the end of a long tunnel.

"Oh, no," I said.

I've always had a fantasy of being the perfect mother. "How lovely, Keri," that perfect mother would say. "I'm so happy for you." But this was real life, and I'm far from perfect, so I answered back, "When? Surely you're smart enough to wait a few years? You're still in graduate school. We have no money saved for a wedding. You're waiting until Ben finishes dental school, aren't you?"

The answer, of course, was "No."

Keri knows me, so she didn't miss a beat. "Actually, we were thinking this May. Since I was born on your birthday, we thought it would be cool to get married on your and Daddy's anniversary."

David's and my marriage had begun with too many debts and too little money. I wanted something different for my daughter. "Keri, you have no idea how much it hurts not to be able to buy the groceries you need, to stand in line at the store trembling at the total."

"Mama," she answered, "you and Daddy are happy. If being poor is part of what got you here, then I want to experience the same thing. I want a marriage like yours."

What could I say back? The truth? The truth is, I wouldn't sell a second of my life with David for any sum of money. I stood in the living room and looked at the young woman whom I call daughter. She seemed very wise, and I was awed by the mystery of being her mother.

Father, trusting those I love to You, I find incredible peace. Thank You.
—PAM KIDD

July 16

*I the Lord search the heart...even to give every man according
to his ways, and according to the fruit of his doings.*
—Jeremiah 17:10

*M*y son was driving me and two of my daughter Tamara's children to
their home where I was going to spend "grandma time." Somewhere
along the way I began handing out saltwater taffy to Caleb, five, and Ruby, four,
in the backseat. The problem was I only passed them the flavors I didn't like.
They got blueberry and licorice and raspberry; I got cinnamon and peppermint
and chocolate. They didn't know the difference, but I did.

I began to wonder, *Is it really sharing if I'm giving something I don't want?
Shouldn't I have a stake in it for it to be true sharing?* We arrived at Tamara's, where
every night Ruby and I read a book about what love is. One page said, "Love is
sharing your umbrella in the rain."

There was no precipitation in Alaska's forecast the evening Tamara walked
into Ruby's bedroom and rained M&Ms, my favorite candy, in my lap. Ruby
was on red alert. Holding out her small hand, she announced, "Don't you know
love is sharing?"

I parted with my M&Ms that night to a gleeful voice inside me that said,
"Now *this* is sharing."

*God, supreme Giver, prepare me for bountiful giving
by first keeping me generous in the small stuff.*
—Carol Knapp

JULY 17

He gently leads those that have young.
—ISAIAH 40:11 NIV

I recently spent an afternoon helping my very pregnant daughter-in-law Alexandra prepare for the birth of her second child. I organized toys while she measured spaces for storage containers that would separate one child's stuff from another's. She penciled some numbers down on paper, made decisions about where to put the tiny new diapers and how to make a single bedroom work for two children.

As we worked, Alex confessed that she was concerned about having enough time to be enough "mom" for a second child. "How will I do everything?" she asked. I admitted that I'd had the same concerns a generation earlier.

Meanwhile, three-year-old Gabriella played nearby, naturally mimicking many of her mommy's actions.

"You weigh thirty-seven, Oma," she told me matter-of-factly as she measured my arm with the tape measure. She then sat down at her little table and began doodling on a piece of paper. "I'm making a meeting," she announced. A short time later, she put her purse over her arm, picked up her baby, stuffed a pacifier in the doll's mouth and headed for the back door. "We need some fresh air," she informed us.

People say she looks just like her daddy, but I can tell you, she walks just like her mommy. As I sat there that day, surrounded by the piles of clothes and toys and the normal happenings in this home, I realized—again—the power of a mother's influence, communicated by simply being Mom. It's one of God's great provisions to moms, a gift that makes us enough to meet the needs of all our children.

> *Lord, help mothers to trust in You, to know*
> *that You are enough to make us enough.*
> —CAROL KUYKENDALL

Commit your work to the Lord, then it will succeed.
—PROVERBS 16:3 TLB

I was blinking the sleep out of my eyes and fumbling around the coffee maker when our son Ian came into the kitchen, much too early, and much too energetically for my sluggish 6:00 a.m. disposition. It was his first day on a new job.

"What do you think, Mom? Pretty neat, huh?" He grinned, and my heart skipped a beat in the sheer joy of being "Mom" to this fine young man. His hair was trimmed; his shoes shined mirror-bright; and his new suit was set off by a classy silk tie, a "just right" tie—and I should know, I bought it!

"Absolutely marvelous!" I replied.

Gulping a cup of coffee, Ian turned, as always, to his dad, his hard-nosed, tell-it-like-it-is dad, for assurance and affirmation. Oh, please, dear Lord, I prayed, no critique, no well-meant advice from this man he looks up to and loves so much, not today. Please, Lord, something upbeat from his dad. I breathed a sigh of relief as my husband put an arm around Ian's shoulder and gave him the words he needed to hear: "You'll ace it, son. You know your stuff."

"Well, here goes!" Ian hugged me just a little too tight, just a little too long. Then with a small, almost imperceptible quiver in his voice, he whispered, "Pray for me, Mom," and I knew he was afraid.

"You've got it, lad!" The Lord must have been smiling; I'd committed this opportunity of Ian's to Him and had been praying for it around the clock for months.

That evening Ian came home smiling ear to ear. "A few kinks to work out," he said, "but Dad's right. I think I'll ace it!"

> *Lord of the daily workplace, Lord of a job well done, I pray*
> *for all those starting a new job today. Settle their shaky hearts. Give them*
> *diligence, dependability, and a determination to make a go of it.*
> —FAY ANGUS

How good and pleasant it is when brothers live together in unity!
—PSALM 133:1 NIV

After packing a bag with toys, diapers, baby clothes, bottles, and who knows how many other things, my son and I head out the door for a weekend in the country. Like most city moms, I have no trouble lifting the hefty stroller up and down the subway stairs, and at Penn Station I purchase a ticket for the train that will whisk me away from Manhattan. After one transfer and more stairs, I settle into my seat for the two-hour trip.

As I look out the window, skyscrapers give way to mountains and trees, and I know that the long, troublesome journey will be worth it. Much more than the country air, it's the family waiting for my arrival that I'm looking forward to. My cousin will honk his horn with a wave, my sister will jump out of the car and tackle me with hugs, and my niece and nephews will run straight to the stroller, shouting my son's name.

When I was growing up in Brooklyn, every day was crowded with the sweet chaos of family, and I'd always envisioned my own children as part of it. But slowly, everyone moved away—my parents to Florida and everyone else hours north of New York City. I miss the family circus and long for my son to experience the abundance of love I enjoyed as a child. So when the voices of my husband and I are not enough and the apartment seems too quiet, I pack a bag and take the train to the love and noise of my family.

Thank You, Lord, for all those who love me and
for Your love that surrounds me wherever I am.
—KAREN VALENTIN

He will teach the ways that are right and best to those who humbly turn to him
—Psalm 25:9 tlb

*W*henever we visit my husband's parents near Lake Erie, my daughter Maria spends hours digging at the beach, piling up mounds of wet sand, and building tunnels and castles. A princess lives in one and her friends in another. Their activities keep Maria busy for a long time.

Lake Erie waves aren't huge, but they're big enough to wipe out a tiny shorefront village. "Start building a little farther away from the water," I told Maria one time, but she assured me everything would be okay. But soon the waves got bigger. "Mommy, Mommy, oh no!" she cried as water lapped the edges of the princess' castle. "Do something, Mommy!" But I couldn't keep the next wave from washing away Maria's afternoon of work. I hugged her tightly and told her we would build another castle together. Still, it hurt, especially since I'd told her not to build so close to the water.

I thought later that Maria's cries to me are similar to my own cries to God when I go my own way, forgetting His gentle guidance. I'm reminded of a work project that I took on, thinking I'd make some quick money, even though in prayer I'd felt a nudge to decline. But I confidently said yes, and then regretted it when the job caused a lot of aggravation. Of course, I ran to God in prayer to fix my mess. Thankfully, He didn't scold me and say, "I told you so." He wrapped His loving arms around me and gave me the strength to finish the job.

> *Open my ears, loving God, so that in prayer*
> *I might not only speak but also listen.*
> —Gina Bridgeman

JULY 21

When I am weak, then am I strong.
—2 CORINTHIANS 12:10

*M*y mother drinks from the same Alice-in-Wonderland teacup every morning. She bought it many years ago when we were on vacation in Florida. My parents had just divorced, and the trip was planned so that we could get away and begin our new lives. Unfortunately, the entire time we were at Disney World it rained. At first we tried to do indoor things, but on the third and final day, we put on raincoats and tried to tough it out. But the wet got the better of us, and after a huge argument over what to do, we decided to leave.

On the way out, we collected gifts for everyone back home. As Mom piled T-shirts and hats onto the counter, she added a half-priced Alice-in- Wonderland teacup as an afterthought.

That evening we drove to the ocean for one last look. The rain had let up and the mosquitoes were brutal, but the water was warm and we stayed to watch the sunset.

"I'm sorry," Mom said. "I guess this vacation wasn't such a good idea." I looked off into the distance and pretended not to hear. It seemed lately all we had was disappointment, and I needed something to be all right. "We tried," she said. "That's the important thing."

When we got home, instead of giving away the cup as she had planned, Mom put it in our cabinet. Soon it became a special part of her morning. Since then, the gold rim around the edge has worn off and the Cheshire cat is missing teeth, yet the cup grows more precious every day.

Lord, so often my weakest moments become my strengths.
Thank You for the little things that help me to remember to push on.
—SABRA CIANCANELLI

JULY 22

And now these three remain: faith, hope and love. But the greatest of these is love.
—1 CORINTHIANS 13:13 NIV

I was visiting my daughter Laura on Whidbey Island in Washington, where she was a part of the AmeriCorps community service program. I wanted to feel close to her, and yet not be too much of a mother—I didn't want to be a walking suggestion box. More than that, I wanted to be able to put aside the differences we have in our outlooks on life.

Laura met me at the ferry, her long, dark hair and sparkling blue eyes standing out in the crowd. We hugged and laughed, then roared away in her noisy pickup. As we talked, I swallowed hard at some of her free-spirited opinions.

We stopped to walk a trail she'd helped build. At the entrance was a kiosk she'd built and painted. "I hurried to get it finished before you came," she said. On it she'd painted a colorful outdoorsy scene with an enormous sun pouring down over all.

"It's beautiful, Laura," I said.

She always did favor the sun, even as a small child. As we walked the trail, I told her a story about her childhood. *Does she even want to hear this?* I wondered. But when I finished, she said, "Mom, thank you. I like it when you tell me things from back then. No one else can give those things to me but you."

The whole week was like that, a twining of old and new. At week's end, when we parted at the ferry, she said, "I love you, Mom. You'll always be my mother."

We laughed and hugged tightly. "I love you too, honey," I said. "I'll be praying for you."

"I'm glad," she said. I could tell she meant it.

As the boat pulled away from its moorings, I waved at Laura, feeling the strong sunshine of her grown-up love—and the grace that allowed me to get out of the way to receive it.

Lord, help me to keep letting go of my daughter, while holding her in prayer.
—SHARI SMYTH

JULY 23

And he turned to the woman, and said unto Simon...I entered into thine house, thou gavest me no water for my feet: but she hath washed my feet with tears, and wiped them with the hairs of her head.
—LUKE 7:44

When I was a girl and my mother's weary feet needed a massage, I usually found something else to do. Then last year I became caregiver to my hundred-year-old aunt. Rubbing her feet during an illness soothed her so much that I offered this act of comfort to others in her retirement community.

I sit on the floor, in the hair salon or in the lounge, and rub feet while people are getting their hair done or working crossword puzzles or reading the newspaper. I rub the feet of guests while we visit after dinner in the living room or watch a movie. I massage the feet of people bedridden from surgery. And when we're together, I finally—joyfully—rub my mother's feet too.

Perhaps the deepest reason I do what I do is that I feel a kinship with the woman in the Bible who, from vulnerability and gratitude, cast herself at Jesus' feet and washed them with her tears. My foot rubs are as close as I can come to this act of devotion.

Lord, thank You for helping my heart find its way to my hands.
—CAROL KNAPP

July 24

For a just man falleth seven times, and riseth up again.
—Proverbs 24:16

$\mathcal{W}$e were remodeling a rental property in the country one summer when we discovered a mud dauber had plastered its nest on the newly painted weatherboarding under the back-porch roof. We certainly didn't want a wasp's nest on the porch so, using a broom handle, I poked the lump of mud until it crumbled down, and swept it away.

A couple of days later we returned to find an even larger nest in the same place. I knocked it down. This went on for three weeks, with the nests larger, thicker, sometimes with tubelike openings to hold the larvae. Finally we found a nest as large as a boy's fist. No holes. The little tubes now held the larvae and all was sealed shut. The nest was finished.

I marveled at the determination of that mother dauber; to repeatedly mix mud just right; carry it, an unbelievably heavy load for her fragile body, in repeated trips to the rainproof shelter; secure it; then shape "beds" for her babies. The determination had to be instilled by God the Creator.

"I give up," I told the absent dauber. "Have your little daubers and be gone! Besides, I'm scratching all the paint off."

I've remembered that wasp's determination—her winning—in times that I've been tempted to give up. When a business failed, when rains washed crops out of our bottom field repeatedly, when I lost weight only to regain it, when a lawnmower wouldn't start, when youths we'd helped start a new life would backslide—until we reached out again. That little dauber taught us that all may appear lost, but you don't give up. You just build all over again because you were created in God's image and have within you what it takes to succeed.

Dear Lord, keep on giving us the courage to stick to the tasks at hand.
—Zona B. Davis

When anxiety was great within me, your consolation brought joy to my soul.
—PSALM 94:19 NIV

*E*lizabeth is away at MathPath, a camp made in heaven for children like her. Yesterday, while I was out, she called home. Amid cheerful chitchat with her dad, she told him that today the camp would be going to a park with a pool. Elizabeth is a city kid whose water experience is with sprinklers; she doesn't know how to swim. Proud of a recent accomplishment, however, she happily said, "Don't worry, Dad. I know how to tread water, so I won't drown."

When Andrew reported this, my heart froze. I am not a worrier by nature, but the thought of a child who can't swim but is confident she won't drown terrified me. I said a prayer, tried to shake off my trepidation and went about the rest of my day. Then last night at two-thirty, three-year-old Stephen pattered into our room because of his own nightmare. He quickly went back to sleep. I did not. I prayed, but I didn't what to pray. My imagination enacted horrifying scenes, each made vivid by the dark room. Ever practical, I made up a mental list of the people I'd have to inform about my daughter's death. I cried. I begged God to keep Elizabeth safe. I remembered every instance in which God had said no to a prayer and pleaded with Him to take this cup from me. I didn't want to add "but Thy will be done." Finally, just before sunrise, I did. And with that, I fell into a brief but exhausted sleep. When I awoke, I e-mailed the camp to have someone keep an eye on Elizabeth at the pool.

Later that evening, the phone rang. "Hi, Mom!" Elizabeth said. "We had a great time at the pool—even though it was only three feet deep."

Lord, help me remember that You hold me just as securely whether or not I worry.
—JULIA ATTAWAY

JULY 26

This is the day which the Lord hath made; we will rejoice and be glad in it.
—PSALM 118:24

It might sound strange, but I find some of my most rewarding reading in a journal that most probably no one else will ever read. It's a diary that my mother kept. The other day I was leafing through it when I came to this:

"Washed the storm windows and carried them down the basement. Cut the canes of the raspberry patch. Swept the floor of my little barn." But it was the concluding sentence that caused me to stare at it, amazed and lost in thought. It said simply, "What a beautiful day this has been!"

How was it, I wondered, that after spending her day at mundane chores such as "sweeping the floor of my little barn," my mother could say, "What a beautiful day this has been?"

And suddenly I knew. It was because she was surrounded by familiar tasks that needed to be done—and she did them with joy.

What a simple road to happiness! Why don't all of us take it—all of the time?

Thank You, Lord, for my daily tasks—each one
an opportunity for the satisfaction of a job well done.
—MILDRED TENGBOM

July 27

For three decades the Nace family has been visiting Yellowstone National Park. Once we found ourselves enjoying a multi-night stay in a rustic cabin nestled within Yellowstone's boundaries.

One morning we rose early and drove out to a lovely picnic area located along the Yellowstone River. After spotting a quiet lagoon, unloading our picnic supplies, and starting the grill, we ventured around the bend to see the rushing river.

Across the river was a huge herd of buffalo, intent on crossing toward us. The mama bisons nosed, prodded, and pushed their babies into the rushing waters. We worried as each of the bawling babies was quickly swept off its spindly legs. Calmly, each mother stepped into the water and swam upriver of her young one, snorting encouragement. Meanwhile the males bellowed support, not stepping into the river to cross until every mother and baby were onshore. The entire crossing lasted nearly an hour, as the dripping creatures ambled ashore slightly downriver of us.

We wondered why the female bison didn't swim downriver of their young to brace the babies upright against their bodies. Later we learned that the mothers had provided their young with the most protection by swimming upriver and breaking the crushing current of the stream.

Father, when I'm facing turbulence in my life, I know
that You're beside me, breaking the current.
—TED NACE

Mortify therefore your members which are upon the earth.
—Colossians 3:5

"*J*ohn, don't pick at that!" Foam rubber poked out of the arm of the sofa, and my son was plucking off small pieces. It was driving me crazy.

Our flowered sofa was already a major eyesore: Nine years of use, one cat and four kids had worn it to shreds. One day about a year ago a frayed spot appeared on one arm. That small spot quickly became a rip, the perfect hiding place for little toys. The rip grew, exposing foam rubber that begged to be pulled and poked and torn. Beneath that was fluff, ideal for a snowball fight when Mom wasn't looking.

At the time, we didn't have money to replace the sofa, so I bought a bedspread to cover its wounds. The spread tended to slip whenever my husband Andrew sat down quickly, and it fell off completely when the kids bounced around on it. I ended up rearranging it a dozen times a day, snapping at whoever messed it up. *This is more than embarrassing,* I thought one day as a neighbor graciously pretended not to notice. *It's mortifying.*

The word mortifying set off a little alarm bell in my head. Didn't Paul say we should mortify our earthly desires? My desire for nice-looking furniture was definitely not spiritual. It was so earthly that it had me growling at the people I love.

I pulled off the bedspread and faced the not-so-ugly truth: Our sofa had been worn out by years of rich family life. From cowboy forts to sickbeds, from pillow fights to snuggly read alouds, this sofa had done it all. Smiling ruefully at my vanity, I turned to my son.

"John," I said, "when we get a new sofa, I'm going to let you completely destroy this one!" His eyes grew wide with anticipation. Now that would make this sofa memorable!

Jesus, appearances aren't everything.
No sofa's going to get me to heaven; only You are.
—Julia Attaway

July 29

*"I am the Lord your God, who brought you out
of the land of Egypt, out of the house of slavery."*
—Exodus 20:2 NASB

*I*t was a gorgeous day, but my feelings didn't match the weather. I'd slammed down the phone after another heated discussion with Jamie, our twenty-three-year-old daughter. As I trudged to the mailbox, the chirping birds and the dancing butterflies irritated me. *Stop being so happy,* I thought.

Jamie seemed determined to forget the truth she'd learned as a child. It was as if she had to prove she could make it without God. And I couldn't change her.

I opened the mailbox. There, on top of a stack of bills, was a small, delicately decorated envelope. Instantly, I knew who'd sent it—Robin, my best friend since high school. She'd drawn a vine of colorful flowers along the edges. In her lovely handwriting she'd written a Scripture that circled the envelope: "Faith is being sure of what we hope for and certain of what we do not see" (Hebrews 11:1, NIV). It was addressed, "To my favorite friend, Julie Garmon."

Robin was walking the same path I was walking with one of her children. As I looked at the envelope, I felt a sweet softness, a moment of understanding, and I remembered my own rebellion. I'd so wanted Jamie to see things my way that I'd stopped trusting God and had closed my heart.

A week later, Jamie and I patched things up. And yesterday, we had another conversation on the phone. "Mom, you know what?" she said. "Everything you need to know in life, you learn in elementary school. Don't take drugs. Eat your fruits and vegetables. Go to church. Make your bed. Things are easier if you live God's way."

"I know," I said. "I've been learning the same thing!"

Father, my rebellion is like Jamie's; I so want things my way. Forgive me.
—Julie Garmon

And we know that all things work together for good to them that love God, to them who are the called according to his purpose.

—ROMANS 8:28

The redeeming part of funeral services for me is the extemporaneous eulogies that come from the congregation. I particularly appreciated the tributes given at a funeral in Ohio that I attended last week. The woman whose life was being celebrated had been a church leader for almost all of her eighty-eight years, and she was saluted for her steadfast faith. Though she herself had experienced many trials, her faith, it was said, never seemed to waver. Romans 8:28 was her faith rock, and she often shared it with those who sought her counsel. That truth gave her strength and courage when questions were long and answers short, she told advice seekers, "and it will do the same for you."

She had taught Sunday school for more than fifty years, and those who had grown in their faith because of her ministry recounted how she had helped them with doubts, illnesses, and family problems. Members of Eve's Circle, a monthly interdenominational woman's Bible study, cited her deep caring, her patience, her gift for listening, and her powerful intercessory prayers on their behalf.

The woman's children also spoke. Her daughter, now a minister, talked about her mother's unconditional love and encouragement. Her younger son, the woman's principal caregiver when she began to fail, described with some humor her disciplinary hand that had guided him on his faith journey. Her older son marveled at her positive attitude and a passion for living that molded his life. She had hoped he would become a minister, but she expressed pride in his chosen work, the writing of inspirational books and articles.

Why am I telling you all this? Because I wanted you to know that this very special woman was my mother, Juna Bauer Beard.

We thank You, Lord, for faithful mothers,
Whose love—save Yours—excels all others.

—FRED BAUER

July 31

Trust and obey,
For there's no other way
To be happy in Jesus.
—John H. Sammis

*W*hen I was a very small girl, Mom took the family to the New York World's Fair. Recognizing the danger in such crowds, she gathered us together at the entrance. "Remember to stick together," she said. "But in case anybody gets separated from the rest of us, stand still. Don't try to find us. We'll come back for you."

Sure enough, it happened. Enthralled by all the exhibits, I lagged behind and suddenly found myself alone. I climbed up on a bench and scanned the crowd. The family was nowhere in sight. Which way had they gone? Terribly frightened, I was tempted to run wildly after them, but then I remembered Mom's words and stood still. For what seemed ages I stood on that bench, straining my eyes in every direction. At last I saw Mom hurrying toward me, the rest of the family following her in a line like baby ducklings. Tears of relief rolled down my cheeks as she threw her arms around me. She had found me, just as she had promised.

In my spiritual life since then there have been times when, feeling separated, I've been tempted to search frantically in all directions for God. But I've learned how much wiser it is simply to be calm, to wait, and let Him find me. "Be still," He said, "and know that I am God." Exactly so!

Lord, give the quietness and confidence that are based on total trust in Thee.
—Betty R. Graham

August

There are friends who pretend to be friends, but
there is a friend who sticks closer than a brother.
—Proverbs 18:24 RSV

*H*i, Pat."

"Oh, hello." Pat looked at me blankly for a second, holding a lunch tray, her handbag slung over her arm.

"Estelle's son," I added. Pat smiled and said, "Oh, yes," then sat down with me at the table in the dining area of the Alzheimer's unit at Claussen Manor, where my mother was a resident. Every morning Pat dressed to the nines, meticulously and tastefully. For each outfit she had a matching handbag, and she took it everywhere.

"How's Estelle doing?"

"She's pretty weak. She's sleeping now."

"Oh, I love your mother. We go way back. We're best friends, you might say. Once in high school we were both interested in the same fellow, even though I think he liked Estelle better than me. It was that red hair of hers, like bronze. Made the boys crazy. Then we decided that we'd rather stay friends than fall out over some dumb boy, so we got rid of him! That was us, inseparable.

"We used to go to church together a lot, too, every day. The nuns made us. Boy, could Estelle sing—not very well, but loud! You couldn't miss it."

It gave me great comfort to know that Mom had a lifelong friend like Pat with her at Claussen. Except Pat and my mother had known each other only a short while. They met at Claussen, though you would not have known it to hear them go on about the old days, the good times they had together as the best friends they swore they were. It made perfect sense to them that they were together. When I happened upon Pat the evening before, standing at the foot of Mom's bed, her friend slipping further away, it didn't surprise me to see a tear slip down her cheek and hear her say, "I'm praying for you, Estelle, just like always."

At first I had been afraid my mother would be lonely at Claussen. But God saw to it that she wasn't. He sent Pat, in her daily best, my mom's temporary lifelong friend.

God, You give us miracles at every turn.
—Edward Grinnan

*Be honest in your estimate of yourselves, measuring
your value by how much faith God has given you.*
—ROMANS 12:3 NLT

"I want that," declared Sophia, my two-year-old granddaughter. She had chosen a *pluot*, a reddish-colored sweet fruit that is a cross between a plum and an apricot.

We were at French Market Produce, a wonderful open-air seafood and produce market. Tables were piled high with dark green seedless watermelons, pink-skinned nectarines, oversized, sweet Vidalia onions, and jars of local honey. And wafting throughout the market was the pungent aroma of boiled seafood.

We bought our pluot and walked over to a bench next to the snowball stand. Sophia took a bite, the sweet juice running down her chin. Minutes later an elderly gentleman sipping a spearmint snowball sat down beside us.

"Whew," he said. "Shopping with my daughter and her boys gets a bit hectic."

"I know what you mean."

"I was going to buy them snowballs. It's something I remember my pop and me doing every Sunday afternoon in the summertime." He shook his head. "But those boys have better things to do."

"Don't sell yourself short," I said. "We're important to our grandchildren, even if they're too young or too busy to know it. Some of my fondest memories are of my grandmother. I remember her helping me get dressed on chilly winter mornings in front of our fireplace. One Christmas she ate all my homemade cookies that my brother and sisters wouldn't eat." I pulled Sophia onto my lap and kissed her forehead.

The gentleman stood up to leave.

"Time to go?" I asked.

He winked at us. "I'll be right back. I know a couple of boys who might just love a snowball."

*Lord of the young and old, help me to see the value
in my relationships with others, especially my grandchildren.*
—MELODY BONNETTE

"See how the lilies of the field grow. They do not labor or spin. Yet I tell you that not even Solomon in all his splendor was dressed like one of these."
—MATTHEW 6:28–29 NIV

*W*hen I was a child, my family lived in a city, not a big one, but a city nevertheless. Outdoors I played on concrete, and the only time I saw a tree was when we took a bus to a small park. Then we moved to a suburb where some of the roads weren't paved and trees were everywhere. I was thrilled!

·Next door to our house was an empty overgrown lot just waiting for a builder to come along. To me it was the most beautiful garden I had ever seen, filled with bushes, , and flowers of every color. I didn't know they were weeds—"stinkweeds," the neighborhood kids called them. I thought they were the kind of flowers people picked to give to someone they loved, and I picked a huge bouquet for my mother. As I carried it home I heard some of the kids making fun of me, although I didn't know why.

My mother must have heard them because she met me at the door and opened her arms wide to receive the bouquet. "What beautiful flowers!" she said in a voice loud enough for the kids to hear. Then she hugged me. When she closed the door, she said, "We must give them some water right away." She found a vase and arranged the weeds as if they were the rarest flowers in the world.

Eventually I learned to tell the difference between a weed and a flower, but to this day I have a deep affection for weeds. I got that from my mother, who cared more about the meaning than the price of things. To her, my wild bouquet told her that I loved her, and that's what mattered.

Lord, help me to see Your love for this beautiful earth
in the wild things You have made.
—PHYLLIS HOBE

AUGUST 4

The memory of the just is blessed.
—PROVERBS 10:7

*M*y bachelor son Phil and I were rolling down an Alaskan highway during my summer visit. "I'll have to clean this messy handprint off your side window, so I can see the scenery better," I said.

There was a pause before Phil replied. "Actually, Sarah made that a long time ago...and I was leaving it for a memory." Sarah, three at the time, is my granddaughter and Phil's niece. I was speechless over his display of tenderness. Here was a guy driving a big four-wheel-drive pickup truck that he likes to keep shined, and its accessory package included five tagalong sticky fingerprints.

Months later, back home in Minnesota, my three-year-old grandson Clay, playing with my loon collection, added a stubby beak to those already broken. He mixed up the birds on the shelf to suit himself, even stacking a smaller one in the hollowed back of a larger one. I won't rearrange the loons or repair the stunted beak. Thanks to Phil, I don't see damage or disorder; I see imagination—and a dear little face engrossed in play. I'm leaving those loons just as they are... for a memory.

Jesus, by Your grace, may the prints I leave behind be the keeping kind.
—CAROL KNAPP

The tongue of the wise brings healing.
—PROVERBS 12:18 NASB

*M*y children grew up with a very noisy, critical mother. I didn't talk; I lectured. And they didn't listen; they argued. So when my twin sons approached their late twenties, I told God I was willing to do anything to be able to communicate effectively with them. He gave me a radical idea: Keep your opinions, warnings, lectures, and I-told-you-sos to yourself. And don't pry.

One scorching July day, I heard the squeak of brakes from the driveway and hurried outside. It was one of my sons. He didn't visit often. He stumbled out of his truck, crying so hard that I wondered if he'd been in an accident. I hadn't seen him cry that much since he was about ten. Now his broad shoulders shook uncontrollably, and his tears formed tiny puddles on the pavement. I reached up to hug him, and even though he towered over me, he crumpled onto my shoulder, his tears soaking my shirt. He let me hold him awhile, then lifted up his head and said, "You haven't called or fussed or nagged or told me how wrong I am. You haven't said anything at all!"

Four small words formed in my melting heart, scurried through my astonished mind, and reached my trembling lips: "I love you, son."

He looked me right in the eyes, sniffed loudly, nodded once, and hugged me so hard I couldn't breathe for a moment. Then, arms tightly around each other, we walked toward the house.

Thank You, Father, for teaching me how to use my tongue—wisely. Amen.
—MARION BOND WEST

AUGUST 6

Whosoever shall say unto this mountain, Be thou removed, and be thou cast into the sea; and shall not doubt in his heart, but shall believe that those things which he saith shall come to pass; he shall have whatsoever he saith.

—MARK 11:23

A small boy working in a Naples, Italy, factory aspired to be a singer, but at the age of ten a voice teacher told him, "You can't sing. Your voice sounds like wind in the shutters."

His mother scoffed at the teacher. She knew that her son loved to sing more than anything else in the world, and she encouraged him to continue. In fact, she made numerous sacrifices, even going without shoes, to pay for his lessons. Her faith was more than rewarded. Not many years later, the world of music owed a huge debt to the mother of Enrico Caruso.

If your mother is living, find a way to express your love for her today. If she is gone, thank God for the part she played in molding your life.

Thank You, Lord, for mothers, whose love excels all other.
—FRED BAUER

But hope that is seen is no hope at all. Who hopes for what he already has?
—ROMANS 8:24 NIV

I t was much more than the relentless heat and humidity that was dragging me down as I drove to our son Chris's house, where we were helping pack up his household goods before he was deployed to Iraq. I was worried about Chris's assignment in a war zone and about the unrealized parts of his future. Would he ever get married and have a family of his own? What kind of job would be waiting for him after he got out of the service?

Suddenly, I noticed the name of a church I was passing: Beauty Spot Church. There was a small cinderblock building in back, and in front was a half-finished sanctuary that dwarfed the original building. There were wallboards around the sides sheathing the metal girders, but the front was still open, and I could see through the supports into the unfinished interior.

As I passed, I noticed a man and a woman walking hand in hand up the dirt mound in front of the building. I was past the church before the couple reached the entrance, but something about them moving toward it struck chords of hope deep inside of me. Life is always filled with things that are on hold, unfinished, and unknown. Only hope can carry us as God takes our hand and walks with us toward His beautiful future.

Dear Jesus, let hope walk with me on the days
I have trouble seeing the dream ahead.
—KAREN BARBER

Do not hide your face from me.
—PSALM 27:9 NIV

I'd brought my three-year-old granddaughter to the beach. Lugging blanket, umbrella, plastic pail and shovel, a thermos of lemonade, and a picnic basket, I found an inviting stretch of sand and gratefully laid down our gear. For me it was a welcome break from weeks of pressure, finishing one demanding assignment and launching another.

For a blissful hour we were absorbed in constructing an improbable castle with an elaborate canal conducting seawater to our moat. We ate our lunch and were collecting shells to beautify the castle walls when I noticed one of our sandwich wrappers blowing away.

"We don't want to mess up the pretty beach," I said as I started after it. This will be a little environmental lesson for her.

I hadn't gone thirty yards when a wail stopped me. "What's the matter, honey?" I called back.

"I couldn't see you!"

"But...I'm right here!"

"I couldn't see your face."

Wrapper and ecological education abandoned, I went back to where a little girl stood with a bucketful of shells and eyes full of tears. *My face!* I thought. She'd seen what I was doing, but that wasn't enough. She needed my face turned toward her, telling her, "I see you. I'm attending to you. I care."

Maybe, I thought as we alternated slipper shells with scallop shells on the grand gateway to our castle, *that's my trouble, too.* Maybe I've been so busy asking what God wants me to do that I've failed first of all to seek His face, to start each day with a relationship, to ask to hear not His orders, but just that He loves me.

Your face, Lord, I will seek. (Psalm 27:8, NIV)
—ELIZABETH SHERRILL

Don't scold your children so much that they become discouraged and quit trying.
—COLOSSIANS 3:21 TLB

’d been having a difficult day, and in every mistake I heard a message of failure. Work returned for improvement: You'll never get it right. Losing my temper with the children: You're a lousy mother. Groceries partly put away and no dinner ready: You plan your time so poorly.

Rummaging in a box of old toys for something to entertain then-one-year-old Mark while I cooked, I found a little blue car. Suddenly I remembered our daughter Elizabeth pushing it along a wooden bench in the tiny church we attended while living in New Zealand when she was three years old.

One Sunday she wandered from our pew to the open door and began singing loudly about the bees buzzing outside, causing all heads to turn. After the service, an elderly woman with regal posture, elegantly attired in a green silk dress, approached us. I feared she would reprimand Elizabeth for disturbing everyone.

Instead, smiling, she sat next to Elizabeth, and in her proper British accent asked her name. "And how old are you?" Elizabeth held up three fingers. "Just three! Goodness! It is difficult for someone just three to sit so quietly." Elizabeth nodded solemnly.

"But, my, you are learning, aren't you? And please keep singing. We so enjoy your lovely voice!" She rose and patted my arm. "She's delightful. She's trying. Each week it will get easier."

As I brought the blue car to Mark, I resolved to be easier on myself and the children. And I could hear dear Mrs. Holland cheering me on: "Keep trying. Each day you'll do better. You are learning."

> *My patient, loving Father, help me to pour out*
> *encouragement on everyone around me, including myself.*
> —MARY BROWN

And when we had taken our leave one of another,
we took ship; and they returned home again.

—ACTS 21:6

*W*hen I attended parent/student orientation with our second son, Chris, at a university clear across the country, I thought I was an old pro at sending a child off to college. After all, our first son, Jeff, had been at college for three years. I settled complacently into my seat for a seminar entitled "Parenting through the College Years" and smiled wryly as the leader began by passing boxes of tissues down the auditorium rows.

The leader played an audio tape of a mother whose son was away at college. She talked about being in the grocery store, reaching for her son's favorite brand of yogurt and then pulling her hand back when she realized her son was no longer living at home. By now, my eyes were burning, and I needed one of those tissues.

After playing the tape, the leader asked for comments. A man raised his hand. "We've sent eight children off to school, and this is our last. Saying good-bye is something you never really get used to. I remember trying to play it cool with my third one. I casually said good-bye at registration. Then something made me turn around and look at my son. He looked confused, like he didn't know what to do next. I walked back to him and did what I'd wanted to do all along. I gave him a hug and said, 'I know you'll do fine.' Don't pretend when you say good-bye. Be sincere about what's in your heart."

As the group walked to lunch, I tapped the man with the eight children on the shoulder and confided, "The only reason I can muster the courage to leave my son here, so far away from home, is that I'm a praying person. I'm trusting that God will be with him. And I'm trusting that God will be with me too."

Dear God, I can't possibly say this good-bye without Your help.
Be with us both while we are apart. Amen.

—KAREN BARBER

I waited patiently for the Lord; and he inclined unto me, and heard my cry.
—Psalm 40:1

*W*henever my husband Norman and I traveled around the country, we met people who gave us new insights about prayer. One of the most unusual came from a woman in Atlanta.

She'd been worried about her son Dan, who lived far away from her. He had three young children and a demanding job that he felt locked into. He commuted to work by bus, and when he finally returned home in the evening, he often dropped into a bar before heading home to his family. He developed a serious drinking problem, and his marriage had worn pretty thin because of it.

If only I could ride the bus with Dan and get him home safely to his family each night, the woman thought. Then she got an idea: *Why not ride the bus with him?*

So the next morning she got on the bus with Dan—in her prayers. She rode alongside him, sometimes reminiscing about things that happened when he was a boy and sometimes silent—just loving him and praying that he would ask for God's help. That night, when he caught the bus for the ride home, she again boarded with him, riding beside him, loving him, praying for him. Twice a day from then on, she'd remind herself, "Now's the time to ride with Dan."

Some months later, visiting her son at Christmas, she learned that Dan wasn't drinking anymore.

"You know, I have a long bus ride back and forth to work," he told his mother. "Somehow, day after day, I thought about my drinking while I was riding the bus. Finally, I made the decision to stop, and once I did, even the bar on the way home didn't tempt me."

This woman reminded me that prayer is a perfect vehicle—for commuting and communing. Prayer, indeed, can get you where you want to be.

> *Thank You, Lord, that "more things are wrought by prayer*
> *than this world dreams of" (Alfred Lord Tennyson).*
> —Ruth Stafford Peale

AUGUST 12

Jesus Christ the same yesterday, and today, and for ever.
—HEBREWS 13:8

*W*hen I was six years old my mother took my brothers and sisters and me to the county fair. I had never seen so much color nor heard such magical music in my whole life. Enchanted, I was attracted this way and that while feasting on a huge cone of cobwebby cotton candy.

As the merry-go-round and other rides zoomed up and over and around me, I suddenly realized I had slipped away from my mother. I searched everywhere through the crowd. The music which had enchanted me became brassy and loud and confusing, and the gaudy colors and glitter tangled my thinking. I ran in circles, crying, looking everywhere for my mother as I bumped into one leg after another.

Just as I turned from a sideshow, I saw her in the crowd. She stood anxiously but patiently right where she'd been all the time. The confusion of the carnival had pulled me away from her. But Mama had not moved.

Now when I'm caught up in the confusion and gaudiness of the world, and I run in circles, I finally discover that God has not moved. He's been there, waiting, all the time. I feel the same relief and sweet sense of security that I felt when I found Mama.

Father, keep me reminded that it is I who moves.
—ORA LINDSAY GRAHAM

Even before a word is on my tongue, Lo, O Lord, thou knowest it altogether.
—PSALM 139:4 RSV

*T*was miserable that bright Hawaii morning, thinking of the family gathered in Kentucky for my mother-in-law's funeral. I'd wanted to leave my job here on Maui, but my husband John insisted I stay.

"It's senseless for you to make an eleven-thousand-mile round trip," he'd said over the phone. "I'll need you more after the funeral."

Perhaps once again a new hymn could cheer me. Something appropriate to Hawaii. Riffling through my hymnal, I spotted the word "ocean." A few lines further, "sunshine." Then, "rainbow." The perfect song for a walk on a tropical island.

Hymnal in my hand, I followed a cow path to a stream tumbling down from the mountain. Turning, I, too, followed the stream to the ocean's edge. Settling myself on a lava outcrop, I scanned the first verse.

> *O Love that wilt not let me go,*
> *I rest my weary soul in Thee;*
> *I give Thee back the life I owe,*
> *That in Thine ocean depths its flow*
> *May richer, fuller be.*

Why, this wasn't a song about exotic scenery! Every line, every word, was part of the commemoration of Mother's life taking place in faraway Kentucky! I sang the hymn over and over there by the sea, and all the way back to the cabin.

That night, John described the funeral. There'd been one disappointment. Apparently his mother had had a favorite hymn, which his sister wanted in the service. "The minister talked her out of it. Said it always made people cry."

The hymn, John went on, was "O Love That Wilt Not Let Me Go." "I don't know it myself, but I feel bad that it was left out."

"No, it wasn't left out," I told him. "It wasn't left out at all."

Remind me today, Lord, that in Your world there are no isolated acts.
—ELIZABETH SHERRILL

*The discretion of a man deferreth his anger;
and it is his glory to pass over a transgression.*
—PROVERBS 19:11

*I*t was midsummer and our family chugged down the highway heading home after a beach vacation. The needle on the gas gauge trembled on the red E and we pulled over at a service station. As the children poured out of the back seat, I headed for the water fountain. I returned to find six-year-old Bob stomping about in a mud puddle beside a leaky water spigot. His legs were splattered with mud and his white tennis shoes were unmentionable.

"Bob!" I screamed, swooping down on him in fury, "get out of there!"

He tucked one black little shoe behind the other and froze. I dragged him out. "You know better than this!" I shouted. "Take those grimy shoes off!" He retreated to the car, his eyes filling with tears. "I'll wash them," he said feebly.

"Off!" I demanded, glaring at him. I dropped the muddy things in the trunk and we piled back in, Bob's lip quivering and my anger seething. We had traveled about twenty minutes when we came upon the most outlandish billboard on the side of the road. I read it, rubbed my eyes, and read it again. Believe it or not, on it was a squishy black mud puddle full of little boys' feet and these immortal words, "Mud puddles are fun... a public service for little boys."

I peeped over the seat at the little wounded spirit in the back, my anger fading into remorse. The poor fellow had wandered into a mud puddle and I'd reacted as if he'd stepped into a smoldering volcano. *A "mud puddle event" and a "volcano reaction,"* I thought. There was a problem. I was sure I was getting a lesson from God that went like this: When annoying little frustrations and problems arise...pause. Don't lose perspective. Don't overreact. It's silly to treat a mud puddle like a volcano.

I leaned over the seat. "Hey, Bob, I'm sorry," I said. "Sometimes mothers forget that a mud puddle is just a mud puddle and mud puddles are fun."

He grinned back. "I know," he said.

Lord, give me perspective as a shield against the annoyances of life.
—SUE MONK KIDD

All men commend patience, although few be willing to practise it.
—THOMAS À KEMPIS

And Lord, please give me patience with Jeffrey..." My prayer was interrupted by a clunk, followed by a splash echoing up the stairway. I charged downstairs to see my two-year-old standing over the toilet bowl, my car keys barely visible in the drain.

"No! No!" My hands instinctively stung his. "Bad boy! You should know better!" I could feel my irritation welling to a crescendo. Why hadn't God sent the patience I'd prayed for?

After a week of the same prayer request, things progressed from bad to worse. Jeffrey seemed well on his way to the terrible twos. What little patience I had was being sorely stretched.

Finally, I admitted my dilemma to a friend. She nodded and replied, "I, too, have prayed for patience."

"I've got to know," I asked. "Did God grant you that serene sense of calm I'm looking for?"

"Yes, but not in the way you think. You see, when you pray for patience, instead of instantly infusing it into your personality, God works in another way. Your problems seem to get worse. But God is only sending you a chance to practice patience. That's the only way you can come by it."

I smiled in recognition that my prayer was being answered! Patience is produced in tiny drops out of the raw material of daily tensions.

From now on, Lord, I will use my frustrations to build patience.
—KAREN BARBER

Christ Jesus...being in the form of God...made himself of no reputation, and took upon him the form of a servant, and was made in the likeness of men.
—PHILIPPIANS 2:5–7

*W*e are halfway through Week Three of the flu at our house. I have had so little sleep lately that the few thoughts that make their way across my weary synapses are mostly about how sleep deprivation is a form of torture.

Last night my feverish baby was unable to sleep except in my arms. Even then, she awoke frequently, crying, "Mama! Mama!" with the high-pitched whine of a toy doll. I held her and rocked her and whispered to her. Sometime in the blur of the early morning hours, I asked God to give me something good to think about.

Nothing dramatic happened. I stroked my baby's hot, smooth skin and idly wondered if Baby Jesus ever had the flu. Surely, He must have been sick sometime. Surely, His mother nursed Him, held Him, comforted Him. Perhaps she stroked His back to ease the aches. My hand lingered on my own baby's back as I paused to think about Jesus with the delicious, smooth skin of a baby. It seemed amazing. God with baby skin. God you could touch. God you could hold tenderly in your arms. God Who is...human.

The baby moved restlessly in my arms. Jesus once weighed twenty-five pounds too. Odd, isn't it, how in some ways it's harder to understand the smallness of God-made-man than the greatness of His heavenly Father?

> *Jesus, help me hold You in my heart*
> *as surely as I hold my baby in my arms.*
> —JULIA ATTAWAY

AUGUST 17

Remember the days of old.
—DEUTERONOMY 32:7 NASB

Recently I asked all of my grown children to tell me their happiest childhood memory. Three of them had to think about it, but not Jeremy. "You'd just come back from a writing workshop in New York," he said with a smile. "The laundry was piled up and the phone kept ringing and you needed to go to the grocery store, but you kept typing. I stood right by you and tried to explain that I needed poster paper for a contest at school. Seems like I stood there all day. All you ever said was, *'Mmm.'"*

I remembered that day clearly. I had wanted to write so much it was like a physical pain. I could feel Jeremy breathing right beside me. His shadow fell across my paper. I prayed, "Please, Lord, don't let him ask me again to get poster paper." And he didn't. What he murmured under his breath was, "Contest ends tomorrow, anyway."

I hit the OFF button on my typewriter and grabbed the car keys and Jeremy's hand. I think I may have even managed a smile. We stepped over spilled orange Kool Aid and piles of laundry. I caught a glimpse of his face. There was a ring of orange punch around his mouth. Whatever he'd eaten for lunch stained his shirt. His shoes were untied. On the way to the store, he told me all about the contest—it was about fire prevention. I tried to listen to him as intently as I've ever listened to anyone in my life. He worked on the poster way into the night.

"Remember, Mom?" my now-thirty-three-year-old son asked. "I won the school prize—five dollars, and I even placed in the state finals! What a memory!"

> *Father, would You help a very busy young mother*
> *to take time today to make a memory? Amen.*
> —MARION BOND WEST

The patient in spirit is better than the proud in spirit.
—ECCLESIASTES 7:8

*R*uby is my Eskimo granddaughter, welcomed to our daughter Tamara's family when she was two days old. Now she is a grinning, bright-eyed four-year-old who says she is "Eksimo." One day, while working with Ruby and her siblings on the subject of patience, I grouped the letters in the word *patient* and converted it to a singsong chant.

"*PA-TI-ENT,*" I called. "What does that spell?"

Ruby enthusiastically shouted, "Patient!"

"What does *patient* mean?" I asked.

In her best four-year-old pronunciation she explained, "It means waiting without *cwying.*" Ruby wasn't satisfied just to know the definition; she wanted to learn to spell the word. She practiced over and over. Her tongue continually stumbled and tripped, but she stayed with it. "PI."

"No, it's PATI," I corrected.

"PATIENP."

"Not quite. It's ENT."

"PATAENT."

"Oh, you're close. Remember, PATI."

Ruby tried once more, heard herself make a mistake, good-naturedly proclaimed, "I messed up again," and started over. The day came when she got it right and we whooped it up. She may not remember her achievement down the line, but I'll never forget the day I watched my granddaughter patiently work to spell *patient.*

Dear God, spelling and definitions are fine, but when it comes
to Your Word, the meaning is in the being and the doing.
—CAROL KNAPP

Lift up your eyes.
—ISAIAH 40:26

*W*ant to take an after-dinner walk?" my husband David asks.

In my best martyred-fishwife voice I answer, "With half the house left to clean?" To further make my point, I yell down the hall. "Brock! Keri! Don't even think of going to bed until your rooms are cleaned!"

"Oh, Mama," Keri, then six, replies, "we were going to catch lightening bugs."

An hour later, I scan my "things-to-do" list, and see that like last week and the week before, the house is reasonably clean. *Oops, the porch.* Broom in hand, I open the door. The whirr of the vacuum and flying dust have dulled my senses. But one whiff of summer and I'm in another time zone. I think of Keri's lightning bugs, and I recall childhood's cool grass under bare feet and the fresh watermelon smell that hung in the air as I ran through the night reaching for stars. Later, the backyard glider would float like a boat adrift on a secret sea, as I watched luminous lights blinking, blinking, inside a jelly jar.

I walk across the porch, sit on the top step. In the simple dark I take stock. Do I really want my children to know me as a grouchy mom with a very clean house?

Summer was offering an alternative. I hurry inside, take four empty jars from under the sink and call my glum family of house-cleaners together. "I have a problem with lightening bugs," I say. "I need to see if it's still fun to catch them on a summer night." And then because confession brightens the soul, I add, "I think it might be more important than a clean house."

It was. It still is.

I'd rather be a lightning-bug chaser, Lord. Help me hold that vision.
—PAM KIDD

AUGUST 20

The Lord said, "...Sarah your wife shall have a son."
—GENESIS 18:10 RSV

*D*ear Tiny Toes,

    I just received your father's call, telling me that you have arrived! Welcome, welcome, welcome, little one! I've hoped and prayed for you for many years, and loved you since your father (John) first told me you were coming to us.

    Here's a true story about your daddy. Auntie Karen was twelve and Uncle Paul, nine, and I thought our family was complete, when I learned I was going to have another baby. Like Abraham and Sarah, I thought I was too old. But the nurse patted my knee and said, "You'll count it a blessing." That's exactly what your daddy has been for me.

    He and your mother (Tasha) have also waited long to have a baby, and I often hinted to them not to wait too long. Then one day a voice in my head said, *Quit bugging them!* I reminded myself it was, after all, his and Tasha's life, not mine.

    Then one April night John called me and said, "We'll be there for Christmas, Mom. We're flying in...." He paused and then added, "Though we've never flown with a baby before." Wild with happiness, I almost dropped the phone.

    So you see, dear one, you have helped me learn to trust. It has taken me seventy-five years to discover this most valuable truth: I am not in charge of my life—or anyone else's for that matter. I have come to trust that life unfolds just as it should, when I trust the Spirit and get myself out of the way.

    Love,
    Grandma K.

> *Lord, help Tiny Toes to follow his deepest truths,*
> *trusting in the Holy Spirit, and wait for the unfolding.*
> —MARILYN MORGAN KING

Happy is he that condemneth not himself in that thing which he alloweth.
—ROMANS 14:22

When I was a child, my parents were divorced and I was placed in a foster home, where the treatment was less than kind. Mother was miles away working as a domestic to earn enough for my care. I was so unhappy and lonely that I began to develop a seriously upset stomach every morning before school. Finally a doctor was called. He suggested that I be removed from school and be sent to a warmer climate.

But how? My father was out of the picture, and my mother was already doing all she could. That's when Aunt Lillian came to my rescue. She worked as a live-in domestic in nearby North Adams, Massachusetts, earning less than ten dollars a week. But she didn't hesitate to quit her job and use her meager savings to take me to her sister's home in Charleston, South Carolina. For five months she stayed with me while I frolicked over the fields and enjoyed delicious meals prepared at hearthside. My health returned and so did my demeanor. We returned to North Adams, and I lived with Aunt Lillian for several years until my mother remarried.

Looking back, I can't remember thanking Aunt Lillian for her sacrifice and her love. She died in 1945, while I was stationed at the Jure Naval Base on Honshu, Japan. I couldn't even go to the funeral. Since then I often wondered how I could repay Aunt Lillian. Then I stumbled upon these words of John Ruskin: "There is only one power, the power to save someone. And there is only one honor, the honor to help someone."

By phone, through letters, in visits, I've tried to help others. Most of those people have never known that I do it for Aunt Lillian.

Good Shepherd, I received life. Let me serve in Your name.
—OSCAR GREENE

And he that sat upon the throne said, Behold, I make all things new.
—REVELATION 21:5

*H*ow did we get from being a cozy family of five to being an unruly crew of ten on our way to a two-week vacation? The short answer is a son-in-law, a daughter-in-law, and three small grandsons heading to a large house in the Loire Valley of France with multiple cribs on site. Everyone got along just fine—except in the kitchen. He wanted to cook spaghetti; she wanted a vegetarian menu. Her two-year-old wasn't allowed any refined sugar; a three-year-old announced he would only eat peanut butter; an emergency bottle of ketchup was located in a local grocery store.

When it was all over and we grandparents were recuperating, life got even more complicated: 1,300 quite wonderful digital pictures showed up in my e-mail from four camera-happy parents. *Grandma*, they thought, *would love to make an album*. The challenge felt daunting, but I found a program, then I clicked and dragged, deleted and pasted through 272 pictures (computers love numbers). One final click and everything flew through cyberspace and was turned into a lovely book with a green linen cover. A few days later, five copies came in what is now scornfully known as "snail mail."

I've always believed in miracles, that there were indeed enough loaves and fishes for the five thousand, and that water turned into wine at the wedding in Cana. But no one expects miracles in the twenty-first century. Imagine how the printers of the Gutenberg Bible would have reacted to my sixty-two-page instant book. But as I turned the brightly colored pages, I realized that the miracle in these pictures was timeless: the love and laughter that binds a family together even when they can't agree on the menu.

> *Lord, may we accept the new and preserve the old,*
> *and use both to strengthen our caring for each other.*
> —BRIGITTE WEEKS

The Lord shall bless thee.... Yea, thou shalt see thy children's children.
—PSALM 128:5–6

*M*om, our pregnancy test is positive!" our daughter Brenda told us on the phone last March. This would be her first baby, due on Thanksgiving Day.

Two months later, at the end of May, my husband opened his birthday card from our daughter Tamara and out dropped a baby shoe! This was her unique method of letting us know when she's pregnant. So far, we had collected three small shoes, so now we were adding a fourth for Tamara's baby due in mid-January.

After another two months, our daughter Kelly and her husband invited us to dinner at a local restaurant. Scrawled in crayon on the paper tablecloth beneath our menus was this message: "Kelly is pregnant!" Her first child would be born in early March. Our trio of daughters expecting babies together—we couldn't believe it!

Next, Tamara phoned from her Arctic Ocean home to tell us they were adopting a newborn Eskimo girl named Ruby Dawn. Now we had one "just arrived" grandchild, plus three more on the way!

This cluster of family birth announcements recalled a typo I'd made several years ago. While writing a friend about my "empty nest," I inadvertently typed, "empty next" instead. It was a prophetic mistake: God always has a "next" for me. And it's astounding how empty climbs to full again, when His hand is tipping the pitcher.

Father, I rejoice with You in the wonder of seeing my children's children.
Fill me with anticipation for the many satisfying "nexts" You have for me.
—CAROL KNAPP

And when he had consulted with the people, he appointed singers unto the Lord.
—2 CHRONICLES 20:21

*O*n Friday, my son Chase left North Carolina for Kansas City, to take part in the Metropolitan Opera National Council Auditions for young singers. He left without receiving the letter that told him where, when, and in what order he would sing. "Just enjoy yourself," I tried to reassure him before he boarded his flight.

Though he said all the right things, we both knew he was nervous. After all, he'd been studying voice for only four or five years. Most of the other singers at the regional competition would be older and more experienced.

Though Chase had done well in elementary school and junior high, the death of his father years earlier seemed to cast a shadow on him. His struggles in high school had left him uncertain about his abilities. I homeschooled him his senior year, and he took courses at the local community college. In a choral-singing class, the director identified Chase's musical gift.

"This is not an entrance audition. It's just for fun," I said to him when he called, hoping Chase wouldn't hear my heart pounding over the phone.

"Keep looking for the letter," he told me.

Soon after his departure, the letter arrived. He was number eighteen out of forty singers and he was to sing at one o'clock.

On Saturday, I waited patiently to hear. There was no word by two or three o'clock. By five, I was no longer able to pretend that I was patient. I called and, after receiving no response, went to a late lunch. When I returned home, there was a message.

"Mom, I won an award. I was the youngest person to win an award and the only one still an undergraduate. I talked to the judges and they said...."

I heard joy and excitement in his voice, but the greatest thing I heard was acceptance and peace.

> *Thank You, Lord, for gifts of creativity and beauty that triumph*
> *over the discouragement and uncertainty of our lives.*
> —SHARON FOSTER

She got him a wicker basket and covered it over with tar and pitch. Then she put the child into it, and set it among the reeds by the bank of the Nile.

—Exodus 2:3 NASB

I don't need any help from y'all. I'm paying for my own college. I've gotten a full-time job. This way, you can't keep butting into my life." Our stubborn daughter packed up her clothes without looking up. "Don't worry about helping me with anything anymore. I can do it myself."

I hugged her stiff body good-bye and didn't walk with her to her car. I didn't trust myself. I thought, *I might race the car down the driveway, begging her to come back.*

For weeks, my thoughts went over that scene, reliving it from every possible angle. I worried about all the things that could happen to her and all the bad choices she might make. One morning, alone in my house, I finally got real with God: "Could You please show me how to let her go? I'm miserable. I'm allowing this to ruin my life."

A Bible story came to me—the incredible faith of Moses' mother. To save her son, she had no choice but to trust God completely and let him go. Knowing all about the dangers of the dark Nile—crocodiles, drowning, starvation—she still turned him loose in his little handmade basket. And I bet that sweet mama let her son go with hope.

Father, I place my grown-up baby down in the Nile.
Only You can follow her along the riverbank.
—Julie Garmon

AUGUST 26

Except ye utter by the tongue words easy
to be understood, how shall it be known what is spoken?
—1 CORINTHIANS 14:9

*W*hen my son Tom decided to trek Brazil for three months, my heart was in my mouth. No news was good news—or so I thought. He didn't tell me about the car wreck until he had been home for a week. Apparently Tom, always a cautious driver, had driven his rental car into the left lane, signaling to make a left turn. The light changed and a driver whizzing past on his left broadsided him and spun the car. Tom wasn't injured, but since he had been speaking Portuguese for only three months, he couldn't make the police understand him. In fact, the other driver convinced officials that Tom had caused the accident. Though the insurance claim was still a tangle, I felt weak with relief that Tom had been spared serious harm in a foreign land.

A month later Tom packed his aging pickup truck to move to graduate school in California. With the precision of a true scientist, he had constructed his itinerary with little wiggle room. I prayed for both his safety on the journey and his peace of mind. Tom was a stickler for schedules and chafed when they went awry. All too soon after he had left, he phoned. Within 150 miles of home, his transmission had gasped its last breath. He had about 2,800 miles left to go, his carefully calculated schedule now useless. I felt myself bracing for a frustrated tirade. Instead, he talked casually about the tow truck driver who had brought him to a garage where the staff dropped what they were working on to help him. The crew had even directed him to a diner with home cooking.

Finally I ventured to ask Tom about his new schedule. "Hey, Mom, not a problem. It will only be two days. Besides, these guys speak English!"

Lord of the Journey, thank You for the beautiful ways
You bless my children as they travel toward maturity.
—GAIL THORELL SCHILLING

O that my people would listen to me, that Israel would walk in my ways!
—PSALM 81:13 RSV

I had phoned my elderly friend Ossie Mobley for a short chat. Just before we hung up, she said in her quiet voice, "Marion, would you have time to say something to Donnie? He just wants to hear your voice. Doesn't matter what you say."

Donnie is sixty-plus, and due to an injury at birth, he's in a wheelchair and isn't able to speak normally. He can make sounds that Ossie understands from a lifetime of caring for her only child. I could hear Donnie in the background, and I pictured him happily anticipating my voice, listening with all his might as his mother held the phone to his ear.

"Oh, yes, Ossie! Of course. I'd love to speak to Donnie. Put him on."

I heard Donnie breathing, waiting, listening for my voice. I had the distinct feeling I was about to learn something. "Hey, Donnie! How are you?" I said. "Did y'all get rain today? We did. I'll bet you went to church Sunday. I need to stop by and see you."

"*Ummm,*" he agreed excitedly. (*I'd really like to see you.*)

"We love *you and Ossie, Donnie.*"

"*Ummm!*" *(We love you too.)*

"Well, bye Donnie. Thanks for talking to me. Bye-bye."

Then Ossie came back on. "Thank you so much, Marion. Donnie sure enjoyed talking to you."

Lord, it doesn't really matter what You say—I yearn
to hear Your voice. Teach me how to listen. Amen.
—MARION BOD WEST

Bring them [your children] up in the nurture and admonition of the Lord.
—EPHESIANS 6:4 RSV

The first thing I notice is the smell of crackling bacon. I open my eyes. I'm really here–vacation at my grandparent's cabin on Lake Weiss in Leesburg, Alabama. The sun gleams from the lake outside my bedroom window. A million birds seem to be singing. Everything an eight-year-old boy could ask of a summer day. I make a break for the front door.

"Brock! It's devotion time."

Oh no. She caught me. I feel like the fish I had hoped to hook. Bebe, my grandmother, reels me in. "We're waiting for you." There she is with my four-year-old sister Keri and my cousins Kristi, ten, and Michele, eight. Girls. How can they act so content, sitting there waiting for my grandmother to read from her daily devotion book?

Looking back on this years later, I have to laugh at myself. I am amazed at my grandmother's patience, trying to instill some good in the heedless little firecracker I was then.

"Brock, the Lord is your Shepherd (Psalm 23:1). Don't forget that, son."

"Oh, Bebe, the sky is so blue today. I'd rather go swimming."

And another time, "'Ask, and it shall be given you,' Brock (Matthew 7:7). The good Lord hears your prayers."

"Yes, Bebe. Isn't this a perfect day for hiking?" And yet over the years those same Bible verses have come to mean a lot to me.

Recently, I found an extra $40 in my pay envelope. It was mighty tempting, but I knew it was a mistake. "A good name is rather to be chosen than great riches" (Proverbs 22:1), Bebe always said. Her words won the day as I headed for the business office. I smiled to myself as I gave the money back.

"Harrison David Brockwell Kidd," I can hear Bebe say, "the Lord loves you."

Lord, it must take the patience of a saint to teach a child. Thank You for the
Sunday school teachers, the church workers, educators, moms, dads, and
especially grandparents who never give up on us.
—BROCK KIDD

August 29

Gray hair is a crown of glory.
—Proverbs 16:31 nlt

*S*ometime back, I read an article on why hair turns gray: It is related to the body's production of something called *melanocyte*. But experience tells me that gray hair is mostly caused by children. Not other people's children, but your own.

Actually, my first gray hair and our son Brock's first step were a simultaneous occurrence. That exact moment also represents a milestone in my faith walk. That's when my prayer-life began in earnest.

Keri, our daughter, on the other hand, didn't contribute much to the "snow on the mountain" until she decided it was time to be a teenager. Less dramatic, but just as heart-stopping, her antics came in spurts, always with the same effect on her mother's tresses: Phone rings. "Hello." "Mama, let me speak to Dad. Now!" Or worse: Phone rings. "Hello." "Mrs. Kidd"—Keri's boyfriend's voice—"let me speak to Dr. Kidd. Now!"

As mothers, we certainly don't want children to be afraid. We want them to develop confidence, believe in themselves. So we pray, and we gray, and we look forward. Which brings me to my final point: What grays my hair builds my faith. I guess that's why a wise man once said: "Gray hair is a crown of glory."

Father, I look past every fear and put my faith
in You. You are truly a mother's glory!
—Pam Kidd

Teach them to your children, talking about them when you sit at home and when you walk along the road, when you lie down and when you get up.
—Deuteronomy 11:19 NIV

After thirty years of parenting, most of them as a single parent, my nest was suddenly empty. Even after I said good-bye to Andrew on the campus of Arizona State University and my nest was empty, my mothering days weren't over by a long shot. Andrew still needed me. Not to send care packages with cookies, clean underwear, and extra dollars stuffed inside a few magazines; no, he needed me to teach him the College Commandments:

1. *Thou Shalt Not Bring Thy Dirty Laundry Home to Mom.* Nothing ruins a perfectly good weekend visit more than the thought of five loads of your jeans and T-shirts languishing on the floor in the laundry room.

2. *Thou Shalt Not Call Thy Mother on the Phone Collect.* If I accept your collect calls, it doesn't teach you anything about fiscal responsibility.

3. *Thou Shalt Not Spend Money Frivolously.* Since your brother and sisters (and now you) got through college with grants, scholarships, loans, work-study programs, and two to three part-time jobs each, in addition to the money I've saved for all of you, it seems that your education is the most important part of these four years and not a car, expensive clothes, or exotic vacation trips during spring break.

4. *Thou Shalt Have Thine Own Checking Account to Pay Thine Own Bills.* Checking account good; credit card bad. A checking account teaches you the value of having money in the coffer to pay for the item before you buy it.

There are days when I still miss Andrew desperately. But there's one consolation. My daughter Julia said it best in a letter she wrote me not long after Andrew started college. At the top she'd typed, "A parent is not a person to lean on, but a person to make leaning unnecessary."

Lord, help my children become strong, hard-working, independent adults so I'll know I did Your work well.
—Patricia Lorenz

Let us then approach the throne of grace with confidence.
—HEBREWS 4:16 NIV

*M*y grandson Cameron loves to play soldier, so for his ninth birthday his mother, my daughter Jenny, decided to give him a military-themed party. The invitations were draft notices and my son-in-law designed an obstacle course for the ten boys who were to attend. My oldest son Ted, who'd served as an Airborne Ranger, painted camouflage on the boys' faces, and they ate MREs in the field. (For us civilians, that's meals ready to eat.) The party was a huge success.

Later that summer, Cameron spent an entire day outside arranging his toy soldiers. When he'd finished, he insisted his mother take a picture, just in case she happened to meet a general. How or when this was supposed to occur was of little concern to my grandson. He instructed his mother to hand over the picture so that the Army could make use of his battle plan.

I enjoyed telling my husband about Cameron's exploits, and I have to admit that we were both impressed. Even at the age of nine, he felt he had something of value to offer others. *We all do*, I thought later, *whether it's a shared recipe or an unexpected birthday card to a shut-in or even what we're convinced is a brilliant business plan.*

So I've made Cameron's message my own: Believe in yourself and in God's ability to use your talents as He sees fit.

*Lord, thank You for the lesson in self-confidence
that my grandson has taught me.*
—DEBBIE MACOMBER

September

I will instruct you and teach you in the way you should go.
—PSALM 32:8 NIV

This past year when I addressed a women's group, I met a lovely lady named Vivian. She explained that my mother had been her first-grade teacher back in the 1940s. "She changed my destination," Vivian said. "Our town was economically challenged, but your mother told us we could change everything through the power of education. I remember running home from school one afternoon to tell my mother, 'We're not poor! My teacher said the whole world's mine because I'm learning to read!'"

From as far back as I can remember, Mother taught me about the joys and rewards of reading. We didn't have much when I was growing up, but thanks to books, we had everything. A poem I saw embroidered on a pillow recently describes my childhood perfectly: "Richer than I, you will never be. For I had a mother who read to me."

I'm buying some books today to donate to a local literacy program. It's one more way I'm learning to say a second thank-you for a mother who taught me one of the great secrets of the universe.

Best of all, reading reveals Your good news, Lord.
The whole world (and heaven) is mine! Thank You.
—ROBERTA MESSNER

*For the Lord seeth not as man seeth; for man looketh
on the outward appearance, but the Lord looketh on the heart.*
—1 SAMUEL 16:7

A month after my nineteen-year-old son was killed in an automobile accident, I waited sadly on a bench in a crowded mall for a younger son to finish his shopping. My depression deepened as I became aware of the hundreds of unfamiliar faces passing by.

It would be impossible for me ever to get to know even this small segment of the world's population, I thought. How can God possibly care what happens to each person in the entire world? On a planet filled with natural and man-made disasters, it seemed incomprehensible that God could concern himself with the heartbreak of one mother crying for her son.

But even as tears began to blur my vision, I remembered what God had told Samuel. He does not see men the way we do; he looks on the heart. I blinked away the tears and tried to picture the heart of each oncoming shopper through God's eyes. Was that sour-faced man worried about his job? Could that whining child need attention? Had that solitary woman also lost a loved one?

My own pain lessened as I felt myself wishing I could do something to bring comfort to all those solemn strangers. By the time my son joined me I knew that, incredible as it seems, God actually does consider the hopes and the fears of each one of us. For I learned that evening that when you look at the heart through the eyes of God, you see with compassion and love.

*Lord, as I look on the outward appearance of others,
help me to look also on their hearts.*
—RUTH HEANEY

The gift of God is eternal life through Jesus Christ our Lord.
—ROMANS 6:23

I spent the summer secretly knitting a sweater for my son to take back to college. Everything about it was designed especially for him: the softest yarn, a charcoal gray color to set off his dark coloring, extra inches to fit his lanky frame. I could almost feel the pleasure he'd take in wearing it.

The day for his departure arrived, and I brought out the sweater and gave it to him. "Thanks, Mom," he said, "but I don't need another sweater." He tossed it onto a chair and left. How hurt I was! And yet, as a parent, I recognized the thoughtless, awkward way that young men have as they walk the road between adolescence and adulthood.

Is this something of the sadness our Father feels when one of His children refuses His gift, the most wonderful gift of all, the promise of eternal life through the simple acceptance of His Son as Savior? This gift is given in love, too, and is tailored to meet our deepest needs. Yet all God can do is offer it. The decision to accept or reject is left to us. What joy in acceptance! What sorrow in the turning away.

Father, I accept Your gift with all my heart.
—PATRICIA PATTERSON

Rejoice with me; for I have found my sheep which was lost.
—LUKE 15:6

*T*hrough circumstances none of my family knew or understood, my mother was separated as an infant from her own mother. I grew up with an ache in my heart for this missing grandmother of mine, and longed for the day when I might find and meet her. Through happenstance, my mother discovered she had a half brother, and for several years we enjoyed getting to know my uncle. From him, we learned a little more of my missing grandmother, for she lived with Uncle Dale six months of every year. But, sadly, she made it clear she didn't want to revisit the past.

The year I turned forty, I felt desperate to meet her; neither of us was going to live forever. Uncle Dale suggested I come for a visit and be introduced as a friend of the family. I'd at least get to see what she looked like, learn what her personality was like, and maybe, if we got on, I could plumb her for stories of her growing-up years.

I talked it over with my children. Phil, then fifteen, gave me a startled look. "But, Mum, if you go as a friend of the family, you'll never meet her as family!"

"Hope deferred makes the heart sick," and in my desperation I'd nearly committed a terrible blunder. Because, of course, Phil was right. I wanted to meet my grandmother, not some old lady.

But if "hope deferred makes the heart sick," so is "desire fulfilled a tree of life" (Proverbs 13:12, RSV). Five years later (and just six months before she died at age ninety-three), Leona Bagley Goodfellow Bent was at last ready to meet me. A miraculous meeting: I found the grandmother I'd been looking for, and she found closure after seventy years of grief. And to think we both nearly missed each other by my giving way to discouragement.

Dear Lord, help me to await steadfastly,
and in anticipation, everything I hope for. Amen.
—BRENDA WILBEE

SEPTEMBER 5

*Many, O Lord my God, are the wonders which
You have done, and Your thoughts toward us.*
—PSALM 40:5 NASB

*T*t was summer in Minnesota, and the birds were nibbling at the feeder—
only not at ours. Seven-year-old Hannah, visiting Grandma and Grandpa,
decided to hang an invader—a fine mesh bag filled with more seed—from the
post. I had doubts about the idea, but it seemed essential to her that we try.
Instead of eating from the bag, the birds were frightened by it and stayed away.
Several days later, with Hannah's permission, I took it down.

Two weeks later, back home in Alaska, where I'd accompanied her, Hannah
was about to don a lavender sundress on a cool rainy day. "Hey, Hannah," I
suggested, "why don't you try the little purple shirt with the heart buttons under
your sundress. It would look cute...and keep you warm."

Hannah had her own ideas—and they didn't include wearing that shirt. Then
I remembered the birdseed bag we had tested at my house. I kindly reminded
her that I'd tried her idea then and was asking her to try mine now. Hannah
popped on the shirt and dress, glanced in the mirror, exclaimed, "Grandma, it
looks great!" and skipped off to play.

We had learned from each other. We had each tried an idea important to
the other. One was successful; one was not. But we had cared for one another
enough to be a team and extend the gift of giving our ideas a chance.

Isn't this what our gracious God asks, that I care for Him enough to open my
life to His ideas? Ideas that always work!

*Dear God, from a far-flung universe to a Savior born among us
to life without end, Your ideas are spectacular!*
—CAROL KNAPP

SEPTEMBER 6

Even a child is known by his doings.
—PROVERBS 20:11

I slumped at the kitchen table fighting back tears. The hieroglyphics in my huge college math book made absolutely no sense. How could I ever become a teacher and provide a better life for my children if I couldn't learn? And as if one math class weren't enough after a thirty-year interval, here I was trying to take two in the same semester!

Just then my son Greg burst through the front door. "Yo, Mom! What's up?" he demanded, blue eyes twinkling with mischief. As he devoured a brownie and made goofy faces, I composed myself. Then I explained that I just couldn't figure out this math problem, fully expecting his sympathy. Greg had always wrestled with school work and never pretended to like junior high.

Instead, he grabbed a pencil and said, "Here, do it like this." I compared the exercise answer in the back of the book with his computation and stared at him in respectful amazement. He was right! I couldn't even match wits with a twelve-year-old!

"That does it!" I growled in a fit of self-loathing. "I'm quitting school!"

For perhaps the first time in his life, Greg stopped clowning and said very solemnly, "You can do it, Mom. I know you can do it. Besides," he looked at me levelly, "if you can quit, I can quit." The challenge was on.

Well, I didn't quit school. By studying extra-long hours and visiting my professor regularly for help, I slogged through those frustrating math courses and earned respectable Bs in both. And now that I'm a teacher, I'm a lot more understanding of students who can't catch a concept the first time around.

Greg would still rather skateboard than buckle down to homework. He isn't a perfect student, but then, neither is his mom.

> *Thank You, Lord, for children who teach us*
> *and challenge us to be our best selves.*
> —GAIL THORELL SCHILLING

O that thou hadst hearkened to my commandments!
Then had thy peace been as a river.
—Isaiah 48:18

*M*y mother and I have not lived near each other for more than twenty years, so when she comes to visit it's always an occasion. I've found, though, that as she grows older, it gets harder to say good-bye. Maybe deep down I'm wondering if we're seeing each other for the last time.

This year she visited me for her eighty-first birthday. Her health is good, and we enjoyed many activities together. But when it came time once again for the airport farewell, I held on to her so long that she finally said, "You have to let me go."

And that's when I recalled the biblical imagery of "peace like a river." I used to wonder why God compared peace to a river because I've seen some very turbulent ones. Then one day I really studied a river and saw how peace and river connect. The river might cut new channels, it might twist and turn, but it keeps moving ahead. Its peace comes from that forward flow.

Mom had her life to live, her friends waiting, her service for God in her small north Idaho community. I had the same in Minnesota. Our forward courses were diverging, yes, but I could be thankful for the days they had intersected.

I drove home from the airport that day, not looking back in sadness and tears and wanting to reclaim what was behind. Instead, I felt carried forward on a current of peace that was taking me exactly where God wanted me to go.

Father, help me flow freely forward, moving in Your current of peace.
—Carol Knapp

SEPTEMBER 8

God hath made me to laugh, so that all that hear will laugh with me.
—GENESIS 21:6

I'd been working on my speech for weeks, maybe years. It was the final night at home for our two daughters before they headed off to college. I wanted to remind them to do their best and to choose their friends wisely and not to dillydally away their study time. I needed to make sure they knew how important it was to attend class and to take careful notes.

I summoned them into my bedroom. "Girls," I began, "there are some things you should remember when you're away at school."

We stood awkwardly in silence for a few moments. Then Katie, the eighteen-year-old, casually stretched out on the floor to hear my lengthy instructions. She's always been the jokester. Twenty-year-old Jamie plopped down next to her, put her hands behind her head and stared at the ceiling fan.

"Let's just talk, Mom. Like we used to," Katie suggested.

"Yeah, that'd be neat," Jamie agreed.

Skip the speech? But do they know enough? Are they ready? I wondered.

Then we did something we'd never done before: I joined them on the floor and the three of us, our feet touching one another's heads, formed a triangle. We talked and laughed about everything from the funny things that had happened during their childhoods to what color toenail polish looked the best and whose Barbie dolls were dressed the finest.

As we said goodnight, I smiled from way down deep. Laughter would always hold us together. The rest, I'd leave up to God.

Dear God, when I'm way too serious and sometimes even try to do Your job, remind me of Your priceless and powerful gift of laughter.
—JULIE GARMON

To the praise of the glory of his grace, wherein
he hath made us accepted in the beloved.
—EPHESIANS 1:6

On a September afternoon I stopped at a store to buy a school folder for my daughter. As my eyes searched the folders, my ears were tuned to a conversation between two young moms.

One was telling the other about her son's game a day or so before. He was devastated because the coach hadn't allowed him to play. Her mother's heart ached, even as she comforted him and assured him there would be other opportunities. The two friends talked on about the pain of seeing their children suffer and then, before parting ways, the mother of the overlooked athlete summed up the issue with one sentence that echoed in my head for days: "I'm just praying that he won't receive rejection."

Receive rejection....

At the age of nine when my best friend Mary found another best friend; when a newcomer to the ministry I worked with was given the position I felt should have been mine; when I wasn't among the handful of people chosen to be at a close friend's bedside when she died from cancer; at those times and so many more, I received rejection. By the time I heard about God's love and acceptance, the wounds had become my weapon—I had learned to reject before I could be rejected.

But that day at the store was the beginning of the end of the power I'd given rejection in my life. In addition to a shiny, green folder for my daughter, I came home with a prayer that I pray every time I feel rejected:

Father, thank You that I don't have to receive rejection
because Jesus received it for me on the Cross.
—LUCILE ALLEN

And Jesus increased in wisdom and stature, and in favour with God and man.
—LUKE 2:52

When our daughter Maria started high school, it was hard for me not to try to relive the ups and downs of my high school years through her. I wanted her not to make the mistakes I made, so I was always giving her advice. "Go to all the football games—don't miss out on things like I did," I told her, even before school started. "Don't go to the dance with a boy you're not crazy about just to have a date" was another bit of my unsolicited wisdom. I couldn't resist it if I thought I could spare her some of the anxiety I had experienced. Finally Maria said to me, "You know, Mom, if I don't learn some of these things on my own, I won't have any advice to pass on to *my* kids!" She was so right. I wanted her to learn from my mistakes instead of making her own.

God's parenting example is clear. He gives me love and direction, but then lets me go out into the world to fall or fly. What an encouragement for any parent to know that even Jesus, in His humanity, was given the freedom to learn and grow. The best I can do for Maria is love, listen, and guide when asked. If she is to grow into the person God created her to be, I need to get out of her way much of the time. Although I'd like to clear the path for her, only she can find her unique way in life.

Lord, give me the wisdom and the strength to know when to keep silent.
—GINA BRIDGEMAN

Put your hope in God.
—PSALM 42:5 NIV

"W hat if this happens again?"

That's the fearful question I carried around in my heart after my husband Lynn suffered a cerebral hemorrhage that threatened his life and required two brain surgeries. It's the same question many of us ask after something fearful happens in our lives.

As I remember back to the terrible day that terrorists attacked our country, I ask myself:

What if...terrorists strike again?

What if...another plane gets hijacked?

What if...something like this happens to me or Lynn or our children and grandchildren or to anyone I love?

As I ask myself these questions, I remember what I kept repeating when similar "What if...?" questions plagued me after Lynn's brush with death. For every "What if...?" question, God gave me an "Even if..." answer:

Even if...I have to face my worst fear, God is still in control.

Even if...things don't turn out the way I want, God's love is still sufficient.

Even if..._____, God's promises are still true.　　　　(write your fear in the blank)

For every "What if...?" fear, Father, remind me of your "Even if..." promise.
—CAROL KUYKENDALL

"Dear woman, why do you involve me?" Jesus replied, "My time has not yet come."
—JOHN 2:4 NIV

*M*om and I were hard at work planning the finer details of my upcoming wedding. As we hurried around town orchestrating transportation for guests, finalizing the reception menu, and making sure someone was at the church early to turn on the air-conditioning (the wedding was in May in Alabama, after all), I began to feel overwhelmed. "Are we doing the right thing?" I asked Mom, waving my hand over the to-do list, which seemed to grow each day.

Mom simply smiled. "The things that you're working on are important: your vows to Brian, taking care of your family and dearest friends, and celebrating the start of a new life together."

"But still," I protested, "I'm starting to feel a little silly."

"Remember the story of Jesus at the wedding ceremony in Cana?" Mom said, her wise smile bringing to mind the ancient story. "I love that story." At the wedding ceremony, Jesus' mother, who, like mine, understood the importance of showing guests a good time at a celebration, went to Jesus, distraught that the wine was running out, and asked Him to do something. And though, as Jesus said, "it's not yet my time," do something He did.

Jesus found the wedding celebration a worthy place for His very first miracle. If He chose to use His awesome power to bless a wedding, why shouldn't I try to do the very best by my dearest friends and closest family?

Lord, thank You for giving me the opportunity to honor the love of family and friends, and to do so while having a wonderful time with my own mom.
—ASHLEY KAPPEL

SEPTEMBER 13

The grace of God means something like: ...Don't be afraid. I am with you.
Nothing can ever separate us. It's for you I created the umiverse. I love you.
—FREDERICK BUECHNER

One of our four children didn't like to go to school from the first day of kindergarten. She didn't want to be separated from me. Many mornings I would have to pull her arms from around my neck and insist she get on the bus. I would smile and wave good-bye. Her small, desperate face would peer at me from the window of the bus as though I'd betrayed her. Sometimes I would say, "Don't be afraid. Jesus will be with you."

The years passed quickly, like thumbing through the pages of a book, and without warning, it seemed, my child who had so wanted to stay close to me and avoid separations had become independent. It was time for her to go away to college and I wasn't ready to face it. Her eagerness to leave home astonished me. Suddenly, I wanted to hold her close and keep her home. If I could have returned to the past for one day, I would have let her stay home from school, holding her close, and we would watch the bus go by without her.

I suppose I succeeded in teaching my child that separations are necessary. And now that she has learned the lesson so well, I have to learn it too. She is the calm, self-assured one and I the almost panicky child. I want to say, "Don't go. Don't go. Stay home a while longer and let's do more things together." But in my heart I know that won't work.

As a five-year-old I made her let go of me, and now I, as a forty-four-year-old, must somehow let go of her. Am I wise enough to learn from my own child? I think so. Although she hasn't actually said so, I seem to hear her saying, "Don't be afraid. Jesus will be with you."

Be with all frightened people, Jesus.
—MARION BOND WEST

I lift up my eyes to the hills—where does my help come from?
My help comes from the Lord, the Maker of heaven and earth.
—PSALM 121:1–2 NIV

*M*any years ago a friend shared her favorite tidbit of wisdom with my five-year-old son. "When in doubt, look up," she advised him. He immediately looked up at the sky. She smiled. "That's right, Christopher. If you're ever in doubt of what to do, just look up. The answer always comes when we remember to ask our Father in heaven."

A few weeks later I took Christopher to the county fair. We rode kiddy rides, visited the pens of farm animals, and finished off the day with some cotton candy. Sunburned and exhausted, we made our way to the parking lot. I dug around in my purse for the car keys. After a few minutes of searching, I peered into the car; my keys were still in the ignition.

"Oh no," I groaned, "we're locked out of the car! Now what?"

"When in doubt, look up," Christopher said.

"Not now, honey," I said. "I've got to figure out what to do."

"Mommy, when in doubt, look up," he repeated.

"Okay, honey," I sighed, "you're right. Let's pray." I took his hand in mine. "Lord, we're stranded here at the fairgrounds. Please help us find a solution to our problem. Amen." Just then, we heard a loud roar overhead. It was a small biplane pulling a banner advertising a locksmith! I quickly wrote down the phone number. "Let's go find a pay phone!" I said.

A few hours later we were back in our car, headed home. I looked into my rearview mirror at Christopher buckled into his car seat, sound asleep. I said a prayer of thanks for this little boy, whose simple faith had led me to just the right answer.

Lord, may I always remember to look up to You for the answers in my life.
—MELODY BONNETTE

September 15

Do not forsake your mother's teaching.
—Proverbs 6:20 NIV

It seems to me more and more, as I shuffle toward half-time in my life, that pretty much all the tools and wisdom and food I needed to try to be a man were given to me, and still are, by my mother. She is eighty-four now and getting fragile and papery, but she's still smarter than I am, and getting pithier too. Recently, when I was swimming in the ocean of distress, I called her up and said, "Mum, what shall I do?"

Her answer was a prayer, a signpost, a handful of holiness. "Be tender," she said.

"Is that it?" I asked. "Is that all?"

"What else is there?" she said.

I hate to admit when she's right, because when I admit it to her she grins that wry grin, but she's right, and I told her so recently when we were walking slowly through the woods.

The woods were all wet and shining, and my children were running ahead. My mother doesn't walk so well these years, and there came a point where she teetered and she took my hand, and we walked that way for a while through the smiling wet woods, and I realized that I hadn't walked hand in hand with my mother for forty years, since she was walking me to school and church and across roads filled with growling huge things that could flatten me. Her hand was so pale you could almost see through it, and we walked slowly because her wheels don't move as they used to, but both of us were so happy we were humming.

I keep thinking that while I'm still crossing roads where growling things are gunning for me, I have the most powerful potent prayers on my side: my mother's love, grinning its wry grin, and her wise, wild words, "Be tender."

> *Dear Lord, thanks for mamas and prayers and rain*
> *and tenderness and telephones in which you can hear your*
> *mum's voice grinning from very far away, but not far at all.*
> —Brian Doyle

SEPTEMBER 16

Let every one of us please his neighbour for his good.
—ROMANS 15:2

*W*hen I was six years old, I decided that my mother was the most generous person in the world. Why? Because she let me lick the batter from the bowl and spoon when she baked sugar cookies. I couldn't believe that anyone would give up that privilege, and I secretly thought that when I was an adult, I would always lick the batter off the spoon when I baked cookies. I didn't care if I ever learned to drive or swim or dance, or did all the other things I thought of as adult, as long as I could lick that spoon.

Well, I am an adult now. At least, I can drive and swim and dance (though not very well). But when my nephews were visiting and we made chocolate chip cookies, I offered them the spoon and bowl to lick. I enjoyed seeing their eyes widen as they scraped off and ate every bit of that batter. And I enjoyed watching them eat it more than I would have enjoyed eating the sugary concoction myself.

So I decided to be generous a few more times that week. I carried my neighbor's groceries up to her apartment even though I was tired after a full day of work. Her glowing face more than made up for the effort. And I picked up the check after my friend Dana and I had coffee and cherry pie at a diner. When she asked why, I said, "Just because." And I felt great, even though my pocketbook was a little lighter.

So I'm going to ask God to keep showing me opportunities to be generous this week. In fact, I think I'm going to bake another batch of cookies with my nephews!

> *Thank You, Lord, for the pleasure of pleasing others.*
> —LINDA NEUKRUG

SEPTEMBER 17

"Is not this the kind of fasting I have chosen...to share your food
with the hungry and to provide the poor wanderer with shelter?"
—ISAIAH 58:6–7 NIV

*M*y daughter Lanea works for the city of Durham, North Carolina, as part of a two-person team on a project called the Ten-Year Plan to End Homelessness. It's been a hot, dry summer and early fall in North Carolina. The entire state has been under a severe drought. In the midst of it, Lanea has sweated, working on a one-day event called Project Homeless Connect to cut red tape and make services available to some of our most needy citizens. She has been planning, meeting, cajoling, coordinating, and talking about the event even in her sleep. "It's so big, Mama. There's so much need," she tells me. I can see that she feels overwhelmed and responsible for everything. As the day draws closer, I can see the telltale signs of stress, but she has worked with the team to secure volunteers, social workers, doctors, and services from public and private organizations. Everything that could be done has been done. What could go wrong?

The night before the event, after months of drought, it begins to rain. The next morning it's still drizzling. We pray. "Well, we have tents," she smiles, trying to sound optimistic as she heads out the front door. When she walks back in the door in the evening, she is glowing. "We fed hundreds of people, Mama! They came in the rain. We handed out toiletries and clothes. There were showers for people and flu shots. There were lines of people to see the doctors and lawyers and to apply for housing and jobs. The barbers and the pet groomers were really big hits!"

I am so proud of my daughter.

Lord, help me to serve You in the way that You desire.
—SHARON FOSTER

September 18

*They helped every one his neighbour; and every one
said to his brother, Be of good courage.*
—Isaiah 41:6

When my son Greg was in kindergarten, he had a classmate named Wayne. Wayne's mother Anna didn't have a car. She walked him to and from school every day, passing our house around 7:45 each morning. After a few days of watching them, I decided I could pick up Wayne for school in the morning and take him home in the afternoon.

Anna didn't have a telephone, so there was no easy way for her to contact me if Wayne wasn't going to school. That meant I'd sometimes drive to her house, bang loudly on the downstairs door so that she could hear me in her upstairs apartment, only to discover that Wayne wasn't going to school that day. Sometimes Anna would wait for me on the days Greg couldn't attend, and I'd feel a terrible pang of guilt as she and Wayne hurried past our house late for school, wondering, I was quite sure, why I hadn't come to pick up Wayne.

Pretty soon, I began to wish I'd never gotten myself into such a predicament. I complained long and often to my husband Larry about the situation, and one night he said rather gruffly, "Would you rather be Anna and have to depend on someone else all the time?" That was all it took. I suddenly realized how difficult it was to be a care-receiver.

Jesus said, "It is more blessed to give than to receive" (Acts 20:35). Being a gracious giver was the least I could do to pass on that blessing.

*Lord, please keep me from losing sight of how hard it sometimes
is to be on the receiving end of my time and patience.*
—Libbie Adams

SEPTEMBER 19

Our world will not be wonderful until we ourselves are filled with wonder.
—JAMES GARROLL

*T*t was a steamy hot day down South—when the sun can burn the rubber off your sneakers. It was also the day the air conditioner quit. In thirty minutes the house was a furnace. "Come on, kids," I called. "I'll turn on the sprinkler for you."

I sat in the pathetic shade of a maple while Ann and Bob danced through the stream of water. Time oozed by like slow, hot tar. I sat there, miserable, immune to everything but the heat and what it would cost to repair the air conditioner. Suddenly Ann squealed. "A rainbow! I made a rainbow!" She had placed her hand over the water causing a fine spray and somehow out of the mystery of sunlight and water drops, a radiant little rainbow arched right out of her hand. My daughter stared at it, her eyes polished with wonder. And watching her childlike fascination, I wondered what had become of my own ability to turn loose of the world's seriousness for just a moment, and find pure simple delight in a tiny arc of color shining in one's hand.

I turned loose and looked around me. I noticed for the first time how the leaves and grass shimmered under a golden blanket of the sun's hot light. I reached down and felt the velvet green shape of one unique clover petal... studied the flitting ballet of a butterfly and listened to the rustling quiet that lies deep in every summer day. And as I did, something began to happen inside me, as if the child in me woke up to a world rinsed with newness. But something more. As I became aware of each creation about me, I discovered the Creator too. Even the tiny rainbow shining in the sprinkler spelled God's name with its colors.

Awaken my childlike capacity to wonder, Lord.
—SUE MONK KIDD

272

SEPTEMBER 20

The four had the same form, their construction
being something like a wheel within a wheel.
—EZEKIEL 1:16 NRSV

*Y*ears back, a TV ad touted Life Savers as "a part of living." In my childhood, the wheel-shaped candies seemed a part of loving. My mother carried a green-on-silver roll of Wint-O-Greens in her pocketbook. She kept the white mints for one purpose: to pull out during church and pass down the pew. Each of us children would peel back the wrap from one candy and hand along the ever-shortening coil. Mom would take one herself before slipping the remainder back in her purse. Even when I visited as a grown-up, if Mom forgot our ritual, during the sermon I would playfully tap her bag and silently tease, *Please.* And at her funeral, I distributed Wint-O-Greens—in memoriam—along the family rows.

Like mother, like daughter. This morning, as I settled in to listen to the sermon, I reached into my purse to retrieve a partial roll of Life Savers. When I didn't find it in its usual compartment, I rummaged feverishly. I didn't relax until my fingers grasped the misplaced mints. I slipped the familiarly shaped candy into my mouth. Of course I tasted the wintergreen flavoring. But today I also savored a suggestion of appreciation: for my mother and little kindnesses she afforded her children; for the family circle that remains unbroken, even though she has passed through this life to the next.

Lord, thank You for my mother's many small gifts,
which I choose to remember as circles of grace.
—EVELYN BENCE

Call upon me, and I will answer.
—PSALM 91:15 NIV

*M*y mind was on my daughter Amy Jo and her four-week-old baby. Brock was golden-haired and healthy and constantly hungry. Every hour he needed to eat. Plus, he cried a lot! So I prayed for little Brock. I prayed that he would sleep that night, that he would rest and be at peace, that his little stomach would stay full beyond those sixty short minutes. Amy Jo's husband was away on business and she was exhausted beyond words. As I prayed, I visualized an angel—complete with giant wings and flowing robe—standing beside Brock's crib, comforting him and singing him back to sleep.

Later, as I climbed into bed, Amy Jo called. "Can you come over? I just need someone else to hold the baby and let me get a few minutes sleep." Gladly, I went.

After Amy Jo nursed Brock, she handed him to me and shuffled off to bed. "Wake me up when he starts crying," she said over her shoulder.

So I began rocking Brock. After a while, I laid him in his crib and patted his stomach. The minutes slipped by and turned into hours. For three hours Brock slept—and so did Amy Jo. Every time he stirred, I prayed and hummed hymns until he was quiet. "That's the most sleep I've gotten in the last month!" Amy Jo said happily when I put Brock into her arms.

As I drove home, the blackness of night giving way to the first hint of dawn, I realized just how miraculously my prayer had been answered. Brock was attended to by an angel that night...an angel named Nana.

How doubly generous, God, to let me be part of Your answer to my prayers!
—MARY LOU CARNEY

"We remember the fish which we used to eat free in Egypt,
the cucumbers and the melons."
—NUMBERS 11:5 NASB

In a casual phone conversation with my seven-year-old grandson Caleb, who lives in Alaska, I mentioned the vegetables I was collecting from farmers' market vendors. "Can you send me some *cukes*?" he asked excitedly. Caleb's mother doesn't garden, and Alaska's growing season is brief for those who do. So I stuffed a box with fat green cucumbers and sent it off.

"How'd you like your cucumbers?" I asked Caleb several days later. There was a dramatic pause, followed by a one-word crescendo: "Awesome!" I was feeling pleased with myself for pulling off the cucumber sensation when he added, "Next time can you send some ranch dressing?"

When Caleb's eighth birthday arrived at summer's end, he received another "grandma box." Inside were clothes, a chess set (he's a very good player) and, yes, more cucumbers—with a big bottle of ranch dressing.

Jesus, may Caleb always love cucumbers and seek joy
in life's small, often overlooked pleasures. Amen.
—CAROL KNAPP

SEPTEMBER 23

Be my Law and I shall be,
Firmly bound, forever free.
—SAMUEL LONGFELLOW, HYMN

 y mother was forever telling me to straighten my shoulders (or my bed); put out the light (or the cat); stop chewing gum (or my fingernails); tone down the record player (or my voice). I guess we all know the routine if we were fortunate enough to have mothers!

I used to think it would be nice to be free. My then-definition of "free" was having nobody telling me what to wear, or what to eat, or that I slept too little, read too much. If I were free, I could eat what I pleased, go without sleep, and let my grades drop to the bottom of the class. I could make all the noise I was capable of making. Imagine!

"I wish I'd been triplets," I once said to my uncle. "Mama would have to divide her fussing time between us."

"She's not fussing, honey," Uncle Henry said. "She's loving you."

That turned my thinking around. Life without the love and guidance of my mother was unthinkable. Who wanted to make noise if there was nobody around to hear it? Why, I might even cry in the night—and she wouldn't hear that either! To this day, my mother must wonder why I rushed out into the yard and hugged her over and over until she gasped for breath.

There used to be times in my adult life when I felt restricted by all the "thou shalt nots" in the Bible. How could I be free if I had to obey all these injunctions from an ancient book? But then I began to see that breaking these laws actually diminished my freedom to live a full and happy life. God knows me best—and what is best for me. Accepting this loving control is my surest path to freedom.

Father, You know best. Guide me with Your loving care.
—JUNE MASTERS BACHER

So do not throw away your confidence; it will be richly rewarded.
—HEBREWS 10:35 NIV

Everything I thought about on my morning walk made me worry. Most of all my husband Gordon had come home earlier saying that he wanted to put his name in the hat for a job in another city. Everything inside of me screamed, *No, I don't want to move again! I don't have the time or energy for it!* As I rounded the curve and headed home, I tried to lift my problems to God, but somehow it didn't seem to do any good.

I collapsed in the living room and opened my Bible to where I had been reading the day before. All at once, a sentence in Hebrews electrified me. I hurried upstairs to copy it down in my journal in capital letters. "DO NOT THROW AWAY YOUR CONFIDENCE."

"Is that the only way confidence can be lost—if I throw it away myself?" I wrote. "That's an amazing thought. Usually I think that overwhelming circumstances or my own lack of ability or the way others have treated me rob me of my confidence. What if confidence is really mine and mine alone either to keep or throw away?"

I'd often mentally substituted the word self-confidence for confidence when reading the Bible. Self-confidence is not always possible, because there are many things beyond my ability and control. But Hebrews says to place my trust and reliance on God, "for he who promised is faithful" (Hebrews 10:23, NIV).

The next morning, as I rounded the same curve in my morning walk, I smiled. What an amazing turnaround my attitude had taken because of that one sentence I'd read the day before. Every time worry or depression crept in, I would simply remind myself, "Don't throw away your confidence."

I began praying for whatever God thought best concerning Gordon's future job, even if it meant laying aside my desire for stability. And I prayed with confidence because I was sure that whatever God's plan, it would be so much better than mine.

Lord, instead of throwing away my confidence,
help me to throw my whole heart into trusting You.
—KAREN BARBER

Thy faithfulness is unto all generations.
—PSALM 119:90

I just wrote the latest entry in my birthday book: Jack Ryan McMahon, a cousin born in Seattle on September 25. The baby who arrived and was duly noted before Jack was Paisley Jean O'Roark, my great-niece born in Columbus, Ohio. And when I flip the pages to January 29, there's my own name, but this entry is in my Grandmother Paisley's neat handwriting. She wrote my name there some sixty years ago.

The book is called *Natal Memories: A Scripture-Text Birthday Book.* As an introductory page explains, it was given to my grandmother in 1947 by Alexander and Elizabeth Fleming, the minister of the church that our family attended in Steubenville, Ohio, and his wife. There's a page for each day of the year with a Scripture verse at the bottom. I imagine my grandmother's concentration and satisfaction as she recorded birthdays of family and friends in a steady and loving hand, and committed many of the verses to memory.

My grandmother died when I was ten years old, and the book must have been swept into a box of her belongings, where I found it many years later and tucked it into a drawer of my own. Recently I discovered it again. And now I'm the one who smiles as I add new births and make note of those who are now here—and were here—and should be celebrated.

Lord, thank You for the little book that somehow anchors the generations of our family in what it calls Your "great unchanging heart of love."
—MARY ANN O'ROARK

I have written unto you, young men, because
ye are strong, and the word of God abideth in you.
—1 JOHN 2:14

For years now, while sitting in church, I've imagined that my grown sons would burst through the doors, find me, and sit down next to me, one on each side. At long last, they'd have returned to God, and I, along with all those who have prayed for them so steadfastly, would rejoice. Actually, Jeremy has returned to the very church my husband Gene and I attend. Each Sunday he sits with us, and I rejoice.

Still, I long and pray for his twin brother Jon to be on the other side of me. When the local newspaper published a picture of Jon at the butcher shop where he works, I studied it long and hard. My eyes lingered on his large, square-shaped hands. The freckles didn't show. He wore a shirt I'd given him beneath his apron. Jon's addictions have taken a tremendous toll, and he rarely communicates with us.

I can't seem to relinquish my prayer of Jon sitting with us. I've placed the newspaper picture of him in my Bible, right by one of his favorite Scriptures: "I am the vine, ye are the branches" (John 15:5). Jeremy continues to sit by me. And in a way Jon does, too, nestled in God's Word.

Because nothing is too hard for you, Father, I'm going
to continue to see my sons sitting on either side of me at church.
—MARION BOND WEST

SEPTEMBER 27

Trust in him at all times; ye people, pour out your heart before him.
—PSALM 62:8

*W*hen my husband Norman and I walked into the house after a full Sunday of church and friends, we found a message to call a doctor at the University of North Carolina Hospital. My heart sank. Our son John was completing his graduate studies at the university.

Norman picked up the phone to return the call, and I stood next to him so I could hear what the doctor was saying. "Your son came in today in great pain. He has an inflamed gallbladder with possible pancreatic complications. We hope to reduce the infection first and operate on him later."

"Well, doctor," I whispered, "John is in your hands, and he is in God's hands. Do what you think is best." We began to pray: for the doctor, for our only son, and for strength from God to help us through.

At 11:15 that night, the doctor called back to tell us John hadn't responded to the medication. "Surgery will be very dangerous," he said, "but it might be more dangerous not to operate."

"Doctor," I repeated, "he's in your hands and God's hands. We'll be with you in prayer."

The doctor had said he would call us after the operation. Four hours passed without a call, then five, then six. We prayed all night long, waiting for the phone to ring. At about 3:30 in the morning, I had a strong conviction that John was going to be all right. When I told Norman, he said, "Ruth, I had the same feeling a few moments ago."

By six o'clock in the morning, the doctor finally called. "John came through the operation successfully," he said. "I think he's going to be all right."

It had been a long time since I had experienced such an overwhelming sense of the greatness and love of God as I did that morning.

Lord, even in the midst of adversity, Your grace strengthens my faith.
—RUTH STAFFORD PEALE

How excellent is thy lovingkindness, O God! therefore the children
of men put their trust under the shadow of thy wings.
—PSALM 36:7

Our daughter Tamara was stranded in Anchorage, Alaska, with a newborn and toddlers Zachary and Hannah, while her husband trained at the police academy. I had come to rescue her.

This day, I took Zachary and Hannah to play in the park. Soon an older woman meandered by with a young child in tow. She nodded and smiled, but didn't seem inclined to chat. Her little charge toddled off across the grass with Hannah.

Zachary and I teeter-tottered while the girls sailed down a small slide beneath the watchful eye of the unknown woman. When I twirled my grandchildren on the tire swing, the other child wanted to swing, too, and the woman came over to help. Haltingly she told me she was from Russia, visiting her daughter.

"Oh," I exclaimed, "you're a *babushka!*"

She laughed, nodding yes.

I pointed to myself. "Me, too," I said.

When Zachary tired of the swing, I went off with him to play in the sand, leaving the Russian grandmother still twirling the girls. Somehow Hannah slipped off the tire and fell backward onto the ground. The Russian grandmother was bending down anxiously over her when I scooped Hannah into my arms.

"It's all right," I said. "She's not hurt."

That's when the thought hit me: Here we are, two grandmothers from countries that used to be enemies, playing in the park with our grandchildren, teaching them to get along, and watching out for them with equal concern.

The two of us left the park, taking our grandchildren in opposite directions. We had met only briefly, but it was long enough for me to gain new understanding of a grandmother's mission: to help shape our world's future by sowing seeds of consideration and respect—starting in the park.

Heavenly Father, with my grandchildren in tow,
lead me in Your path of loving-kindness.
—CAROL KNAPP

Every way of a man is right in his own eyes.
—PROVERBS 21:2

*W*e had seven more stops to go on the subway when three-year-old Stephen decided that he wanted to put fresh blackberries into the roll he was munching. I looked at his yellow shirt and beige shorts, and suggested that berries and clothing shouldn't mix. "But I won't stain them! I *have* to put berries in my roll!" Stephen wailed. "I have to!"

We were heading for a rut that we'd already visited several times that day. I took a deep breath and squatted down in front of Stephen's seat. "Buddy," I said, "I think you've got to be a bit more flexible here." "But I can't bend my legs that far like my stretchy rabbit can!" he protested. *Hmm...wrong word. Let's try again.* "Okay. I can see you have an idea about the blackberries that you like a lot. But you need a backup plan. A lot of times in life your first idea won't work. In fact, it's usually good to have a whole bunch of other ideas. That way you don't get stuck."

Stephen pondered my words. His eyes narrowed suspiciously as he weighed the sense of my words against his impulse to reiterate, "But I have to put berries in my roll!" another five hundred times. I took advantage of his indecision to point out that the lady across the aisle had purple hair. The distraction worked, at least for a moment. Then Stephen noticed his blackberry-less roll.

"Mommy," he said, "I want those berries to *smush* into my roll." I groaned inwardly, thinking of the remaining three subway stops that would be filled with wailing. I opened my mouth to speak, but Stephen continued, "Can I have the berries when we get to the playground?"

Lord, I guess I don't really HAVE to do everything my way.
I could do it Your way instead.
—JULIA ATTAWAY

This is my memorial unto all generations.
—EXODUS 3:15

Last week I tried to sharpen a mechanical pencil. Last year I sent my youngest grandson a card that read "To My Great Niece." And no family gathering passes without the Halloween story: I filled a bowl with candy, turned on the porch light, and waited expectantly for trick-or-treaters—on the last day of September.

But there's a reason I'm not always attentive to details: family tradition. My mother once gathered a colorful fall bouquet for the dining table, only to discover (painfully) that she'd picked poison sumac. My sister Amanda bought and wore a belt several times until a church friend pointed out that the "lovely designs" were skulls and crossbones. Amanda hadn't noticed; she was wearing the belt upside down. But good traits run in our family too. My banker-grandfather made an all-day trip to return mortgage papers to a struggling farmer after an overzealous employee at the bank refused a fifty-dollar seed loan without them. Grandma taught me about Jesus by patiently teaching me hymns of faith. Daddy bought gasoline so our pastor could make hospital calls. Neither friend nor stranger ever left our house hungry. At Mother's funeral a friend remarked, "I always envied the love in your family."

Some family traditions, like inattention to details, should end with me. But others—compassion, patience, generosity, hospitality, love—need to be cultivated, cherished, and passed on. I hope that my children and grandchildren will continue to laugh and forgive my foibles. I pray that they will nurture and keep the spiritual gifts lived out and handed down from previous generations.

Thank You, Lord, for the blessed heritage that is mine!
—PENNEY SCHWAB

October

OCTOBER 1

To search out a matter is the glory of kings.
—PROVERBS 25:2 NIV

*W*hen our son John headed off to college, I knew there would be independence issues—mine. I've always depended on him for all things electronic. Before John left, I lamented, "What am I going to do without you? I've always relied on you to help me when I don't know how to do something on my computer."

"Do what I do," John replied. "If you can't figure something out, look it up on the Internet."

I was stunned at this simple remedy, which I'd never thought to try. I'd always figured there was something in the younger generation's blood that made them computer whizzes. John had been gone only a week when I couldn't figure out how to make my e-mail program send an automatic reply saying that I was out of the office. I clicked every bar and looked at menus with no luck. I was about to call John, but instead I tried what he suggested: I typed my question on the Internet search page. A few more clicks and I had printed out instructions. I followed the steps. *Bingo!* My auto-reply was all set up.

I guess it's never too late to learn more independence and resourcefulness. Even if you have to learn it from your own teenage son!

> *Father, for too long I've relied on others to take care of parts*
> *of my life that I should be handling myself. Help me take*
> *practical steps toward healthy independence.*
> —KAREN BARBER

OCTOBER 2

*Not that I have already...been made perfect, but I press on
to take hold of that for which Christ Jesus took hold of me.*
—PHILIPPIANS 3:12 NIV

O ne Saturday, as I was clearing off a cluttered bookshelf, I came across the baby books I had kept for my two sons Greg and Jeff. I had recorded detailed information about each of them, noting everything from their first faltering steps to their high-school graduations.

I was young and inexperienced, and I felt inadequate as a mother. To compensate, I expended a vast amount of energy trying to become the perfect parent. I couldn't be perfect, of course, yet even now, browsing back through the books, I could feel the old lingering sense of guilt and regret.

Later that same day, while rummaging through a box filled with odds and ends from one of the bedroom closets, I came upon an envelope containing two little badges. The first one had been given to Jeff by his second-grade teacher Mrs. Parker. It bore a whimsical smiley face and a shiny gold star, and proclaimed in big black letters, "JEFF IS A GOOD LISTENER." As I looked at the badge, I remembered how hard second grade had been for Jeff, and how I had always seemed to be lecturing him about his behavior in class. Most days, I felt, I had been impatient and demanding.

Then I took the other little badge out of the envelope and turned it over in my hand. It had been unevenly cut out of green construction paper, and written on it in a child's scrawl was, "Momy is a good listener." I smiled. Here was my own personal badge of recognition, lovingly crafted by a seven-year-old, who obviously hadn't shared his "Momy's" opinion of herself.

Greg and Jeff have grown into fine young men. As for the "perfect parent," I've learned that there is no such creature. With God's help, I do the best I can, and in His grace He forgives me the rest. The real accomplishment is in learning to forgive myself.

> *Thank You, Father, that through Your love I can
> forgive all imperfections, even my own.*
> —LIBBIE ADAMS

OCTOBER 3

When I am afraid, I will trust in You.
—PSALM 56:3 NIV

I've been living with this "what-if" fear, which I sometimes think about in the middle of the night. When our children started leaving home and going off to college in faraway places, I began dreaming that someday, when they got married and settled down, they would live close enough so that I could be involved in the lives of my grandchildren. I imagined myself watching a grandchild perform in a preschool program or play in a soccer game, or making cookies for an after-school visit. As that season of life draws nearer, however, my adult children are still living in faraway places, and I've started to fear that things may not turn out the way I dreamed.

"I don't want to be the kind of grandma who has to carry little presents in her purse to coax her grandchildren into liking her when she gets off the airplane to visit," I whined to my husband Lynn recently.

"You're racing ahead of yourself," he told me gently. "Relax and trust God."

His words reminded me of a story in Corrie ten Boom's book *The Hiding Place*. She, too, dealt with "what-if" fears, and her father helped by asking her about riding to Amsterdam on the train.

"When do I give you your ticket?" he questioned.

"Right before we get on the train," she answered.

"Exactly," he reassured her. "And God in heaven does the same thing. He gives us what we need when we need it. So don't run out ahead of Him, Corrie."

Maybe my grandchildren will live within driving distance, maybe they won't. But that time hasn't come. I don't even have any grandchildren yet; the train hasn't pulled into the station. But while I'm waiting, I don't have to run ahead and squint to see the train way off in the distance. I can relax and trust God, knowing that He will give me whatever I need when I need it. He will give me my ticket when the train pulls into the station.

Father, I pray for greater trust to believe You...and act like I believe You.
—CAROL KUYKENDALL

OCTOBER 4

"Teach them the good way in which they should walk. "
—1 KINGS 8:36 NASB

This past summer I sat in the audience as my son debuted as a chorus member in his first professional opera with the Cincinnati Opera Company. As I watched Chase, I strained to try to pick out his tenor voice from the others.

He is a man now, but summer still reminds me of when he was a boy. Summer is the sound of motorboats on the lake and lawn mowers in the yard; it's the smell of new grass and sweet flowers. Summer is my memory of my young son pushing a mower across the yard. I didn't know how to raise a son, how to help him be a man. It was not my plan to raise him alone. I did not anticipate his father dying in a motorcycle accident. "God, You've got to help me. I can't do this alone." When I finished my prayer, it came to me that we should read the accounts of King David's life. Even as I thought it, I shook my head. The last thing a boy would want to do was sit on the couch and read the Bible with his mom.

But, surprisingly, Chase agreed. Over a period of weeks we read together, taking turns and then discussing what we learned. "There are all kinds of men in the world. Saul was one kind of man, and David was another. You get to choose what kind of man you'll be." That was the beginning, and then there were karate lessons, kickboxing lessons, ballet, football, skateboarding and snowboarding, and lots of conversations and carpools.

Chase survived. He thrived. Now, he is a man. He is driving me places and teaching me new things—about opera, about how men think, explaining Bible passages to me, and about how he will raise his son.

Lord, encourage all those who are raising children.
—SHARON FOSTER

OCTOBER 5

It is not good...to be hasty and miss the way.
—PROVERBS 19:2 NIV

Recently, my son Ross and I watched a terrific TV special highlighting baseball's twenty-five greatest moments. The one among them that has particularly stayed with me happened in game six of the 1975 World Series.

Boston Red Sox catcher and Hall-of-Famer Carlton Fisk hit a dramatic home run in the twelfth inning to beat the Cincinnati Reds, keeping alive the Sox's hopes of a Series victory. Fisk hit the shot straight down the left-field foul line toward Fenway Park's legendary wall, the Green Monster. After jogging a few steps from home plate, he waved his arms at the ball as if coaching it to stay fair—which it did—to win the game. (But the Sox lost the Series.)

It's not the home run, but Fisk's comments that were so poignant. Asked many years later about that night, he remarked that since it happened so early in his career, he thought he'd likely have more such moments. But that turned out to be his only World Series. The moment had passed so quickly, and was never to come again in his twenty-four-year career.

To me, that's an important truth about all of life. My daughter Maria asked if we could read a chapter of *Charlotte's Web* tonight. "It's late," I told her, "and I want to get in a load of wash." *There's lots of time to read,* I thought. But who knows? God has blessed my life with abundance, but not with any guarantees.

Besides, that exact moment with Maria will never come again. The days will pass in a blur and soon she and her big brother won't have time for me. What once seemed like an endless road, dotted with those "Mommy, watch me" moments stretching into eternity, will too quickly reach an end.

So I have to go now. I have a date with a girl named Maria and a spider named Charlotte.

Open my eyes, Lord, to the all-time great moments
in my life, so I don't miss a single one.
—GINA BRIDGEMAN

OCTOBER 6

If ye shall ask any thing in my name, I will do it.
—JOHN 14:14

Four of us from our Victim's Impact Panel spoke to the people arrested for drunk driving this month. A highway patrolman gave details about several of the alcohol-related fatalities he had handled. I told them about working as an emergency medical technician at a car wreck where three young men were killed. Mary Jo, the president of our Mothers Against Drunk Driving chapter, spoke next. She told our forty listeners about her mother who was killed on Ute tribal land by a drunk driver.

San Jean was our last speaker. She is a courageous Ute woman who always begins by saying, "I'm here not to speak of the dead, but to speak for them."

The audience response varies from month to month. We didn't seem to be getting through to them on this night. San Jean's eyes were shut while Mary Jo shared memories about Jenny, her mother. San Jean's sister is the drunk driver who killed Jenny. I don't know if San Jean's eyes were shut out of respect for Mary Jo's mother or if she was praying. I know I closed my eyes and prayed for San Jean and Mary Jo. And I prayed that our stories would reach, and change, our seemingly unmoved audience.

When we finished, we met in another room to wait for the written comments. Before the people who were arrested are allowed to leave the courtroom, they have to fill out a comment sheet. The comments on that night were the best ever. We were mystified, but encouraged. I told my wife about it the next day—how we felt that our presentations are becoming more polished, and that is why we affected this group so much.

While I was talking to her, however, I remembered my prayer for San Jean and Mary Jo's mother. "It's the first time I prayed for help during one of these," I admitted.

> *Dear God, thank You for the times You hear my pleas for help.*
> *Now help me to make prayer my first, not my last, resort.*
> —TIM WILLIAMS

October 7

God has given each of us the ability to do certain things well.
—Romans 12:6 TLB

*M*y daughter Amy Jo had passed the bar exam, and she and I had driven down to Indianapolis for the swearing-in ceremony. After today, Amy Jo would be licensed to practice law in the state of Indiana—to stand before judges and plead cases, to write briefs and give counsel, to protect people unjustly accused, to "defend the Constitution of the United States against all enemies."

A gavel pounds and the court is called to order. The judges file in—their billowing robes somehow even blacker than the sea of business suits that surrounds them. The soon-to-be lawyers shuffle in, pausing at the microphone to say their names to the judges before whom they will practice. They are nervous, serious, well-groomed. Finally, Amy Jo appears. She's easy to spot: blonde, beautiful, poised—and seven-months pregnant. Her black jacket buttons spread neatly across her wide belly. Inside, my grandchild is also a witness to this auspicious event. "Amy Jo Redman," she says confidently into the mike. I smile, remembering the ten-year-old girl who asked one rainy afternoon, "Mom, do you think I'm smart enough to be a lawyer?" My answer: "Certainly!"

Later, I applaud (perhaps a bit too loudly) along with other proud families. Someday, my grandchild may wonder if he or she is good enough or bright enough or talented enough to follow a dream. When that time comes, I'm sure Amy Jo will know just what to say. She is, after all, pretty smart.

Every good and perfect gift comes from You, Lord. Thank You
for dreams—and for the intelligence and perseverance to pursue them.
(And thanks for soon-to-be grandchildren too!)
—Mary Lou Carney

OCTOBER 8

And Hezekiah spoke encouragingly to all the Levites
who showed good skill in the service of the Lord.
—2 CHRONICLES 30:22 RSV

*P*romptly at 6:00 a.m., our hungry children stampeded into the hotel restaurant, then-five-year-old Elizabeth skipping with excitement and Mark toddling to catch up with her. Their shrieking drew head-turning from our fellow diners.

"*Shh! Shh!* Inside voices," we hushed. But the children were pumped with excitement for our big airplane trip home. We constantly reminded them to lower their voices. I began to lose patience, barking at Elizabeth to sit still and shouting as Mark sent a fistful of pancakes flying to the floor.

Business people surrounded us, conducting meetings before catching their planes, and constantly glanced over at our rambunctious, noisy table. Finally Alex led the children out. Kneeling by the high chair, picking up pieces of strawberries and pancakes, exhaustion overcame me. I felt like a failure as a mother and dreaded trying to control the kids on the long flight ahead.

Rising, I found a silver-haired man in a navy blue suit standing before me. *Oh, no, he's going to chastise me for the kids' noise!* Instead, he smiled. "I just wanted to tell you how I enjoyed watching you young folks with your children. It's so refreshing to see parents who care so much."

Amazed, I stammered, "Thank you."

Somehow this man had seen love coming through our dealings with our children, even through our mistakes, and made a point to tell me. As I walked to our room, I felt invigorated, ready to tackle the challenges ahead that day. And during the coming days, as I attempted to teach and discipline the children, his words stayed with me, reminding me to be "a parent who cares so much."

Lord, thank You for the power of encouraging words.
Show me today someone who needs to hear them from me.
—MARY BROWN

OCTOBER 9

"My body also will live in hope."
—ACTS 2:26 NIV

*Y*our son Jeremy's been in an auto accident. Come to the emergency room," said the voice on the phone.

My husband Gene and I rushed to the hospital, more than an hour away. Jeremy, severely depressed, had been in two other accidents recently. "He has a broken right hip and two bad breaks in his left femur," a doctor explained after sewing up Jeremy's face. We left the hospital about one o'clock that morning as Jeremy slept soundly following surgery.

Two days later, another call came from a different hospital. "Come now," we were told. Jeremy's twin brother Jon had been admitted in serious condition with a rare bacterial infection. The hand surgeon explained that he could lose fingers, his whole hand, his arm, or even his life.

Back at home one day after visiting both my sons, I was overwhelmed with fear and discouragement. I'd planned to ignore the mail, but a lumpy envelope addressed in a child's handwriting caught my eye. It was from my nine-year-old pen pal Avie.

Inside was an ordinary stone, covered with a scrap of green-and-white-checked cloth and tied with a bright green ribbon. "This is a prayer rock, Miss Marion," Avie wrote. "Put it under your pillow tonight and it will remind you that nothing is impossible with God." I put the stone under my pillow and, amazingly, that very night my discouragement lifted and I began to hope.

After surgery, Jon went into intensive care and remained in the hospital for eleven days. He may need more surgery someday, but he's alive—with two hands. And his brother Jeremy seems to be viewing life differently—with hope.

Father, let me never forget that hope sometimes comes in unusual ways.
—MARION BOND WEST

OCTOBER 10

Share with God's people who are in need. Practice hospitality.
—ROMANS 12:13 NIV

For more years than I can count, my wife Shirley and I have taken part in the Church World Service-sponsored CROP (Communities Responding to Overcome Poverty) Hunger Walk to raise money to help stop hunger in our community and around the world.

My mother conducted her own version of CROP when I was growing up. We lived a couple of blocks from the Wabash railroad tracks and hosted people passing through town regularly. The hobos who rode boxcars in those days always seemed to find their way to our house. Someone once told me that migrants would leave a mark on trees or sidewalks identifying a place where hungry people would be fed, but I could never find any such mark.

Mama never turned anyone away. It was the same when friends would show up unexpectedly around dinnertime. "Put an extra leaf in the table," she would whisper to my brother, my sister, or me, and then she would stretch whatever she was fixing—stew or tuna fish casserole or pot roast—to accommodate the number of plates. She didn't have to coach us to pass up the potatoes if they were in short supply or go easy on the gravy. We knew the routine, even to the point of fibbing that we weren't hungry.

The Bible often commands us to practice hospitality, suggesting in one place that by doing so we might have "entertained angels unawares" (Hebrews 13:2). Whenever I'm inclined to be less than generous with the bounty God has provided, I remind myself of something my mother told me as a child, maybe when she was feeding strangers on the back porch: "No kindness, no matter how small, goes unnoticed by God."

Lord, school us in the doing of kindly acts,
Regardless of station or side of the tracks.
—FRED BAUER

OCTOBER 11

Wisdom and knowledge shall be the stability
of thy times, and strength of salvation....
—ISAIAH 33:6

*I*t's six weeks into school, and friends and neighbors are asking, "How are the kids adapting?" No matter how many times I'm asked the question, I pause. It's hard to articulate how different life is after eight years of home-schooling. "I think they're all doing well," I begin slowly. Academically, this is true. It's also true that the teachers are full of compliments about how well the children fit in. Yet something feels vaguely amiss, and I've been struggling to put my finger on it. Partly it's our new schedule. In the mad morning rush to get lunches packed and hair brushed, and to find the shoe or homework that's not where it's supposed to be, there isn't time to savor one another. There's a whole lot of Martha and too little Mary in our lives right now. I haven't quite figured out how to get our day focused before we're all out the door.

There's also a sense of dislocation now that everyone is centered in a different place. At 6:45 a.m., Elizabeth heads off to high school. John's bus arrives at 7:30 a.m. to take him to the Bronx, and then the no-longer little girls, Mary and Maggie, begin their trek up to the church school with Stephen and me. It feels as if we're scattered about on different paths, when we used to be companions throughout the day. The children miss being with one another. They miss spending time with me. I miss them.

I know by faith that God is with us in our new schedule as much as He was in the old. But we Attaways are used to recognizing His presence in familiar routines that no longer fit on the daily agenda. Part of what's new this year is finding other ways to spend time with the Lord. We're learning to seek Him where we are, even if we're not in the usual places.

> *Lord, help me distinguish between what's uncomfortable because*
> *it's different and what's uncomfortable because it's not Your will.*
>
> —JULIA ATTAWAY

OCTOBER 12

I will not leave you comfortless: I will come to you.
—JOHN 14:18

After my mother died, I did pretty well with the big events like Mother's Day and Christmas. But what I missed most were the articles and coupons Mother snipped from the newspaper for me. She had a knack for knowing when I needed one of Erma Bombeck's humorous columns or when I was about out of peanut butter or when a Dilbert cartoon would be perfect for a presentation at work.

Then fall arrived, the kind of crisp, cool day when Mother and I would sit and talk together on my screened-in porch. As the mailman drove up to my rural mailbox, I walked down to meet him, thinking a new Country Home magazine might take my mind off things.

Among the bills and usual junk mail was a fat envelope with three stamps on it from an address I didn't recognize. When I tore it open, some small pieces of paper fluttered out. The note inside read: "Forgive me, but I feel as if I know you from your writing in *Daily Guideposts.* You had the devotion for today, and as I read it, I sensed God telling me that you could use a little encouragement. I'm sending along some things I thought you might enjoy."

There were coupons, a bookmark, a church bulletin and a newspaper clipping about some quilters. And, oh yes, a vintage Erma Bombeck column.

Thank You for the little things, Lord, that bring such big comfort.
—ROBERTA MESSNER

Cast thy burden upon the Lord, and he shall sustain thee.
—PSALM 55:22

*T*his is the part of parenting I'm not good at: waiting for my teenager to come home from a party on a Saturday night. I was good at soothing hurts and listening to those preteen woes, but I'm not good at waiting. It's nearly eleven o'clock, Ross's curfew time, so he should be home soon. Sitting upright in the reclining chair in the family room, I'm trying to distract myself by watching TV. A news promo says there's been a bad accident but doesn't say where. I know Ross is a good driver, careful and smart about all that he does. Besides, I can't do anything sitting here at home.

Suddenly I'm reminded of something my friend Nancy said the other day as we talked about our children. When I asked why she seemed unfazed by their problems, she said, "I guess I just don't pay attention to things I have no control over."

Tonight, that thought keeps echoing in my mind. Isn't that really the source of my anxiety? Paying too much attention to something I should be letting God pay attention to, trying to control what only God can control? I finally realize that all I can do is turn to God and say, "Here, You do it. I can't manage this."

His response? *Then don't. I will.*

Watch over him, Lord, I pray. Take away my fear. And I keep praying until I hear Ross's key in the door.

Lord, help me recognize those times when I can do nothing but turn to You.
—GINA BRIDGEMAN

How good and pleasant it is when brothers live together in unity!
—PSALM 133:1 NIV

I held my breath. My cousin Jayme was playing in the championship soccer game for girls ages twelve and under. The score was tied 0–0 as the buzzer sounded, signaling the end of the game, and remained scoreless through two overtimes. Now Jayme and nine other girls from her team would be chosen to take penalty kicks. The other team picked their ten kickers, and the twenty girls moved into the middle of the field to prepare themselves for a tense fifteen minutes.

The two soccer teams echoed each other, missing and scoring in tandem, until the final pair of girls moved to the line. Kelly, a teammate of Jayme's, set her ball and backed up. She ran forward, kicked and watched as the goalie dove on top of her shot. *Blocked.*

My aunt excitedly grabbed Jayme, who had been chosen to kick in the seventh spot, and exclaimed, "Oh, I would've been so nervous if that had been you out there!" Jayme shrugged, still focused on the one kick left that would decide the game's outcome, and replied, "It doesn't matter who kicks first or last, Mom. We win as a team and lose as a team."

The final shot soared past Jayme's goalie and the horn sounded the opposing team's victory, but my aunt never noticed. Tears came to her eyes, not because the team lost a championship, but because Jayme, only eleven, understood that there are more important things in life than scoring goals.

*God, thank You for the reminder that my focus belongs
on the game, not just the final score.*
—ASHLEY JOHNSON

"Seek the welfare of the city...and pray to the Lord on its behalf."
—JEREMIAH 29:7 NASB

O f all the racket a city dweller like me has to put up with, sirens are probably the worst. Sirens are designed to be impossible to ignore, and though I've become pretty good at pushing them into the background, there are still times when an ambulance or fire truck sounds like it's right in my living room.

That's what happened last night. Several police cars decided to stop outside our apartment building, sirens bleating, right under our windows. The sirens woke Millie, our golden retriever, who went into a barking frenzy that woke up my wife Julee, who shook me awake to tell me to make Millie quiet down. I lurched into the living room where Millie was barking at the window, her breath fogging up the glass. "*Shhh*...hush!" I said, dragging her away. She got loose and resumed her barking vigil. Finally I pulled the blinds, and she stopped. All the while the sirens continued. My head started pounding. How would I ever get back to sleep? I peered through the slats in the blind. Nothing seemed amiss on the block.

A memory of my mother came back to me: Whenever she heard a siren, even a distant one, she stopped what she was doing and said a quick prayer. We'd tease her sometimes, telling her it was probably just a couple of police officers hurrying back from their lunch break. But I came to admire Mom's Johnny-on-the-spot faith: Sirens mean people in distress, and people in distress need prayer.

The sirens had stopped by now, and Millie had unceremoniously taken my place in bed (she likes that nice warmed-up spot). I didn't have the heart to remove her. Besides, I wasn't going to get back to sleep now. I would sit for a while waiting to hear another inevitable siren come through the night. And I knew what I would do.

Lord, my mother taught me well. The world is full of opportunities to pray.
—EDWARD GRINNAN

I will never leave thee.
—HEBREWS 13:5

I'm writing this by the light of the clown night lamp I bought so my two-year-old granddaughter would feel safe. Dawn has never been away from her parents overnight before, but I've told her I won't leave her, and she's learned that she can trust me.

My mind is filled with unknowns about Dawn's future and the world's. Like a child away from home, I sometimes long for the comfort of familiar ways. But One Who loves me has told me that He will never leave me, and I've learned that I can trust Him. That trust may be the best legacy I can give my little Dawn. Perhaps it will be a night-light for her in this still-new twenty-first century.

My dear Dawn,

I still remember lying in bed with you that night when you were two years old and how I prayed for your future. How quickly that future has arrived! The world you have inherited is full of violence and suffering, with airplanes flying into towering buildings killing thousands, bloody wars in many parts of the world, millions of people dying of AIDS. But there are also new heart surgeries adding years to people's lives, amazing technologies allowing instant contact around the globe, a new physics that touches the realms of mystery and spirit. And most important, my dear Dawn, the same loving and changeless God is in charge, the One I trusted when you were two, the One we can trust forever. And I will always believe in you.

Much love, many prayers,
Gram

*Great Creator, thank You for being our changeless
certainty in a world of unknowns.*
—MARILYN MORGAN KING

October 17

For now we see through a glass, darkly; but then face to face:
now I know in part; but then shall I know even as also I am known.
—1 Corinthians 13:12

*G*randma Johnson was a tiny, energetic woman with a truckload of determination. Every member of the Johnson clan has stories to tell of her feistiness. My father talks about how his mother came to New York City, alone, in the early 1920s to earn a Master of Fine Arts degree. My mother saw Grandma's single-minded drive when she came home one day to find Grandma intently painting the inside of some dresser drawers, oblivious to the three young children she was supposed to be looking after. My own memories of Grandma's visits include the time she took over my high school swim team's annual dinner, unperturbed by the fact that she was a complete stranger and that others had already planned the event. Strong-willed, determined, controlling—whatever you wanted to call her—Grandma Johnson was a force to be reckoned with.

Then while I was in college, Grandma became quite sick. She needed full-time care, so my parents moved her halfway across the country to live with them. She was in her eighties, and no one expected a full recovery. But her health slowly returned, and as it did, Grandma's arresting eyes mellowed into a softer, warmer blue. Her commanding arm now reached out primarily to clasp a hand gently in her own. She was gentler, sweeter, a pleasure to be with. It was as if her illness had released her from her need to be in charge, and the effect was transforming.

Surely there had been love there all along, yet something had obscured it. Perhaps our own prickly reactions to her had made us incapable of seeing it.

Dear Lord, thank You for grandparents, in all their wonderful,
human and sometimes frustrating complexity.
—Julia Attaway

OCTOBER 18

May the Lord cause you to increase and abound in love for one another.
—1 THESSALONIANS 3:12 NASB

I'd been feeling left out of my own family. Our daughters, in their twenties, were out on their own, and Thomas, our sixteen-year-old son, preferred his father's company to mine. If Thomas and his dad weren't playing basketball or baseball or fishing, they were talking about sports.

Thomas and I had been close when he was little; he loved to go to the library with me. But books weren't important to him anymore. One Saturday night I peeked through the den window and saw them at it again—playing basketball. Thomas had grown a tad taller and a bit quicker than his dad. I decided to go outside and watch. Opening a lawn chair, I sat down under the lights.

"Want to play, Mom?" Thomas asked. He made a difficult-looking shot.

"You *really* want me to?"

"Yeah, let's see what you've got."

The coolness of the evening and the feel of the basketball in my hands took me back to when I was a teenager. After supper, my dad and I would shoot baskets in the driveway. I never played organized sports, but for those few minutes we were a team—Daddy and me. He's in heaven now, but under the stars with my husband and son, I remembered our sweet time together.

My long-lost dribbling rhythm returned that night, and I even made a few baskets. The guys *oohed* and *aahed*, but something bigger happened: I rediscovered the common ground I had shared with my father and now shared with my almost grown-up son.

Father, continue to show me how to connect with those I love.
—JULIE GARMON

OCTOBER 19

You shall have a song as in the night when a holy feast is kept; and gladness of heart.
—ISAIAH 30:29 RSV

I stood looking out of the open bedroom window of my sister's home in Virginia. The beauty of the Shenandoah Valley sunset should have filled me with peace. But I was too worried about events back home in Louisiana to appreciate the scene before me.

My son Christopher was enlisting in the Army. Tomorrow was the day that he would report to the Military Entrance Processing Station, where he would be assigned a job and sworn in. I was feeling anxious, wishing I was close to him. This trip to visit my sister had been planned long before I knew he would be joining.

Dear Lord, I prayed, *take care of Christopher. Touch the people who will be helping him decide on his career in the Army. And, Lord, give me peace.*

I turned to walk away but stopped short. A bugle was sounding outside the bedroom window. It was a familiar tune, but I didn't recognize it at first. Then it came to me. Someone was playing "Taps!" I knelt down and placed my arms on the windowsill. As I closed my eyes and listened to the melody, I felt my anxiety leave.

The next morning at breakfast I said to my sister, "Sandi, I know this sounds crazy. But last night I heard 'Taps' playing outside my window."

"Oh, I forgot to tell you!" she exclaimed. "The Massanutten Military Academy is across the street. Every evening the recruits gather on the campus and the bugler plays 'Taps.'"

The next day I checked my e-mail. I had a message from a fellow history teacher. It began: "Just thought you might be interested in this:

> Day is done, / Gone the sun,
> From the lakes, / From the hills,
> From the sky. / All is well.
> Safely rest. / God is nigh."

It was the words to "Taps."

Dear Lord, You are my strength, my wisdom, my peace.
—MELODY BONNETTE

Love never ends.
—1 CORINTHIANS 13:8 RSV

*E*very year my mom opens up *Daily Guideposts* with anticipation—and dread. She enjoys reading the entries of all the contributors, but she makes a point of finding my devotionals first and telling me how much she likes them.

But dread, you ask? She's afraid I'm going to write about an incident when I was a kid and she got upset—a momentary lapse, let's say, in her parenting skills. So let me see if I can banish the dread once and for all.

Mom, I can't even begin to thank you for all the things you did right as a parent. You were patient, enthusiastic, fun, and full of praise. Thanks for teaching us how to play tennis, write thank-you notes, listen to music, and be a supportive friend. If we all have such good friends today, it's because we grew up watching you be such a good friend. If we all have good marriages, it's because we grew up seeing how you and Dad talked through your differences. You were a great Sunday school teacher, homeroom volunteer, art museum docent, and general organizer of a house with four children going in a thousand different directions.

I hope when you read this you'll know I mean every word. Happy birthday, Mom. You're the best!

> *Dear God, let me never grow tired of telling*
> *the people I love how much they're loved.*
> —RICK HAMLIN

OCTOBER 21

For whoever would save his life will lose it;
and whoever loses his life for my sake, he will save it.
—LUKE 9:24 RSV

O ver the last few years I've watched my youngest son step deeper into danger for God.

Blake's first trip was to Guatemala as a high-school kid, to help build a hospital. A second trip took him to Kenya to learn firsthand how hunger can be relieved. The following year, six months after Muslim terrorists bombed Catholic churches in Indonesia (and six weeks after our government advised Americans to leave the country), Blake went in with a college group to talk to Muslims about Christ. Last summer he went to China to smuggle in Christian literature. "Going in, we'll scope out four towns," Blake explained. "Coming out, it'll be hit and run, hit and run, hit and run, hit and run—then get the heck out before we're caught!"

The night before he flew to China, I asked him one more time why he couldn't content himself with hauling rice bags and digging wells. "Why must you go places where you can be killed for talking about God?"

For six weeks I prayed daily, hourly, for Blake's safety and the effectiveness of his mission. I sensed danger the final two weeks and urged my friends to pray nonstop. Sure enough, the police were following Blake and his group from town to town and finally stormed their hotel room late one night. Blake was the only one with literature still on him. He dodged into the bathroom and tossed it from the window.

Today Blake is living with me, working locally for Habitat for Humanity. I treasure each day, a God-given respite before He moves Blake on.

For He will move Blake on. And Blake will go. Because, as he said in that last conversation before leaving for China, "Jesus is right. When we give up our life, Mom, only then do we find it."

Dear God, please give me the strength to give up my son permanently
to this troubled world, that Your love might profit.
—BRENDA WILBEE

But though God has planted eternity in the hearts of men, even so,
man cannot see the whole scope of God's work from beginning to end.
—ECCLESIASTES 3:11 TLB

I'd never ridden a four-wheeler before. I climbed up onto the back and held on tightly to my twelve-year-old son Thomas's stomach.

"Mom, just relax. You'll be fine."

"Are you sure you know what you're doing?"

"Yes, ma'am." He clicked the gear with his foot.

"Is your helmet fastened right?"

"Yes, Mom. Let's go. You'll like it." He drove me around our wooded property. Ah, Thomas knows me pretty well. He's not going fast. He reached ahead and carefully pushed back tree branches so they wouldn't slap us. As Thomas headed downhill, he drove slowly as though leading an old horse down a rocky cliff. He wound around and stopped at the little creek. We didn't talk—we didn't need to.

I relaxed and thought back over the past year. So many changes: My grandparents had both died; our middle daughter left for college. Thomas seemed to be taking charge, riding me around, leading the way. I began to trust his skills. I admired his confidence and kindness.

My thoughts raced ahead. Years ahead. *One day I'll be really old, Thomas will be grown and even have children of his own. I don't want anything else to change. Talk to me, God.*

A truth came just as gently as the leaf floating down the creek. When the end comes, there will be a place prepared especially for me, a perfect place. I will love my new home even more than the majesty of these woods. No fear. Like Thomas, my Shepherd will be right beside me.

Oh, Lord, You know the outcome. You won't leave me.
It's going to be good, isn't it?
—JULIE GARMON

OCTOBER 23

My health fails; my spirits droop, yet God remains!
He is the strength of my heart; he is mine forever!
—PSALM 73:26 TLB

There is no doubt about it: My state of well-being is most decidedly affected by barometric pressure. On a bright, sunny day, I'm full of bounce and ready to cope with almost anything, whereas stormy weather has me drooping around, trying to conjure up energy that simply isn't there. I've spent a lifetime being "under the weather."

My mother used to put her hand on my forehead, pull out the thermometer and, unless I had a raging fever, tumble me out of bed with the cheery comment, "Ah, you're just a bit under the weather. Get up and get going. You'll be just fine."

Likewise, Mère Francesca, mistress of physical education at the convent school I attended, wouldn't let a bit of rain (or sleet or snow) keep us indoors. "Cold?" she'd say. "Run around. That'll warm you up." And she had us sing this ditty:

> *Whether the weather be cold,*
> *Whether the weather be hot,*
> *I will weather the weather,*
> *Whatever the weather,*
> *Whether I like it or not!*

These days, whenever I'm feeling under the weather, I roll out of bed and resolve to "weather it." Generally, by the end of the day, I surprise myself by how well I've coped.

> *On those days I droop both physically and emotionally,*
> *rev me up, blessed Holy Spirit. Strengthen and energize me.*
> —FAY ANGUS

OCTOBER 24

Be of one mind, live in peace; and the God of love and peace shall be with you
—2 CORINTHIANS 13:11

*M*y father works quite a bit with the St. Peter Indian Mission School at the Gila River Indian Community south of Phoenix, Arizona. One day when my dad was planning to take down a load of donated books, I decided to go, too, and take along our then-four-year-old daughter Maria. But that morning, Maria came to me with a worried face.

"Mommy, I don't want to go see the Indians," she said. "I'm scared." I knew what was going through her mind: stereotypical images of fierce Indians from television and movies.

"Oh, you'll like them," I told her. "They're just kids like you and your friends."

But she wasn't sure, and didn't say much in the car on the ride down. When we arrived at the mission, the kids swarmed around my dad. We had walked only a few steps from our car when they spotted Maria, and a curious group gathered around us.

"What's her name?" a girl asked shyly, and when I told her, several kids responded by saying, "Hi, Maria. How are you?" Maria clung to me tightly, unsure of how to react.

"Her hair is so pretty," said a girl with long, shiny black hair. "Can I touch it?"

"Sure. She'd probably like to touch your hair too," I said, and the little girl reached out to stroke Maria's sandy-blond head. They both smiled.

"She's like a little doll," another girl said, and they all giggled.

Later that day Maria danced and played a game with them, then we all ate lunch together. On the ride home I asked Maria what she thought of the children. "I like them," she said. "Can we go see them again?"

I'm thinking of this today because it's United Nations Day, a day to celebrate the idea that if even the most diverse of God's people can meet face to face, they can't deny their similarities. Their swords become plowshares, as their fear becomes understanding, love, and, naturally, peace.

Dear God, help me to bring Your peace everywhere I go.
—GINA BRIDGEMAN

OCTOBER 25

We consider blessed those who have persevered.
—JAMES 5:11 NIV

*W*hile visiting my daughter Lindsay in Southern California recently, I joined her on her brisk daily walk, pushing the stroller and her nine-month-old daughter up and down the hills in her neighborhood. As we walked, she talked about her post-pregnancy diet and exercise. After listening for a few moments, I offered my own reflections on these topics.

"I've decided that I've reached an age where I can quit worrying about fashion and figures," I told her. "I'm going to start wearing loose, comfortable clothes and sensible shoes. I'm not going to worry about how much chocolate I eat anymore or whether I'm holding my stomach in all the time."

I was on a pretty good roll when Lindsay cut me off abruptly. "You can't throw in the towel, Mom!"

"Why not?" I asked.

"Because that means quitting. Giving up. It means you don't care. And you can't care for others when you don't care for yourself."

When I returned home to Colorado a few days later, I brought along Lindsay's "Don't throw in the towel" advice. I even looked up the origin of that phrase. It's a boxing term: a fighter's manager throws in the towel to signal that the fighter is giving up, quitting.

I face lots of temptations to "throw in the towel": on a relationship that feels tedious, on reading through the manual that will tell me how to use my new digital camera, on doing a project on my computer or an exercise program that is sometimes painful. And then I remember Lindsay, persevering with that stroller up those hills, pushing through the hard places. "You can't throw in the towel," I hear her say.

That's why I'm sitting here at my computer...and holding my stomach in. Because I can't quit.

Lord, throwing in the towel comes easily for me.
Persevering does not. Help me push through the hard places.
—CAROL KUYKENDALL

The Spirit of the Lord God is upon me...he hath
sent me to bind up the broken-hearted.
—ISAIAH 61:1

$\mathcal{H}$ ow's John doing?" a woman from my prayer group asked. I hadn't touched base with her in a while. We changed my son's anxiety medication over the summer, and instead of improving, my twelve-year-old spent two weeks in the hospital.

"He's up and down. Some days he seems fine, and he is. Other days he seems fine, and a minute later we're wondering if we should call 911." There was a pause in the conversation. Then, gently, my friend commented, "The unpredictability must be hard."

It was my turn to pause and collect my thoughts. "Yes," I said, "but I don't focus as much on that now. What I'm finally beginning to grasp is that part of the point is learning to say thank you each day my son is alive." Still another pause. "It took me a long time to get there," I added.

"How do your other kids handle it?" my friend asked.

"They pretty much know to go to another room and entertain themselves when John starts to blow. They enjoy him when he's able to be fun and keep themselves safe when he's not."

"I'll keep praying for you."

"Thanks. It's hard, but it's harder to be John. He's a great kid with some really difficult problems. He thinks he's horrible. I wish he could know fully just how precious he is to God—and to us."

My friend nodded. There wasn't much else to say, but a lot to pray for.

Lord, people suffer. Let me hold them up to You before I cry out for myself.
—JULIA ATTAWAY

OCTOBER 27

Except ye be converted, and become as little children,
ye shall not enter into the kingdom of Heaven.
—MATTHEW 18:3

One red-and-gold autumn day my six-year-old son's spaniel, Captain Marvel, got sick. The vet said it was a severe infection and administered a shot. But Captain Marvel only got worse. For two days he whimpered in his doghouse, refused food and water, and couldn't get up. My son hovered over him like a sad little cloud. I was sure the poor dog was dying, so... back to the vet. This time he offered to put the dog to sleep. I refused.

No, Captain Marvel would die in his own bed.

I broke the news to Bob gently. He ran to the doghouse, fell in a pile of shriveled leaves, and prayed this simple prayer. "God, please make Captain well." Then he rubbed Captain's ears. "You'll be fine," he told the dog. But I felt nervous. Now how would I explain the dog's death?

Early the next morning as I shuffled past the patio glass, I saw a streak of brown and white fur flash across the yard. There was the dog racing for his feeding bowl as though in a dog-food commercial. Captain Marvel was alive, well, and hungry.

Was it those few seconds between a trusting little boy and a tender-hearted Father that had made the difference? Was it a child's simple trust? Perhaps I'll never know the answer. But how I yearn to find my own childlike faith again.

Uncomplicate me, Lord, so I can come to You in total trust.
—SUE MONK KIDD

Sing to the Lord a new song, for he has done marvelous things; his right hand and his holy arm have worked salvation for him.

—PSALM 98:1 NIV

*I*t's seven thirty at night and the fourth time today I've stood in front of the sink, washing dishes. Our dishwasher broke a few weeks ago and has yet to be replaced. Tonight, I'm not only washing the dishes, I'm also grumbling about it.

It feels as if I'm always washing dishes; my hands are wrinkly and dry. And although our family routine is supposed to be "the cook doesn't clean up," I was both chef and maid tonight.

In between cooking and cleaning, I entertained three-year-old Caeli, did some laundry, and put Caeli and her five-year-old sister Corinna to bed. The last thing I want to be doing now is staring at the wall behind the sink again and adding more wrinkles to my already dry hands.

Wait. I always tell the girls that grumbling is a choice, that instead of complaining about the situation, they can choose to sing a new song. One of my favorite hymns, by Charles Wesley (1707–1788), pops into my mind: "And can it be that I should gain an interest in the Savior's blood. Died he for me? who caused his pain! For me? who him to death pursued?"

Ninety minutes later, I'm still humming that song. Wouldn't you know it? I actually ended up enjoying my quiet time in front of the sink and the rest of my nightly tasks.

Funny how a tiny change of heart can change an entire evening.

Father God, thank You for those gentle reminders of what really counts, especially when my own heart wants to grumble.

—WENDY WILLARD

Eye hath not seen, nor ear heard, neither have entered into the heart of man, the things which God hath prepared for them that love him.
—1 CORINTHIANS 2:9

When I was a child my mother made the most wonderful chocolate cakes from scratch. She used only the best ingredients: fresh eggs from Grandmother's hens, milk right from the dairy, the silkiest cake flour, pure vanilla, rich unsweetened chocolate melted slowly in a double boiler. We waited while she brought it all together in the *whirr* of the mixer. Finally we moved in for a taste of thick, smooth chocolate batter.

Two of us got a beater, one a spatula, while the other four spooned up the extra batter left in the bowl. Every drop was a foretaste of what was to come: a moist, three-layer chocolate cake that melted in the mouth.

It's been many years since I've eaten the batter while waiting for the cake. But the taste of it and the yearning for the cake are still on my tongue. It calls to mind another taste that fills me with longing for heaven—the taste of joy.

It comes to me in a brilliant sunset, a soaring note in a symphony, a baby's smile, a hug from a friend, my husband's face across a crowded room. I can't summon it, I can't hold on to it, I can only receive it as a foretaste of what God is preparing for me in my real home.

Lord Jesus, thank You for foretastes of eternal joy.
—SHARI SMYTH

Behold, children are a heritage from the Lord, The fruit of the womb is a reward.
—PSALM 127:3 NKJV

*M*ama! you say the weirdest things!" my daughter protests, and I laugh while she groans.

"What did I say so wrong?" I feign innocence, pouring it like syrup on pancakes. Lanea is now twenty-seven and I'm forty-six, but we giggle long distance on the phone like schoolgirls—schoolgirls talking way past their bedtimes. We gab each night, mostly about nothing, but each word says we love each other. Each conversation is a choice to be friends.

It was so difficult to leave her when I moved to Chicago. I packed way too quickly, laughed too loudly, and left too many things behind. We drove to the airport pretending that my excitement over my move was also hers and that neither of us was fearful in any way.

We hugged good-bye at the curbside check-in, and I saw the same look on her face she's probably seen a thousand times on mine. Looking down at me from her six-foot height, her expression said, *Are you sure you know what you're doing?* When the woman checking me in told me that my flight was delayed because of snowstorms in Chicago, Lanea's doubtful expression became more pronounced. Her eyes widened and one of her eyebrows lifted higher. "I'll be okay, baby," I reassured her.

She hugged and kissed me again, waved, and then drove away, looking like a mother dropping off her child at school for the first time.

My oldest baby is grown up, and I am far away. To my mind, our separation was as much about giving her a chance at independence as any adventure I might be having in the big city. I can laugh with her now and not worry how each sentence, each word, will affect her future. Now each time I call and we laugh and giggle, she knows that while I'll always be her mother, I'm also her friend.

Lord, thank You for giving us the courage to be friends.
—SHARON FOSTER

OCTOBER 31

They that dwell under his shadow shall return...and grow as the vine.
—HOSEA 14:7

*W*hen my children were small, I was the magical elf of our pumpkin patch. In mid-August, when the pumpkin vines began setting on fruits about the size of apples, I would sneak into the garden with a nail, stick or barbecue skewer, and scratch each child's name on a baby pumpkin. The scratches made a thin mark, but didn't otherwise damage the fruit. Better yet, the tiny globes remained invisible beneath the broad, scratchy pumpkin leaves and my work went unnoticed.

Over the next few weeks as the pumpkins swelled and turned first ivory, then yellow, then brilliant orange, the scars would grow, too, stretching with the shell and forming a brownish welt. By harvest time each fifteen-pound pumpkin would be personalized with a two-inch-tall name—a source of infinite amazement and speculation.

After the first September cold snap, I would casually suggest, "Maybe we'd better go pick those pumpkins." My four children would rush to the dead garden and easily spot the orange pumpkins glowing like lanterns amid the leaves blackened and shriveled by frost.

"Mom," Tess would suddenly shriek, "it has my name!" The enchantment never failed. As the older children caught on, they still let Trina, the youngest, delight in finding her special pumpkin without spoiling my secret. Even when all the children were old enough to solve the mystery, they would remind Mom to "go name the pumpkins" as soon as they first bulged on the vine.

I haven't grown pumpkins for years now and half of my children have left home. Very often I wonder whether my relationship with God has made any difference in their lives. Did I pass on my faith—really and truly? Did I make an impact? Then I pause to consider the faint etchings on those tiny pumpkins—and know that in God's good time, for my children, too, there will indeed be a joyful harvest.

> *Lord of creation, thank You for the miracle of growth,*
> *in my garden and in myself.*
> —GAIL THORELL SCHILLING

November

NOVEMBER 1

A gracious woman retaineth honour.
—PROVERBS 11:16

I suspect that everyone knows someone in the category of a saint, someone whose example of suffering and service is an icon for the rest of us.

"She was a saint" could be said about my Grandma Schantz, who lived in a little brown house in Springfield, Ohio, where I was born. She had deep-set French eyes filled with kindness, a mischievous smile and a laugh that filled the house with music. Because of Grandpa's disabilities, Grandma worked in an electric motor factory till the day she died. She had everything but money, yet her hallmark was generosity. When we went to see her, she fixed all our favorite foods. And always she had something for us boys. "Here is some copper wire I salvaged from work. You boys can use it for your amateur radios." She saved old postage stamps and cigar boxes for us to keep them in.

Sunday night was the highlight of our week, when my dad would take all of us for a drive around town. Sooner or later we would end up at the A&W Root Beer stand, where teenage girls would bring trays of frosty mugs to our windows. The sassafras fragrance of the liquid would attract bees and butterflies.

"How about some popcorn for these boys?" Grandma would say. "I'll pay for it." She knew my parents would never buy such a luxury. To this day the smell of popcorn or the taste of root beer floods my brain with memories of Grandma.

She is just one of millions who quietly go about making the world a sweeter place for all of us. They are the kind of people who, without a word, make me want to be a better person.

Lord, You gave me my grandma's eyes. Now may I see as well as she did.
—DANIEL SCHANTZ

NOVEMBER 2

The Lord gave, and the Lord hath taken away; blessed be the name of the Lord.
—JOB 1:21

*T*he letter lay, fragile and stained, on top of the pile. It was hard going through my mother's things. Missing her was still so new. I looked at the date. It had been written by a friend to my mother in 1939, shortly after my father died.

"Dear One," it began. "It hurts so terribly, doesn't it? Accept the pain if you can. Say, 'Yes, because I have loved and now lost, I must cry for a while. I must hold this ache of loneliness within myself and say, this is the price I pay for having loved. I will accept this price and pay it in gratitude for the love I was blessed to know, for I would not have wanted to be without that love. I will pay this price, God, and I thank You for the wonderful years we shared.'

"I think He must have cried on the day that His Son hung dead on the cross, don't you think so? Don't you think that because He, too, is familiar with tears, dear friend, He is especially close to you right now?

"I weep with you, and my love surrounds you. Please write and let me know your plans, and if there is anything at all I can do to help."

I folded the letter and slipped it back into the envelope, grateful for this healing message from the past. Thank you for the wonderful years, Mom, I whispered. Of all the women in the world, I'm so lucky you were the one God gave me. Yes, it was worth the price.

> *Thank You, God, for giving her to me. And*
> *for giving me Your Son. Such gifts are eternal.*
> —DORIS HAASE

NOVEMBER 3

Six days you shall labor and do all your work,
but the seventh day is a Sabbath to the Lord your God.
—EXODUS 20:9–10 NIV

I was having Sunday lunch with friends, celebrating the baptism that morning of their daughter, when the waitress came in. "Emergency phone call for Mary Lou Carney," she said. My chicken salad stuck in my throat as I ran to the nearest phone.

"Honey," my husband said, the fear in his voice as clear as the phone connection. "It's Brett. He's been hurt."

Our son Brett has always been oblivious to danger, whether riding his three-wheeler or rock climbing, walking rafters in the houses he builds or driving his pickup truck on icy roads. "What happened?" I asked.

"Power nailer. He has a nail buried in his leg. He's in the emergency room now."

I headed for the hospital, praying all the way. "Please, God, let him be okay. Prevent infection. Help him bear the pain. Send a good surgeon." But on another level, I was fussing at Brett. Why did he have to work today? If he'd been in church, this wouldn't have happened.

I rushed into the emergency room and was shown to a small, curtained area where Brett lay, a morphine drip hanging from his bed. A dent just above his knee made it clear where the nail—complete with brass barbs—was buried. All thoughts of lecturing him about keeping the Sabbath vanished as I took his hand.

Brett looked up and managed a smile. "Grandpa always told me not to work on Sunday."

I squeezed his hand...and bowed my head in gratitude to One Who never takes a day off from watching over His children.

You are faithful, O Father, even when we are not. Forgive us for stealing from Your ordained day of rest. Slow us down enough to bless us.
—MARY LOU CARNEY

His divine power has given us everything we need for life and godliness.
—2 PETER 1:3 NIV

"Here you go, Mom!" the nurse said. It was two hours after my C-section and I was about to see my son for the first time. His high-pitched cries grew louder as the nurse brought him to me. *Oh no,* I thought, *what have I gotten myself into?*

"Here's Mom," the nurse said putting him into my arms. A wrinkled red face looked up at me. As I laid his head on my chest, the word mom stuck in my mind. I didn't feel much like a mom. Would I be a good one? Would I have the answers, know how to stop his crying, be able to put him to sleep?

He was warm in my arms, snug in a white-pink-and-blue-striped blanket. He squinted up at me. I was so caught up in looking down at this baby I had imagined and anticipated for months that I didn't notice the silence.

"Isn't that something," the nurse said. "He hasn't stopped crying since we took him from the OR and now look at him, so happy. He knows his mama."

A calm reassurance covered me. *Trust this,* I thought. *Trust this beautiful little boy who knew you as his mother even before you did.*

Thank You, Lord, for giving me all I need to be Solomon's mom.
—SABRA CIANCANELLI

NOVEMBER 5

For of all sad words of tongue or pen,
The saddest are, "It might have been."
—JOHN GREENLEAF WHITTIER

*I*n times of stress and trouble everybody in our family sought out my maternal grandmother. Her uncommon common sense never failed to cut problems down to size.

At one period in my life I left a good job to start my own business. It took all my savings and investments. In a little over a year the business was failing. I was desperate. At home I made myself and everyone else miserable with my lamentation about what I should have done and what I ought to have done.

One evening my grandmother took me to her room and closed the door. "Now," she said gently, "tell me all about it." I recited my woes, hashing over things I should or I ought to have done. "I'm just unlucky," I said finally.

She put her hand over mine. "Not unlucky. Your trouble now is that you're possessed by two little demons." Her eyes twinkled.

"Aw, c'mon, Grandma," I objected. "There aren't any demons today."

"Indeed there are demons today," she continued, "and two have you in their possession. Their names are 'Shoulda' and 'Oughta.' They're sly and they sneak up on you. They paralyze you and destroy hope. To get rid of them, all you need do is simply to refuse to call their names. Then you can clear your mind for positive action."

Grandma was right. Those two demons try to hinder all of us.

Lord, preserve us!
—CHARLES M. DAVIS

NOVEMBER 6

It is for freedom that Christ has set us free. Stand firm, then, and do not let yourselves be burdened again by a yoke of slavery.
—GALATIANS 5:1 NIV

*T*he Americans are coming!"

The news was exhilarating *and* frightening. As a refugee child of almost ten fleeing from bombs and enemy gunfire, I was painfully aware that not all people were friendly. What will these soldiers be like? Will they send us to prison? Will they make us go back to Russia? But soon we children knew that we had nothing to fear. These soldiers treated refugees with dignity and respect. They easily parted with a meal so we had something to eat. What's more, they gave us chocolate bars, a treat beyond our imagination.

When the order did come for our family to return to Russia, an American officer listened carefully to my mother's explanation of why we couldn't return. "The Communists will send me to Siberia," she said, "and my children to an orphanage. That's what they've done to many of our relatives and friends." Because of the officer's intervention, we were allowed to remain in Austria. Three years later, a young man from Pennsylvania, working with the American Mennonite Central Committee, reconnected us with some of our relatives. Then the committee made it possible for us to immigrate to America.

The first time my mother was able to vote, she could hardly believe it. She'd lived under Communism, Fascism, and now democracy. To be able to come and go as we pleased, to worship in whatever church we chose, to pursue higher education—all this was ours! And all because more than two hundred years ago, some men got together to write these famous words: "We hold these truths to be self-evident, that all men are created equal, that they are endowed by their Creator with certain unalienable Rights, that among these are Life, Liberty, and the pursuit of Happiness."

Dear Father, thank You for the freedoms we enjoy.
May we never take them for granted.
—HELEN GRACE LESCHEID

NOVEMBER 7

Ask, and it shall be given you.
—MATTHEW 7:7

*O*ur daughter Jennifer, a senior in high school, asked for the umpteenth time, "Mother, do you think there might be some way I could have a car to drive to school?"

I gave my usual reply, "No way in the world." I didn't think she was ready for the responsibility of owning a car, and she didn't have a job at the time, so it was out of the question. "You can drive the blue goose." The goose is our twenty-year-old car. Sometimes it runs fine. Other times it won't budge out of the carport.

On the day before school was to start Jennifer said, "Mother, I'm going to ask God for a car. Will you pray with me? I want one by tomorrow."

Exasperated, I said rather harshly, "There's no way that you can have a car. Daddy wouldn't even consider it. Forget it. It's the goose for you."

"Will you pray with me?"

"It's impossible."

"I thought you said that with God all things are..."

"Yes, I know, but this is... oh, all right. I'll pray!" Sometime during the morning I finally prayed about the car. During the day Jennifer would gaze out the window and say, "Can't you just see it sitting out in the driveway waiting for me?"

I looked out the window. "Nope, all I see is the blue goose waiting for you."

"Well, I've asked God for a car," she said softly.

Toward evening Jennifer came home from a friend's house, her face all aglow. "Mama, Daddy, you'll never guess what! Donna's grandmother gave her a car, but she's not yet old enough to drive it. Her mama says I can drive Donna's car and keep it here if I'll pick her up for school each day and take her home. She only lives a few streets over."

My husband and I agreed to the plan. And that night, looking out from the upstairs bedroom, I stared at the little red car sitting in the driveway. I had to smile at the car, and at the faithfulness of my Father.

Father, forgive me when I limit You by my own doubts.
—MARION BOND WEST

The right word at the right time—beautiful!
—Proverbs 15:23 MSG

I desperately needed a few words from my son Jon. For months he'd been in prison and didn't answer my letters. He had been struggling with addictions, and I felt relieved that he was now safe, following rules. But I hounded him in my letters: "Why don't you write?" There was no response. But he finally phoned one day to tell me he could receive small amounts of money to be spent at the prison store.

I wrote back with fifteen statements I'd come up with. Each contained a blank for him to fill in. "Complete these, Jon, by simply filling in the blanks, mail the sheet back to me, and I'll pay you two dollars for each answer." In three days a letter from my son appeared in our mailbox! I kissed it, standing there in the sweltering August sun, and marveled over his handwriting. Then I traced my address with a finger, smiling. Here's a sample of the words he wrote.

1. Mostly I feel: *excited about what the future holds for me.*
2. What I anticipate is: *more funny times with Jesus.*
3. The most important thing I've learned during the past months is: *that you can never give up on your dreams.*
4. One of my favorite biblical truths is: *how Paul got his vision back after being blinded.*
5. My strong points are: *my good looks.*
6. The last funny thing I recall is: *me and my detail officer laughing about this questionnaire, Mom.*
7. The best part of each day is: *when I get to shower after working all day in the sun.*

Oh, Father, I'm singing, "Beautiful words, wonderful words,
wonderful words of life" (Phillip P. Bliss).
—Marion Bond West

If at first you don't succeed,
Try, try again.
—WILLIAM E. HICKSON

*S*ometimes when everything seems to go wrong in my life and I'm ready to lie down and quit, I remember a scene from my childhood. I'm five years old and plagued with a stuffy cold. It is before the days of recliners, but Mama has fashioned me one by putting blocks under an old cane-bottomed rocker, and immobilizing it in a tilted-back position in front of a crackling kitchen-stove fire.

Putting a warm flannel poultice on my chest, she wraps me snugly in a colorful quilt.

While she busies about the kitchen she lures me into a game of "count the squares."

Mama calls out "red!" and I try to count all the red squares in the quilt. But before I reach the number ten, I complain I've lost my place.

"Okay, then we'll just start over," Mama says. She reheats the poultice and places it gently back on my chest again.

"But, Mama, I can't remember which number I was on," I complain. "I don't know how far I've gone."

"Never mind," she says. "It doesn't matter how far you've gone. You can always start over."

Mama was only trying to keep a fretful child occupied, but in the process she taught me a lesson close to the heart of Christianity. No matter how far you go astray, in the eyes of Jesus it's never too late to start over.

Dear Lord, thank You for this new day and the fresh starts I can make in it.
—ORA LINDSAY GRAHAM

Each of you should look not only to your own interests,
but also to the interests of others.
—PHILIPPIANS 2:4 NIV

"What did you do today?" I asked my son Brett, who had called me on his way home from work. Brett was quiet for a moment before he answered.

"Raked leaves, mostly."

Raked leaves? It seemed an odd thing for him to do in the middle of the week, when he's usually busy with construction work—often supervising his crew as they tackle a remodeling job, tear off an old roof or frame up a new house. Maybe it had been at one of the rental properties he owned.

"Where?" I asked. Again, that small silence before he answered.

"Near one of my duplexes. This lady was out raking her big yard—from her motorized wheelchair. So I went and got my tractor and leaf collector and did it for her. She tried to pay me, but I told her I didn't want any money. That I was... well, behind on my good deeds."

If you ask me what my son does for a living, I'll tell you about his construction business, about his ambition and work ethic and attention to detail. But if you ask what makes me most proud of my son, I'll tell you a story about the day he raked leaves.

Dear Jesus, when You were among us, You went about doing good.
Let us never forget to do the same in Your name.
—MARY LOU CARNEY

NOVEMBER 11

Ye are bought with a price.
—1 CORINTHIANS 7:23

I'm sad to say that I didn't even realize it was Veterans Day until my daughter Keri and I came upon a roadblock in downtown Memphis, Tennessee.

"What's going on?" we asked the attendant at the entrance to the parking garage.

"Why, the parade's coming," he answered. "You know, it's Veterans Day."

I don't suppose we would have ever thought to stay if it weren't for this man perched atop a doorstep. He was looking down the empty street as if something very important was about to happen.

"Keri, how would you feel about staying for the parade?" I asked.

"Sure, Mama, I love parades."

So we chose a sunny spot on the edge of the sidewalk and waited. Others gathered around us: a group of preschoolers, an elderly couple, several men wearing VFW caps. Then came the crash of a cymbal, the roll of a drum, and finally the parade spread out before us. A band marched by, then another. Girls twirled batons and drum majors pranced. Next came convertibles marked POWS and PEARL HARBOR SURVIVORS and PURPLE HEART HONOREES, followed by rows of robust wheelchair vets who tossed candy to the cheering crowd.

Then an old sailor came by, all alone. He marched with such purpose that he might as well have been a one-man parade. A survivor of World War II, he was dressed in an old, blue wool uniform with bell-bottom trousers. Something in his face said he was marching for other sailors, the ones who never came home. Overcome by his silent testimony, I couldn't suppress my tears. I caught Keri's eye. She was crying too.

Later that evening I heard Keri tell her new husband Ben, "When we have children, let's make a pact always to take them to a parade on Veterans Day. I think it's important."

> *Father, today we come to You remembering the sailors and soldiers*
> *and all the rest who willingly gave their lives for our country,*
> *and in the process assured us the freedom to turn toward You.*

—PAM KIDD

And this I pray, that your love may abound yet more and more.
—PHILIPPIANS 1:9

*W*hen my mom was in the early stages of Alzheimer's and still able to live on her own, my wife and I flew out to Michigan to spend a week with her. We brought along our young cocker spaniel Sally, whom Mom took to instantly. Satisfied that Mom could look after Sally, Julee and I felt comfortable spending some time seeing relatives and doing a few touristy things around Detroit. We noticed right away that Sally had taken an unusual liking to Mom. Whenever we went back to the house, Sally wouldn't leave her side.

"What a great dog," I said to Julee.

However, a couple of days into our visit, Julee and I noticed that the dog food we had brought along was disappearing. I took Sally aside and looked her right in the eyes. "What's going on here?" I asked, not actually expecting to get an answer.

You can probably guess. Mom couldn't remember from hour to hour if she had fed Sally, and Sally was always up for seconds. So Mom would feed her again. We put a note on Sally's food, telling Mom not to worry about Sally's meals; Julee and I would take care of it. That was the end of Sally's amazing gourmet vacation, and I think she held a little grudge over the fact that her scheme had been found out. But here's the good part. Even after Sally got back on her regular feeding schedule, her devotion to Mom didn't abate. She seemed to know that Mom needed all the extra care and attention she could get.

When we left at the end of the week, Mom cried. "Thank you for coming to visit me, Sally," she whispered, hugging her close. "I hope you come back soon."

Your love takes many wondrous forms, Lord,
even a cocker spaniel with a big appetite and a bigger heart.
—EDWARD GRINNAN

But solid food is for the mature, for those
who have their faculties trained by practice.
—HEBREWS 5:14 RSV

*M*om, let's take cooking lessons." That suggestion from a twenty-four-year-old guy more likely to be listening to rap than spending time in the kitchen came as quite a shock.

"Why would you want to do that, lovey?" I asked.

"Well," he answered bluntly, "you can't cook and neither can I, so Dad cooks for you, and I just eat expensive junk food. We should both give it a try."

So we did, taking an eight-week course in basic cooking techniques. I was definitely the oldest student, and my son was the only male among bright, energetic young women. I was skeptical at first, but Daniel loved every minute of it, energetically carving up a raw chicken with a vicious eight-inch chef's knife. The only part he didn't like was chopping garlic cloves, until the teacher told him lemon juice would remove the pungent aroma from his hands. I enjoyed learning about different foods and listening to the witty and talented teacher. But even more I enjoyed watching my son.

After about half the classes were over, Daniel actually cooked dinner for some of his friends and invited me. As he brought the platter of chicken Marsala out of the kitchen to the astonishment of the assembled youth, there was such a look of pride on his face that tears suddenly stung my eyes. My troubled, angry, disaffected teenager had turned into a self-confident young man who was proud of his achievements and actually enjoyed his mother's company.

"We had fun, didn't we, Mom?" he said as he set the platter down. "And, by the way, I'll make the pies for Thanksgiving—and the pastry."

Thank You, Lord, for young people who bring light and laughter into my world.
—BRIGITTE WEEKS

You brought me out of the womb.
—PSALM 22:9 NIV

The year was 1939, and Rose's third pregnancy had been a real concern. No baby's heartbeat could be detected, no movements felt.

As her due date drew near and then passed, she traveled down the fifteen miles of washboard road to be near the small rural hospital on the Canadian prairie. The young examining doctor, his brow furrowed, had a hasty consultation with the old general practitioner before he told Rose what would have to be done.

"An immediate Caesarean section is the only answer, but I must tell you that it will be the first major surgery ever performed in this hospital. We expect your baby to be stillborn, and your chances of survival are not that good either. I'm sorry, but I advise you to call your husband to come and say good-bye."

On the morning of September 4, under the bright lights of the operating room, Rose heard the two physicians arguing.

"We cut here, or not at all," insisted the young graduate doctor, tracing a line down Rose's lower abdomen. He had spent long hours the night before in his study, and the procedure described in his surgeon's textbooks was stamped on his memory.

Tension gripped the room as the old doctor considered all the risks involved. Then quietly, graciously, he laid aside his scalpel.

Moments later, the lusty cries of a healthy eight-pound baby girl startled the worried nurses. Little did they know that Mom and I would go on to enjoy each other's company for another fifty-seven years.

Lord, whenever I think I have all the answers, remind me of that old doctor whom You graced to step aside to let another be Your instrument.
—ALMA BARKMAN

NOVEMBER 15

When one door closes, another opens but we often look so long and so regretfully
upon the closed door that we do not see the one which has opened for us.
—ALEXANDER GRAHAM BELL

As a child, Evelyn Sass had a promising singing voice and was often called upon to sing the solo parts in church and school productions. With her teacher's encouragement, she began to dream of a musical career.

Then, suddenly, in her early teens, through a series of illnesses, Evelyn lost her hearing totally. The dream of becoming a singer died. She became depressed and withdrawn, spending long hours alone, until one day her teacher came to visit.

"You know, Evelyn," the teacher said, "God gave us five senses. You still have four of them. I challenge you to concentrate on one of these. See if you can't develop it beyond the norm so that what you gain in one offsets the loss in another."

Evelyn did. She chose sight, and she worked and worked at it until she had developed such a remarkable skill at lipreading that in 1930 she won the National Lipreading Tournament held in New York City. In addition she went on to have a successful business career, married, and bore a daughter—me.

I'm proud of my mother—and I know what she went through because I also have a hearing problem and rely on lipreading. And like my mother I have come to know that there are many doors in this life. What a waste of time it is to keep on staring at a door you know cannot be opened. And how exciting it is to find the one that God swings wide for you!

Father, thank You for opening my eyes to the
thrilling opportunities You set before us.
—ELEANOR V. SASS

A time to keep silence, and a time to speak.
—ECCLESIASTES 3:7

*W*hen all of our family was at home, there were six of us plus our two dogs, and the noisy chaos often made it hard for me to pray. Then I read about Susanna Wesley, the mother of John and Charles, who had a large family—nineteen children, ten of whom reached adulthood. When she wanted to pray, she'd pull her ample apron up over her head as a signal to her family, who would quiet down or leave the room.

So I made a little sign that read: *Quiet please. Silent Prayer.* I punched holes in the top corners and tied a string into them, so I could hang it over the door of the master bedroom. Then I'd go in, prop myself up in bed and drop into silence. After resting in the arms of the Holy Spirit, I'd be ready to listen to the family's problems and complaints, hear about the happy events of the day, and help harmonize any discord among them.

So my question today is, "What causes that transformation to happen?"

Silence has its own magic.
When you let yourself fall into the vastness,
your soul is held and embraced by the Spirit,
and all of the day's tangles and wrinkles
are combed out and ironed to smoothness
so that your heart and soul and spirit
are tranquil and ready to speak
from that place deep
where the Wise One dwells within.

> *Holy One, please help me to value silent prayer enough*
> *to make time for it, no matter how chaotic my life might be.*
> —MARILYN MORGAN KING

All good gifts around us
Are sent from Heaven above;
Then thank the Lord, O thank the Lord
For all His love.
—MATTHIAS CLAUDIUS, HYMN

The blustery day only added to the high spirits of the children, making them as restless as the wind. The day worsened as the older boys, four and six years old, fought or begged to go to the beach and the baby fretted with teething difficulties.

For the tenth time, it seemed, I said, irritably and too loudly, "Please go outside." Then as they finally did go, I yelled after them, "But stay close to the house." We lived beside the large parking lot of a grocery store and I worried about their safety.

Thankful for the peace, I hurried about catching up on chores. Suddenly I realized that things were too quiet. I ran to the door and saw all three boys playing quietly in a large box which was not there earlier.

"Look, Mom," Clay shouted. "Jesus sent us a box."

At first I was tempted to explain that the wind must have brought it from the store. Then I was ashamed. How seldom I give Jesus credit for the everyday pleasures of life. A child's expression of gratitude caused me to say a prayer as I went back to my work with a light step.

Thank You, Jesus, for children, the wind, and boxes.
—RUTH DINKINS ROWAN

So teach us to number our days that we may get a heart of wisdom.
—PSALM 90:12 RSV

*M*y father quite literally counted his days—27,834—and died with a heart of wisdom. "He had no regrets," said a family friend at the memorial service, unintentionally giving me a magnifying glass through which I could see all too clearly my own.

One regret eclipses them all: I gave my children the wrong father. And over the years, while counselors, doctors, and ministers tried to help me analyze why, the fact remains that I did, and there are days when I find myself paralyzed by regret.

But then Evelyn Rose, my first granddaughter after four grandsons, arrived. I looked into her face and beheld a soul untouched by regret, with a whole life stretching before her. She was an empty book, a clean slate upon which she could write anything. *Dear God, don't let her reach middle age burdened by regret.* An odd sort of optical illusion occurred, for I began to see my face in hers— seeing myself as God does. I, too, have a whole calendar of days stretching before me, a clean slate upon which I can write anything.

Evelyn Rose was born on September 28. In a way, so was her grandmother. In the days that followed, I turned a corner. I joined a new church, made new friends, had my first party in my new home with a group of writers living within ten minutes of me, and took under my wing a single mother whose struggles eclipse my own.

It won't be said at my funeral that I had no regrets, but it can be said God let me begin again.

Dear Lord, teach me to count my days—19,878 so far—
making each one wisely count for You.
—BRENDA WILBEE

*Train up a child the way he should go: and
when he is old, he will not depart from it.*
—Proverbs 22:6

*S*o now the youngest child has gone.
Each of my three left for good reasons–education, travel, career. But I am anxious. How will they fare without me? God, did You really intend for motherhood to be such a dead end?

Now what? My future seems as empty as this house. I pause to pick a few dead leaves off the plants that decorate the dining-room window and notice the philodendron has bits of root peeking through the drainage hole of its clay pot. Just to have something to do, I carry it out to my work table in the kitchen.

I tap the pot sharply on the edge of the table. The whole plant, roots tightly massed into a hard ball, slips into my hand. I gently place it on the table and reach for a hammer. Three quick blows shatter the small clay pot into shards. These I place in the bottom of a larger pot for drainage, add a layer of fresh soil, center the philodendron, pressing the roots down firmly, adding more soil to cover, tamping it down to hold the plant securely.

I think of my mother. She taught me how to transplant, showing me how the original pot, broken to bits, could serve as a foundation for the plant's new growth.

I think of my children. And then I smile. Yes they, too, are transplanted. The container that once held them so securely—our family life together—is broken now. But the fragments will always be the foundation for new growth. My children will flourish, I know. And so, thank God, will I.

Lord, as we grow, help us to remember that our roots are secure in Thee.
—Marilyn Connell

Blessed is he whose transgressions are forgiven, whose sins are covered.
—PSALM 32:1 NIV

*F*orgives neglect" reads the description for the sunflower seeds in my wildflower catalog. Looking over catalogs of seeds and bulbs is one of my favorite things to do. There's something peaceful and hopeful in looking forward to a field filled with blooms.

Growing up, I spent fall and winter evenings sitting on the couch next to my mother, her nose deep in a bulb catalog and a pad resting beside her so she could jot down her order. A single mother with four children, Mom always made time for a flower garden. And when the bulbs came in the mail, together we would push them into the earth. "They'll be beautiful," Mom would say. "Just wait."

Months later, a cold winter behind us, the bulbs I had forgotten about would begin to sprout. I was too young to understand exactly why those spring blooms meant so much to my mother. She kept watch as the pale green shoots rose from the cold ground. Each bloom was too precious to cut.

Forgives neglect. I couldn't get past those words. Tiny seeds that would grow to the king of flowers, standing strong, heavy head filled with hundreds of small blooms that follow the sun—even if I neglected them.

I circled the sunflower seeds in the catalog and pictured exactly where they'd sprout and flourish in my backyard.

Lord, thank You for my mother's love for flowers and for the sunflowers that remind me of Your boundless forgiveness.
—SABRA CIANCANELLI

NOVEMBER 21

Since my youth, O God, you have taught me,
and to this day I declare your marvelous deeds.
—PSALM 71:17 NIV

Last Thanksgiving my children and I joined my friend Portia and her new family and reminisced over past Thanksgivings, including the year we ate beans and rice in our trailer in rural North Carolina. Several days later, alone in our hotel room, my daughter Lanea, my son Chase, and I made a list of the things we had to be thankful for.

It was quite a list: Chase had healed with no visible scars from the head and face wounds he received in a skiing accident. Lanea had started graduate school and had her first apartment and car. Our Chihuahua Punkin had been returned to us after three weeks of futile searching. I had completed my first novel. Portia had celebrated her first anniversary as the wife of a widowed minister and stepmother to his children. Our extended family was well and blessed. My brother Newton was thriving after surviving a bout with cancer, and my mother was recovering from hip replacement surgery. And finally, the lingering grief that we had felt since the death of Chase's father seemed to leave us.

After we finished our thanksgivings, we sang a song in which the singer professes that he came to God and got just what he wanted. He sings about miracles, healing, and deliverance. It's a simple chorus, and we sang it over and over. As we sang, a look of surprise came over fifteen-year-old Chase's face. "I just realized," he said, "we really did get what we wanted!"

I smiled and added one more thing to the thanksgiving list: My children have grateful hearts.

It's true—we got just what we wanted.

God, thank You that every day truly is a day of thanksgiving.
—SHARON FOSTER

NOVEMBER 22

In every thing give thanks: for this is the will of God in Christ Jesus concerning you.
—1 THESSALONIANS 5:18

*I*t's Thanksgiving morning. The kitchen table is piled with unpeeled potatoes, and I am missing my mother.

How many potatoes did Mother peel in her lifetime? I breathe in the earthy smell of the unwashed skins and hear Mother say, "Mary Lou, run down to the basement and get us some potatoes for supper."

Mother loved feeding people—and not just family and friends. I remember many Thanksgiving meals when, as we cleared the table, Mother would say, "Let's make up plates for the Georges." The Georges were the poor family at the end of the road. Some years it wasn't the Georges, but it was always some hard-luck case that had come to my mother's attention.

I pick up the knife and begin peeling the potatoes. It's Thanksgiving and time I started giving thanks.

My daughter and son-in-law will be arriving later with my two grandsons. They live only a mile away. Thank You.

My son and his wife will come with little Isabelle Grace—it's her first Thanksgiving. Thank You.

My mother-in-law, widowed several years ago, will contribute deviled eggs and cranberry salad to our feast. At eighty, she's still able to drive herself and help babysit her great-grandkids. Thank You.

I'll give my sister a call to wish her a happy day. She's the only one who shares my childhood memories, and I cherish our relationship. Thank You.

My husband will say a simple grace. We've been married for thirty-eight years. Thank You.

I'll place a mountain of steaming mashed potatoes in the middle of the table and hear Mother say, "Good girl. You used real butter and lots of it." And I'll know that Mother will be a part of this holiday and all the ones to come. Thank You.

> *Sweet Jesus, thank You for the godly ones who have come*
> *before us and for the reunion You have planned for us in heaven!*
> *—MARY LOU CARNEY*

That I may publish with the voice of thanksgiving,
and tell of all thy wondrous works.
—PSALM 26:7

*E*very year at Thanksgiving, my mother's boss gave her a large turkey, so she was the one who brought the cooked bird for assorted aunts, uncles, and cousins to devour at Aunt Paul's house in Brooklyn.

When we arrived at Aunt Paul's on Thanksgiving afternoon, Mom would join the crowd of cooks in the kitchen, while my cousins and I filled up on candies, nuts, and other goodies. It was a wonder that we had any appetite left for dinner.

But appetite I certainly had, for turkey and the trimmings. Especially the trimmings, including Mom's wonderful stuffing, made of corn flakes, olives, celery, onions, butter, and spices from a recipe she claimed to have found on a corn-flakes box. I would have been happy to eat turkey and Mom's stuffing every day for a solid month. But no one else felt that way. So one year the aunts got together, and Mom was instructed to deliver the uncooked turkey to Aunt Frieda or Aunt Naomi. They could be trusted to stuff it safely, if heavily, with bread and liver stuffing. The family was delivered from corn-flakes stuffing. And I was heartbroken.

Mom's been gone for twenty years now, but I still long for her stuffing. Every time I tell people about it, though, I'm greeted with puzzlement, or even revulsion. My wife Julia had the same reaction when I told her the story. That's why I was surprised, a few weeks before Thanksgiving last year, to see an e-mail on our computer from a cereal company. Not knowing for whom it was intended, I opened it. "Dear Mrs. Attaway," it read. "We have checked our records from the 1950s, but we were unable to locate the stuffing recipe you requested."

Julia stuffed our turkey with challah bread and chestnuts. She loves it, and it's delicious. But to me, knowing she had been willing to forego it so I could again taste my mother's stuffing, it was as sweet as manna from heaven.

Dear Lord, thank You for food, family, and friends, for blessings without number.
And especially for the memory of my mother's stuffing.
—ANDREW ATTAWAY

Therefore, since we are surrounded by such a great cloud of witnesses...
let us run with perseverance the race marked out for us.
—HEBREWS 12:1 NIV

I do not sew. Not even a little bit. But I lost buttons this week—from my coat, my jeans, and my favorite sweater—and I have to try.

I stand on a stool and stretch to reach Grandmother's sewing basket on the top shelf of the guest closet. I pull back the lid and see bright spools of thread lining the bottom in colorful disarray. "Always keep a good supply of thread laid by, so you can match your cloth." Grandmother's voice is so clear I want to turn to see if she is peeking over my shoulder.

I settle into my reading chair and begin to thread my needle. I can almost feel Mother's hand on mine, guiding it toward that silver sliver's eye—the way she did the summer I was eight and tried to make clothes for my doll. After a few initial fumblings, my needle slips in and out of the buttons, attaching them securely. Suddenly, my hand becomes my sister's as she sews rows of buttons on the sleeve of my wedding gown—a gown she made for me by cutting up her own wedding dress.

Later, as I tuck the sewing basket back on that remote shelf, I feel connected to the women in my family in a way I haven't in a long time; connected to their resourcefulness, patience, generosity. And if my clumsy attempts with a needle and thread are what prompts this closeness, I'm almost eager for my next loose button!

Thank You, Lord, for the threads that bind me to my past
and to those I love. May I learn from them even now.
—MARY LOU CARNEY

If...you seek the Lord your God, you will find him if you look for him.
—Deuteronomy 4:29 NIV

*M*y four-year-old son is busy. He climbs on furniture, has trouble sitting still for more than five seconds, and runs everywhere. Most of the time I don't mind Trace's activity, but when he wiggles and giggles and squirms during church, I lose my patience. Not only does he talk nonstop to anyone who dares to sit next to us, but he also dances during hymns and stands on the pew and says, "Amen!" as loudly as he can. I worry constantly that he is distracting the other worshippers.

"Church is a time for quiet reflection," I whisper.

One Sunday our pastor asked Trace if he'd be willing to light the candles during the opening prayer. I was about to decline (picturing candle wax dripping down the aisle) when Trace said, "Please, Mommy, I know I can do it." He looked so excited that I didn't have the heart to say no.

The candles got lit. But it took two trips because Trace walked so fast the first time that the flame on the candlelighter went out. And he managed to get everyone laughing when he skipped back to his seat. *That's the last time I let him do that*, I thought.

Three days later I was getting the mail when I noticed a card addressed to Trace from Nancy, a member of our church. "Dear Trace," it said, "Thank you for the wonderful job you did helping your church family last Sunday. We all love the joy and enthusiasm you bring. You are a blessing."

Dear Lord, help me to remember there is a place for all of us in Your family.
—Amanda Borozinski

NOVEMBER 26

Thanks be unto God for His unspeakable gift.
—2 CORINTHIANS 9:15

Our daughter's earliest prayers were simple "thank you" prayers, and she fell into the habit of beginning every prayer with the words "Thank You, Jesus." By the time she was five, her prayers were more complex, including petitions for herself and others. But she still insisted on the same formula, with the result that her prayers sounded rather awkward: "Thank You, Jesus, for letting me play with Katy tomorrow." "Thank You, Jesus, that You will give Grandpa and Grandma a safe trip." "Thank You, Jesus, that You will help Mommy's cold get better."

I wondered if I should teach her that not every prayer had to begin that way. Yet as I listened to these prayers, I realized that she was teaching me. She had complete confidence in Jesus and believed He had already taken care of all her needs. Trusting in him, she was, as it says in Ephesians, "giving thanks always for all things"—even before they happened!

Thank You, Jesus, for answering the prayers that I have yet to pray.
—CAROL ZIMMERMANN

"Freely you have received, freely give."
—MATTHEW 10:8 NIV

*M*y friend Barbara stopped by today to finish up some pillows we've been designing. As I walked her to her van, I stopped by the mailbox under the arbor. Inside was the newest issue of Mary Engelbreit's Home Companion. One look at the red and green cover promising Easy Ways to Make a Home for the Holidays and Tasty Treats to Make and Give, and I was secretly planning my escape. There's nothing I look forward to more than sitting down with a cup of coffee and the latest issue of Home Companion.

"Is this the magazine by that greeting-card artist?" Barbara asked. "I went to the grocery store to get the Christmas issue and they were out. The bookstore too."

My mind traveled back forty years. My grandmother had just retrieved the holiday issue of Good Housekeeping from her mailbox. I grabbed it from her ottoman as soon as I spotted the cover announcing an article on making gingerbread houses. A few minutes later when Mother came to pick me up, Mamaw handed me the magazine. "You take it, honey. I can look at it later," she said. I murmured a brief thank-you and slid it under my arm, even though I could see the yearning in Mamaw's eyes and remembered the cup of coffee waiting for her on the kitchen table.

All afternoon, I kept thinking about that look in Mamaw's eyes. She ran a little alterations shop from her dining room, and there wasn't much money for extras. Her favorite magazine was her only extravagance, but she had let me enjoy it first.

I handed my new Home Companion to Barbara. Sometimes the best way to say a second thank-you for a long-ago deed is simply to repeat it.

> *Heavenly Father, thank You for Mamaw and all the models*
> *of unselfishness who've taught me the importance of giving.*
> —ROBERTA MESSNER

NOVEMBER 28

I have given you an example.
—JOHN 13:15

*M*y mother stoked up the fire in the kitchen stove with the wood she had carried in herself. She washed dishes with the water she had pumped from the well in the front yard. On wash day she scrubbed the family's overalls and hung them over the page-wire fence to dry. For meals she cooked countless variations of salt pork and potatoes, and people knew they would always be received with a warm welcome into her drafty old house on the Canadian prairie.

The linoleum was worn through where a welcome mat should have been—a silent testimony to the countless visitors who dropped in for food, friendship, and fun. They never seemed to mind her threadbare sofa and mismatched dishes. They pulled the odd assortment of old wooden chairs up around the table at mealtime and enjoyed the hospitality as if they were members of the family.

I thought of her today as I fussed with Thanksgiving preparations. Would these dishes match that tablecloth? What could I use as a centerpiece? Supposing more company came than I expected, would there be enough turkey and cranberries and pumpkin pie? And I really should have cleaned the rug and freshened up the kitchen curtains and....

In my mind's eye I could see my mother in her bib apron welcoming people through that scarred old kitchen door. I picked up the phone and dialed our son's number. "Hello, Lyle. Is there anyone you know who's alone for Thanksgiving? There might be? Well, bring them along for supper! See you all later!"

And then I began to peel a few more potatoes.

Thank You, God, for a mother who valued people instead of things.
—ALMA BARKMAN

Thou, Lord, hast helped me and comforted me.
—PSALM 86:17 RSV

*M*other was old and frail when she moved down to Staten Island, New York, to live with my brother, but she had always been so strong I assumed that she'd live for many more years. So I was unprepared when I got the call from my brother: "Oscar, it's Mother."

Ruby and I drove to Staten Island, and the next day I found myself sitting at my mother's funeral. Mother was a bright, well-educated woman. She had studied to become a registered nurse, but because of the Great Depression and the lack of opportunity in our small town, she could only find a job as a domestic. Her workday was spent in her employers' kitchens.

As I sat in the pew I wondered, had she really been happy? Did she feel fulfilled? Did she feel that service to others was its own reward? She never complained—never gave a hint of resentment. But did she wish things had been different?

Then the priest moved forward from the altar and spoke about her, calling her Mrs. Morgan (she had changed her name when she married my stepfather years before). I was taken back to the kitchens where she had worked, where she ran things with the efficiency, warmth, and professionalism of a registered nurse. I thought of all those people who feasted on her rice, lima beans, French fries, and chicken, and listened to her advice—all those households where she had made a difference. One woman in town was so notoriously difficult they said no one could work for her. Mother did for twelve years. And she was called Mrs. Morgan. Respected and admired, she was always Mrs. Morgan.

At once I was comforted and reassured. What might have been a job for some, Mother turned into a calling. It was not the career she planned on or studied for, but she made it something worthwhile.

> *Heavenly Comforter, help me make the most*
> *of all the opportunities that come my way.*
> —OSCAR GREENE

And suddenly there was with the angel a multitude of the heavenly host.
—LUKE 2:13

om had just arrived at our home for a holiday visit. As she stared at an angel ornament on my tree, she said, "My mother saw an angel when I was a girl." Then she told me this story:

"When I was young, I had severe asthma. One night I couldn't breathe. Mama was begging and praying that I wouldn't die. Suddenly she looked up in the open doorway to the hall and saw a beautiful dark-haired woman. The woman didn't say a thing. She just smiled and gave a friendly wave. Afterward Mama told me, 'I think it was an angel telling me that you would live and grow up to be a woman like the one I saw standing in the doorway.'"

Mom's story has challenged my conventional ideas about angels. Her angel looked like an ordinary person. Mom's angel didn't do anything remarkable; she didn't even say anything. Yet in the hour of deepest need, my grandmother had drawn strength and hope from this being who did absolutely nothing except stand there and wave. Sometimes the whole mission of angels is simply to appear.

Angels are spiritual beings who are invisible except when they choose otherwise; we humans are visible beings whose spiritual side is invisible until we choose to let it show. This Advent season, I can imitate the angels by letting someone glimpse my spiritual side. Maybe it will be seen as I drive to church or when I help a person in need. Maybe it will be heard when I sing a carol or write a Christmas letter telling about the wonderful things God has done for me during the past year.

This Advent, let's be angelic. Let's become visible!

> *Lord, I pray that Your light will so shine in my heart*
> *that it will be seen by everyone I meet.*
> —KAREN BARBER

December

Abram said to Lot, "Please let there be no strife between you and me, and between my herdsmen and your herdsmen; for we are brethren."
—Genesis 13:8 nkjv

I was perplexed when my friend Donna said to me, "My family's going to have a 'Bob Hope Christmas' this year!"

"What on earth is a 'Bob Hope Christmas'?"

"You know how Bob Hope was always away from his family on Christmas, entertaining the troops? Well, what about his own family celebration? When did he do that?"

"I never really thought about that. Whenever he got back, I guess. Whenever he could...."

"You see!" she said triumphantly. "That's a 'Bob Hope Christmas.' When I first got married, there was so much hustle and bustle seeing both families—each in a different city—that it took the joy out of celebrating. And then after the kids came along, it became really hectic. Sometimes we had to spend the whole day traveling. And we occasionally had two turkey dinners!

"So I decided that when my kids had kids, we'd have a 'Bob Hope Christmas.' It's important to their in-laws that the children spend the twenty-fifth with them, so I tell my kids that we'll do Christmas whenever it's convenient.

"I go to church on the day itself," Donna explained, "but as for the rest of the celebration—"

"A Bob Hope Christmas," I mused. "Sounds like a great new tradition."

Dear God, let me do what I can to assure that holidays are a time for restoring and reinforcing relationships, not hurt feelings and petty squabbles.
—Linda Neukrug

DECEMBER 2

And blessed is she that believed: for there shall be
a performance of those things which were told her from the Lord.
—LUKE 1:45

*C*hristmas was approaching, and I had been invited to give an informal talk for a small group of friends from church. We met one evening in Kathy's home on Big Lake in Alaska—gathered around her dining table, snow piling up outside.

After dinner I brought out my scribbled notes, and we began to think about Mary, the mother of Jesus. Who was she? What must it have been like for her to bring God's own Son into the world? Each of us had sons, and we knew that close mother-child bond. None of us felt so far removed in age or place or time that we did not long to see into Mary's heart and know her more. Most of all, we hoped to find mirrored, in her heart, images of Christ that would inspire and motivate and comfort us, that would help us to grasp that we, too, are among those to whom the promise of a Savior is given.

That night Mary's awestruck voice seemed to call to me from the Scriptures: "Join with me in receiving the amazing benefits that Jesus, the Savior, gives. Don't be hesitant or unbelieving. You, too, are included." And so, during this Advent season, it is my hope that through a closer look at the events of Mary's life recounted in the first chapters of Luke, each one of us will be better able to recognize the images of Christ in Mary's life in our lives also. Then, placing our praises alongside Mary's, we can truly say, "My spirit hath rejoiced in God my Savior" (Luke 1:47).

Jesus, You are come as the fulfillment of all God's promises—
born into this world to fill our needy hearts.
—CAROL KNAPP

DECEMBER 3

And Miriam answered them, Sing ye to the Lord,
for he hath triumphed gloriously.
—EXODUS 15:21

*O*h, no, here she goes again.

The *she* was my mother, and I was the twelve-year-old boy standing next to her in the pew on Sunday morning. Mom loved to sing in church. Fortunately, it was the only time she sang, because my mother couldn't carry a tune to save her life. Yet sing she did, as if there were no tomorrow. Whatever the diametric opposite of perfect pitch is, she had it, the uncanny ability not to go anywhere near the right tone.

It was bad enough going to church with your parents (I always tried to go to a different service so I could sit with my friends), but to have that kind of attention drawn to yourself was utterly mortifying. And people did cast slightly alarmed looks in our direction, to be sure. Even when I decided to attend the "guitar service" (it was the sixties, after all), my mother followed, eager to learn a new sort of music to mangle.

I was an altar boy, and I remember serving Mass with Father Walling when my mother would launch into song. He'd wince ever so slightly, and I would imagine that he could barely restrain his hands from flying up to cover his patient, suffering ears. Instead, he would quickly summon me with the cruets of wine and water.

All protests from my siblings and me fell on (tone) deaf ears. "You are supposed to be singing, not listening," she'd say, completely unsympathetic. "Besides, I'm sure God doesn't mind my voice one bit." I envisaged God frantically putting in cosmic earplugs.

Well, today it pleases me to no end that my mother really didn't give a hoot about what anyone thought of her singing. She was singing to God, not to us, and she believed that whatever came out of her mouth came out of her soul, and it was music to His ears. And now that she is gone, I miss her awful caterwauling more than I ever could have imagined when I was that self-conscious boy. But I know she is in heaven, singing, and God doesn't mind one bit.

My praise, Lord, is never on pitch until it reaches You.
—EDWARD GRINNAN

Every man shall give as he is able.
—DEUTERONOMY 16:17

*M*y mother-in-law was an alcoholic. She loved her grandchildren, but her addiction made it hard to express that love. Every fall, for a dozen years, we went through the same heartbreaking scenario. In September she would call Carol and ask, "What can I get the boys for Christmas?" Carol gave her mother lists of things the boys liked and sent her samples from catalogs. She went so far as to suggest an 800 number to call with the exact item number of the Lego or Playmobil toy or football jersey.

Finally, about a week before Christmas we would get another call. "I'm so sorry," my mother-in-law would say, "I just haven't had time to get anything for the boys. Let me send you a check. You get something nice and put my name on it." Because we wanted the boys to know their grandmother loved them, we obliged. But it was painful.

Then one summer she did something very brave. She went into a rehab program and stopped drinking. That fall there were no calls from my mother-in-law about what the boys wanted for Christmas. No matter. We were busy rejoicing in her recovery. What we didn't know is that her body hadn't really recovered from the ravages of her disease. After only three months of sobriety, she had a massive stroke and died two days before Thanksgiving.

That December was a sad one, full of regrets. What if she had stopped drinking earlier? What if we had urged her into rehab years ago? We asked ourselves a thousand "what ifs?" Then, before Christmas, a big package arrived in the mail. Carol looked quizzically at the return address. It wasn't from a mail-order company she knew, and a phone call to California assured her that it hadn't come from my family. When she opened the box she discovered a present for the boys, ordered by their grandmother. The one present my mother-in-law had bought before she died. A gift that meant more than words can tell.

Lord, help me give in return for all I have received.
—RICK HAMLIN

DECEMBER 5

Thanks be to God for his indescribable gift!
—2 CORINTHIANS 9:15 NIV

This week my daughter Elizabeth and I have been eating breakfast by candlelight. I realized we hadn't lit the Advent wreath on Sunday, and it seemed a nice idea to light it Monday in the early morning darkness. Something about the flickering warmth of candles brings my thoughts around to mystery. Nowadays we illuminate our world brightly and crisply, and it gives us the illusion that we know much more than we do. We operate as if everything is seeable and knowable, or at least *should* be seeable and knowable. But much of life isn't so luminous; people most surely are not!

Gazing at Elizabeth eating her gingerbread in the soft glow of the candles, I remember things that I don't remember under electric lights: the stories of Milky-Milky (a cow) and Walky-Walky (a horse) that I told at bedtime when she was a preschooler, her ocean-themed birthday party when she was four, comforting her the first time she forgot to do her homework, her excitement when her much-beloved mentor Alison arrived at our house to teach her math. By candlelight, it's easy to appreciate that there's a certain miracle in the fact that this marvelous being across the table is my child. How did that happen?

Perhaps part of the reason I've been silently waxing nostalgic during breakfast lately is that Elizabeth is applying to college a year early. Last night we heard from MIT. Among my future memories will be the shout of joy that burst from her as she read that she'd been accepted. *This is my child. What a gift. What a gift.*

Oh, Jesus, the Father's beloved Son, what a gift You are!
—JULIA ATTAWAY

DECEMBER 6

*T*oday I threw away a pair of house shoes. They were ratty, really, the insides threadbare and tattered. In several places the sole had completely separated from the shoe. Their blue fake-fur lining was matted and mashed down. So why have I kept these slippers so long? Because they were a gift from my mother who's been dead thirteen long years. They look exactly like something she'd have picked out: Purple flowers cover the entire shoe, and they are very, very warm. These house shoes—now so battered from wear—were one of her last gifts to me, and letting them go is like losing yet another bit of her.

My mother was not a collector of precious things. When I cleaned out her house, I took her china, her books, and her wedding ring. I also inherited several quilts she had made. I cherish these things. They were hers. Now they are mine. But these house shoes touch us both. Mother picked them out for me. I wore them with gratitude and, after she passed, with a sense of finality. When they wore out, there would be no other pair coming from her. Still, they are a mess. If Mother were here, she would laugh at my sentimentality. "Goodness, Mary Lou, get those filthy things out of the house. And get busy doing something worthwhile."

Whatever you say, Mother. Still, I hope the trash truck comes soon. I've already begun to reconsider.

> *Remind me, Lord, that nothing is ever lost as long as
> I know where it is...and I know Mother is with You.*
> —MARY LOU CARNEY

DECEMBER 7

And Mary said, "Behold, I am the handmaid of the Lord;
let it be to me according to your word."
—LUKE 1:38 RSV

*W*hen Gabriel told Mary that she—a virgin—would conceive a son by the power of God, she quickly said yes. How did she arrive at that moment of complete surrender? How did she become so perfectly the Lord's "handmaid," as she so humbly calls herself? Could it have been without pain and tears and self-denial? In the house in Nazareth, did she feel the cold shadow of the Cross?

One Sunday afternoon before Christmas several years ago, my husband Terry and I were sitting in our living room, watching a football game on television. As we sat there, one of our children quietly told us some devastating medical news—a checkup had revealed a serious, perhaps fatal illness. We were stunned.

That night I lay in bed in agony. Christmas was supposed to be a celebration of birth—of life—and I had just learned that my child was probably going to die. Not even tears could relieve the pain in my heart.

From out of the dark the Lord brought to my mind two Bible verses: Philippians 4:6–7 (RSV): "Have no anxiety about anything, but in everything by prayer and supplication with thanksgiving let your requests be made known to God. And the peace of God, which passes all understanding, will keep your hearts and your minds in Christ Jesus."

Deep in the night, I had a crucial decision to make: I could bow to God's Word and find peace as His obedient daughter, or I could surrender to my fear.

I chose to believe what He told me. I repeated that verse many times in the following months. And hardly understanding how it happened, I learned in my own small way to become a "handmaid"—to accept God's will for me, even if it led to a cross.

O God, Mary sets me an example of obedience.
When my understanding fails me, let me repeat her yes to You.
—CAROL KNAPP

DECEMBER 8

The Lord is able to give thee much more than this.
—2 CHRONICLES 25:9

*W*e live a four-hour plane ride from most of our family. But neither distance nor time can stop the outpouring of love of grandparents for their grandchildren. You should see the Christmas gifts waiting for my three-year-old son. Piles of brightly wrapped boxes of every imaginable shape and size tower above him.

One morning another package arrived at our door. I started to complain to my husband. "Don't you think this is a little much?"

Jacob just looked at me and smiled. "What did you say you were thinking of making for breakfast?"

"Hotcakes," I replied, pulling a glow-in-the-dark frog and a toy car from the box with a sigh.

"Mmm..." Jacob said pouring coffee.

As I got out the big metal mixing bowl, the flour, eggs, sifter, and buttermilk, my mind began to drift. My mom was a single parent for a while when I was growing up, and I ended up spending a lot of time with my grandparents. I played all sorts of wonderful games with my grandfather. He possessed a mind and a heart full of stories. He taught me to embrace my imagination. My grandmother had wonderful recipes. She shared with me the basics of cooking that I relied on when I was married. To this day, whenever I make hotcakes, I think of my grandmother lovingly guiding and instructing me. I remember feeling so proud the day she asked if I would make the hotcakes while she set the table.

Jacob's simple question reminded me that glow-in-the-dark frogs, stories, toy cars, piles of presents, and hotcakes are all ways for grandparents to say the same thing: "I love you."

Lord, help me to remember that love is a gift.
—AMANDA BOROZINSKI

December 9

We have different gifts, according to the grace given us.
—Romans 12:6 niv

*W*hile my boys were in college, they struggled with what to buy their grandparents for Christmas. They wanted my mom and dad to know how much they loved them, but finding a gift within their price range became more of a challenge each year.

Then one Thanksgiving, my father casually mentioned how much he had loved decorating the house with lights every Christmas. He couldn't any longer and that saddened him.

Shortly afterward, Ted and Dale came to me with an idea. As their Christmas gift to their grandparents, they wanted to make the three-hour drive to their house and decorate it for Christmas.

I pitched in and purchased the necessary supplies, and the boys spent two days stringing up lights and boughs all around the outside of the house. Every bush, plant, and tree trunk was wrapped in lights. My dad beamed with pride that his house was the most brilliantly lit home in the neighborhood.

Ted and Dale had such a good time with my parents, and each other, that they returned every couple of months and completed necessary tasks around the house that my father could no longer manage. My parents treasured this special gift more than anything the boys could have purchased.

I learned something valuable from my sons that year: An extra toy under the tree for the grandchildren won't mean half as much as playing a game with them or holding a special tea party complete with fancy hats and gloves. The gift of my time will be remembered long after they have outgrown their toys.

Lord Jesus, at the first Christmas You gave us the gift
of Yourself. Help me to make myself a gift to others.
—Debbie Macomber

This is My commandment, that ye love one another as I have loved you.
—JOHN 15:12

*T*he telephone rang early on a dismal morning in December, and a lilting voice greeted me, "If it were your birthday, I'd say, 'Happy Birthday,' but since it isn't, I'll just say, 'I love you, Mom.'"

Suddenly the gray day was radiant. My heart leaped with joy. My daughter had no particular reason for calling long-distance except to say that she loves me!

"Love" is so easy to say—and so often left unsaid. When was the last time you spoke words of love to your mate? To your children? To a friend? The Bible tells us that "a flattering mouth worketh ruin" (Proverbs 26:28) but genuine affection, freely given, can cheer the saddest heart.

Try it today. Don't presume family and friends know that you love them. Tell them. It will brighten their day and yours too.

Lord, keep us aware of Your love for us and help us to share it with others.
—DRUE DUKE

And the leaves of the tree are for the healing of the nations.
—Revelation 22:2 niv

"I don't want to go get a Christmas tree!"

John's angry shout filled the family with tension. It wasn't clear—it's rarely clear—what had brought on his blast of anger. John's mood swings are sometimes sudden. In the past week he'd been feeling down, and I was girding myself for a rough Christmas.

Ten minutes and many deep breaths later, the family tumbled out into the night. There was no way of knowing whether it would be a peaceful evening or not. At least the cool air felt good.

The place that sells Christmas trees was eight blocks from our apartment. Two-year-old Stephen chattered happily as he rode in our collapsible laundry/grocery cart. Mary spied the shadow of the moon grinning faintly behind its glowing crescent. My husband Andrew pointed out the spire of the Empire State Building lit up in red and green, seven miles to the south. John was reserved.

The Christmas tree vendor, in town from Vermont for the month, still had an ample selection. The fresh pine scent was invigorating. We decided on a tree, and it was straight-jacketed in plastic netting so it would fit into our cart. Stephen gladly gave up his place there and walked, talking, the whole way home.

John read a book while we trimmed the tree and set up the crèche. Maggie asked if she could sleep on the little sofa. Stephen wanted to sleep near the tree too. So did Mary. They trotted off to retrieve pillows and blankets.

"Can I sleep on the big sofa?" John sheepishly asked.

I looked searchingly at my son, my constant challenge, and nodded. That's when I knew that however his feelings might shift, whatever the ups and downs, whatever tomorrow would bring, this was still a season of hope.

Jesus, sometimes I wish You'd just fix what is wrong.
Help me, instead, to trust in what is eternally right.
—Julia Attaway

He has put down the mighty from their thrones, and exalted the lowly.
—LUKE 1:52 NKJV

O n an upper branch of the Chrismon tree is a fish. Within the fish are the letters used to spell *icthus*, the Greek word for fish. They are also the first letters of the Greek words for "Jesus Christ, God's Son, Savior." In the early church, when believers faced persecution and even death for proclaiming Christ, the fish became a secret sign of the Christian community.

My mother believed in community. Her first project after we moved to a small town in Oklahoma was organizing a Christmas pageant that brought together Catholics, Protestants, and people who didn't publicly profess any faith.

The pageant became an annual event, and the role of Mary became a popularity contest. Then Mother was elected to head the casting committee. She didn't ask for a list of cheerleaders or class officers; instead, she asked the committee to reflect on the character of Mary and choose accordingly. They did. Judy, a sweet-faced country girl with a radiant smile and flowing hair, got the role.

Was there a fuss? You bet. Mother held her tongue until the day she was cornered by the irate mother of an angel. The woman listed several reasons why the committee's choice was wrong: Judy wasn't one of the "in" crowd, her family had too many children, and they didn't attend church regularly. She ended her tirade by saying scornfully, "Judy is *poor!*"

"So was Mary," mother said.

I believe in community. I believe especially in Christian community, in the fellowship of believers. But I wonder: *Does my community include the lonely? The rejected? The poor?*

> *Lord of all, this Advent season and throughout the year,*
> *help me widen my circle to include all Your children. Amen.*
> —PENNEY SCHWAB

The light shines in the darkness, and the darkness has not overcome it.
—JOHN 1:5 RSV

*W*hen my son Ross asked what I wanted for Christmas, I told him I didn't need anything—just having him home from college was present enough. Then my daughter Maria was hospitalized for treatment of a chronic health condition, and shopping was forgotten, along with decorating, baking, and everything else. I felt particularly bad because we had promised Maria that this year we'd put up lights, something we hadn't done for years. But that wasn't going to happen. My husband Paul and I were struggling to keep things going at home and work while I spent nights with Maria in the hospital.

The Sunday before Christmas, Paul and I had spent the day at the hospital, and then I headed home to change clothes and pick up some things for Maria. As I turned the corner at the end of our street, I couldn't believe what I saw: Our house was covered with lights! Dozens of red, green, blue, and yellow bulbs ran along the perimeter of the roof, across the top of the garage, and through the bushes by the front door. Ross and his friend Sarah had spent the day hanging the lights, as well as putting up our tree and many of our favorite decorations.

It was the best present anyone could have given us, and it didn't cost a thing, except one entire Sunday afternoon when two teenagers could have been doing something else. Instead, they created the most beautiful light display I had ever seen. And when Maria returned home two nights before Christmas, she thought exactly the same thing.

Dear God, help me to give more of myself to those
I love, for often it's the only gift they want.
—GINA BRIDGEMAN

DECEMBER 14

When his mother Mary had been engaged to Joseph, but before they lived
together, she was found to be with child from the Holy Spirit.
—MATTHEW 1:18 NRSV

*M*y mother was the one who brought Christmas. She kept the anticipation and, yes, the anxiety simmering from Thanksgiving weekend, when the first decorations were hauled from the attic to be modestly distributed in bedrooms and more lavishly laid in the living and dining rooms, to New Year's Day, when the tree came down.

Mom taught my sister Lori and me to give up candy with her during Advent to show that "we're waiting for Jesus," though my father was exempt from what seemed a monumental sacrifice. And she was in charge of the candles—not only the electric candles that glowed in each window, but also the Advent candles, the focus of our grace before dinner on every Sunday in Advent.

To appease my father, with his abiding fear of fire, no live greenery surrounded the candles; even plastic pine cones were unacceptable, "just in case." The four candles were set in a simple metal holder on the kitchen table. But unlike Advent candles in every other household and church in our community, Mom's candles were not purple and pink. Traditionally, purple candles are lit on the first, second and fourth Sundays in Advent to symbolize waiting for Jesus. The pink candle is lit on the third Sunday as a foretaste of our joy in His nearing birth. But my mother's metal wreath held four white candles.

There were two reasons for Mom's unconventional choice: First, she believed our whole time of waiting for Jesus should be joyful. And reason number two? Purple and pink clashed with the rest of her decorations.

Jesus, let the pure light of Your coming birth
burn away my worries and distractions.
—MARCI ALBORGHETTI

Joy to the world! The Lord is come;
Let earth receive her King;
Let every heart prepare Him room
And heaven and nature sing.
—ISAAC WATTS

There was a war on, and I had four little boys to raise by myself. Money was always short, even for necessities, so I took a part-time job as a waitress, and used my tips to buy toys and clothing at the dime store, which I passed each day as I walked home. I would pick the presents out very carefully, after much deliberation, because I knew I really had to stretch the nickels and dimes, or the boys would be disappointed on Christmas morning. I would daydream how their little faces would look, as they found the gifts from Santa. I would smuggle the packages into the house, and hide them in a box in my closet.

A week before Christmas, I came home to find the sitter taking a nap, and the children squealing with delight. They had found the box, and the presents were scattered all over the house, the new clothes tossed to one side, in favor of the toys.

"Look, Mama, look," yelled the boys. "Santa was here; come and see!"

I was so upset I sat down on the bed and started to cry. I felt that our Christmas had been spoiled.

Just then, my mother came by to help me get the boys ready for bed, as she did each night, even though she had a job to go to each day, and a house to keep up. She took the situation in at a glance.

"Merry Christmas, boys. *Ho, ho, ho!*" she sang out. "Santa really did come last night, didn't he? Now isn't that nice? He brought the presents early, and now we can have a whole beautiful Christmas Day all to ourselves, just us and Baby Jesus to celebrate His birthday."

Forgive me, Lord, if I have turned the sacred birthday of Thy Son into
a tinsely, commercial holiday. Let me give gifts of loving, and caring,
and sharing, instead of plastic trinkets. And, please Lord, let the Holy Spirit
of Christmas have room in my heart all year long, not for just a day.
—PAT SULLIVAN

But grow in grace, and in the knowledge
of our Lord and Saviour, Jesus Christ.
—2 PETER 3:18

O n a two-shelved rack on my kitchen wall is a collection of tiny teacups. There is one from each tea set my daughter received during her childhood Christmases.

The smallest one is unbreakable, of painted metal. It was the first. The second Christmas and the third are also represented by metal cups, successively larger. Number four is a red plastic, followed next by a delicate pink plastic. By the sixth Christmas, she understood being careful of breakage and the first china cup appears, small and heavy. By the next year, the cup was slimmer, thinner, more delicate. The last one is a beauty. It is hand-painted, almost transparent, the top-of-the-line quality.

The evidence of her growth and development is reflected in those cups, from days of clumsy grabbing at the metal ones to an ease of handling the most fragile.

I hope that as my Heavenly Father surveys the collection of days I offer him throughout my life, He will be able to discern in me just as steady growth and development in His will.

Father, we do wish to grow steadily and we pray for Your help to do so.
—DRUE DUKE

DECEMBER 17

Every good gift and every perfect gift is from above.
—JAMES 1:17

O n a long-ago Depression Christmas I opened an enormous box, certain that the tricycle I had yearned for was inside. But there was no tricycle, just another box! I unwrapped it thinking "Well, it'll be something very special, anyway." But all I found was another box—and another and another—each smaller than the last. Finally, I opened the last one. There was a pair of woolen mittens my mother had knitted. My disappointment was keen, but as I looked at them more carefully I discovered that these were no ordinary mittens. They had gauntlets at least six inches long, and wide enough to pull up over my snowsuit arms so the snow couldn't get inside and chap my wrists any more! I'd asked for a pair like that but had forgotten—and here they were! I knew the love that went into those mitts. I rushed to Mother and gave her a big hug and kiss and said, "Oh, thank you, Mom. They're just what I wanted!"

Well, I'm fifty-three now, and I've learned that the gift of life has come to me from my Heavenly Father, wrapped much the same way. When I started out, I dreamed of all the wonderful things I was going to accomplish. But, year by year I've been unwrapping my gift of life, one "box" at a time, and again and again I've been disappointed many times. I haven't accomplished very much, I'm not famous, my seventeen-year marriage has ended in divorce. But I haven't opened the last box yet!

My excitement mounts. What will I find? If I'm wise, I will look it over very carefully and receive it joyfully because it is my Father's loving gift.

Oh, thank You, Heavenly Father!
—JEAN DEAN

DECEMBER 18

The Lord is good unto them that wait.
—LAMENTATIONS 3:25

I'm thinking back to Christmas Eve 1983, Wyoming. My daughter Tess, four, sleeps in her peppermint-striped pajamas. On the sofa eleven-month-old Greg snoozes on his daddy's chest. I'm rocking six-week-old Tom, singing lullabies by firelight. My living room is rich in miracles this holy night.

After years of infertility, I now had two baby boys this Christmas Eve: Greg, adopted in January when he was three days old, and Tom, born to us in November. Last Christmas Eve my heart ached with longing. When I asked Tess what she wanted for Christmas, she said, "A baby brudder"—the one present we could not promise. Despite years of prayer, it appeared that we would never give birth to a child. God must have something else planned, I told myself.

Then a mere three weeks after Christmas 1982, our caseworker phoned, "You have a son in Rock Springs!" Our family felt complete—we had a daughter and a son. Who could want more? I stopped feeling sorry for myself and plunged into joyous, full-time mothering.

Now here I was with a toddler and two babies, one asleep in my arms. As I rocked him, I wondered what Mary sang to Baby Jesus in that stable long ago. I wondered how many mothers and fathers would sing lullabies to their babies on this holy night. I wondered how many would sing songs about the special baby who will guard their children forever.

Only embers glowed in the fireplace as I finished singing "What Child Is This?" Tom didn't understand the song yet, of course, but he would. I thought, *I'll keep singing to my children at home, at church, and in the car, not just on Christmas, but every day. God has blessed me beyond my wildest imaginings; I have only begun to sing my praise.*

> *Infant Jesus, in the tumult of Christmas,*
> *hear the lullabies of love from the stillness of my heart.*
> —GAIL THORELL SCHILLING

December 19

I received a Christmas e-mail update from a friend of mine living in Boston. It has not been a good year for her. Her father died from cancer, she broke up with her boyfriend, and now she has found out she's pregnant.

This is ironic, because she is deeply religious. But she didn't use the word *ironic*; she used the word *shame*.

During the difficult visit to the obstetrician, she had many questions, but she couldn't stop crying long enough to ask them. Finally she confessed that she had always viewed pregnant single girls as either "incredibly stupid or incredibly selfish."

The obstetrician was quiet for a moment, then said, "Or they're incredibly human."

It was exactly the right thing to say—for her, for me, and now for you. My friend is carrying a child; you and I are carrying all sorts of things, too, but our baggage is less obvious. Some of what we carry is stupid and selfish, but what she carries is incredibly human. You would think we'd see the irony of that, but we do not. We march on doggedly, blind to our own faults and only too eager to shame others for their sins.

Maybe my friend should name her child after the obstetrician, but I've already thought of other names. I think the baby should be called Wonderful. Or Counselor.

Sorry, I'm getting my Advent stories of young girls in difficult circumstances mixed up.

Lord, no matter how faithful I may think I am, I'm human too.
Keep my friend and her baby and all of us close to You.
—Mark Collins

Have they not heard? Yes verily, their sound went into all the earth,
and their words unto the ends of the world.
—ROMANS 10:18

*B*y hovering near the Christmas tree for hours, I had become a master at recognizing those pesky presents by the time I was seven or eight. As soon as I picked one up and gave it a little shake, I knew exactly what it was: an ornament. Back then I saw those neatly wrapped, lightweight boxes as necessary evils that I had to tear through and politely thank my grandmother Bebee for before I could get to the good stuff. Every year she gave ornaments to each of us grandkids. They came from her travels with my grandfather, and over time we'd received tree-hangers from all over the world. There was a wooden Great Wall from China, a tin Big Ben from London, and crudely carved mangers and stars from places I'd never heard of. On the back of each was the year and the place it came from, neatly written with a black marker.

All these years later those same ornaments have taken on a unique importance as my son Harrison and I decorate our tree. They remind me, of course, that I was always in my grandmother's heart as she traveled far and wide. But somehow they've also become symbols of the greatness of God, as they bear witness to the impact that Christ's birth has had on our world.

"Where is this one from, Daddy?" Harrison asks for the umpteenth time.

"That's a Taj Mahal from India," I reply, imagining the little shop in Agra that Bebee must have visited to find such a treasure.

"India?" Harrison replies with amazement. "I didn't know people that far away knew who Jesus is."

Isn't it wonderful to know they do?

Father, Your Spirit fills heaven and earth, and
Your Word truly reaches the ends of the world.
—BROCK KIDD

DECEMBER 21

My voice shalt thou hear in the morning, O Lord;
in the morning will I direct my prayer unto thee.
—PSALM 5:3

"Ten o'clock and I'm already behind," I muttered. Not a single gift wrapped; cookies for the neighbors just a lump of dough in the fridge; too late to send cards and letters to arrive on time. And this afternoon at four, my first granddaughter would be baptized. I was hosting the dinner afterward and had only just slid the ham into the oven. The casseroles weren't made, the house was a mess—and the kids were still sleeping!

"Up and at 'em, boys!" I rolled Tom and Greg, both sixteen, out of bed. The racket woke up Trina, thirteen, who had given her bed to company and slept on the sofa. Over cheerless bowls of cereal, I recruited my morning help.

"Tom, you can vacuum the living room. Trina, please unload the dishwasher. Greg, you can empty the trash and clean the small bathroom. I'll peel the potatoes for the casserole."

My children wearily gathered dishes and slouched off to their assignments. Satisfied that we were proceeding on schedule—my schedule—I returned to the potatoes.

A few minutes later Greg reappeared. Maybe he can't find the sponges or cleanser.

"Mom, what's the date today?"

"December twenty-first. Why?"

He showed me the spiral-bound desk calendar with a prayer and inspirational thought for each day that we kept by the bathroom sink.

"Oh, I just need to fix this. It says August seventeenth." He turned the pages, grinned and sauntered off, reading the prayer for the day.

I paused in my potato peeling and considered the bathroom...toothpaste splatters on the mirror, wet towels on the floor, clutter on the counter. And the first thing Greg focused on was a calendar?

And a prayer—a perfect way to start a messy project and a busy morning!

Thank You, Lord, for children who remind me of what is truly important.
—GAIL THORELL SCHILLING

DECEMBER 22

And this shall be a sign unto you; Ye shall find the babe
wrapped in swaddling clothes, lying in a manger.
—LUKE 2:12

*I*t was my mother's first time back to church following a stroke that had paralyzed her right side. As we pushed Mom's wheelchair up the narrow side aisle, I searched for an inconspicuous spot where no one would notice her eye patch or her slouch.

Unfortunately, as Dad parked Mom's wheelchair in the aisle, the children participating in the Christmas pageant began marching up the aisle behind us. Dad had no choice but to push Mom toward the specially built plywood stage. Finally, Dad veered aside and parked Mom in the only available spot—right next to the grand piano.

As the program began, the children playing Mary and Joseph knocked on the door of a cardboard-box inn and the innkeeper bellowed, "There's no room for you here! The only place I can offer is the stable." I wondered if Mary and Joseph felt awkward and out of place as I did, with Mom sitting up front in the curve of a grand piano.

After church as I hurried Mom out, a woman stopped us, leaned down with tears in her eyes and said, "We're so glad you're back. You're such an answer to prayer."

Suddenly I remembered that many people at church had been praying for Mom. If I'd succeeded in keeping Mom neatly tucked away in an obscure corner, they might not have seen her and been able to share in the joy of her return.

Father, the cries of a newborn heralded the coming of Your kingdom; thank You
for using the weak things of this world as signs of Your powerful presence.
—KAREN BARBER

And they came with haste, and found Mary,
and Joseph, and the babe lying in a manger.
—LUKE 2:16

t was 7:30 p.m. on Christmas Eve, and our college-age son Chris, who'd just flown in from California, was going out to buy gifts for the family. "Why bother?" I told him. "You're not going to find anything. The stores are all closed."

I was still skeptical when he returned proclaiming, "Mom, I got some good stuff. You all are going to love what I got you!"

When Christmas morning arrived, we were indeed surprised by our gifts. I certainly didn't expect to unwrap a new pair of windshield-wiper blades. "I really needed these," I admitted, remembering how my windshield was always smeared.

"The gas station was open Christmas Eve," Chris said.

My husband was surprised to find a gift certificate to our favorite Chinese restaurant. Chris's brother John received passes to the movies.

I don't remember any of the other gifts we gave or received that year, but Chris's still stick in my mind—gifts I assumed would never materialize. They reminded me that the shepherds set out in the middle of the night, and followed their hearts and found Jesus. Yes, my best present that Christmas came disguised as a pair of windshield wipers. Chris's last-minute gifts showed me that a seeking spirit will always be able to find God's treasures.

Father, this Christmas as I thank You for the gift of Your Son, help me
seek out the gifts and graces I need to keep growing spiritually.
—KAREN BARBER

DECEMBER 24

Grace be with you, mercy, and peace, from God the Father, and
from the Lord Jesus Christ, the Son of the Father, in truth and love.
—2 JOHN 3

*T*t is Christmas Eve, and five of us file into church. My daughter Charlotte says in her practical way, "Take the end seat, Mom. You'll be the only person who has to get up." The others nod their heads in agreement. This is the place I would wish to be on Christmas Eve, but I am honest enough to realize that my family is here mainly to please me. For a moment, I wonder deep down whether I should have left them to their DVDs, VCRs, PCs and other acronymic pursuits. Never mind, it is Christmas.

The overflowing church is glowing with candles and flowers. The handbell choir is ethereal and the children's choir irresistible. The organ fills the air with the sound of trumpets, and we launch into "Hark, the Herald Angels Sing."

When the appropriate moment comes, I rise to go forward for Communion. It's a big church, so I have a ways to walk. I'm almost at the chancel steps when I feel a touch on my arm. I turn in surprise. There, right behind me, is Daniel, my baby, but now a grown man a head taller than I. We kneel together at the altar rail and receive the bread and the wine. As we rise and move to the side aisle, Daniel puts his arm around me and whispers, "I love you, Mom."

No moment in any church at any time was more holy—or more joyous.

Thank You, Lord, for the touch of grace, sent
without fanfare and received with gladness.
—BRIGITTE WEEKS

DECEMBER 25

And yet I am not alone.
—JOHN 16:32

Our family opens gifts on Christmas morning—quietly, with coffee and quiche before the children were born; with bewildered toddlers, who preferred the boxes to the gifts; amid preschooler pandemonium. Then, as the children grew older, we could take turns and savor the experience. A lighted Christmas tree, soft carols, and a special coffee cake add to the festivities.

But in 1996 my daughter Tess, seventeen, was in Spokane, Washington, about one thousand miles away. She couldn't come home. Then a few days before Christmas, she injured her knee. Overwhelmed with pain, loneliness, and memories of happier holidays, she called crying on Christmas morning.

"Oh, honey, I wish you could be here too. Did you like your presents?"

"No. I'm too depressed to open them."

"Well..." How to comfort long-distance? "You aren't alone now! We're here. Kids, get on the bedroom phone. Tess is going to open her gifts!"

Tess stopped sniffling and dug into the box. First she opened the red fleece cloche hat and mittens. "So soft. They fit great, Mom."

Then the surfboard-shaped pillow her brother had sewed in home economics class. "You really did this? Way to go, Tom!" Now there was energy in her voice.

Next, slippers. The harp tape. "I love them!"

Sounds of paper tearing. "What are you opening now, honey?"

"A book—must be from Mom!"

A squeal. "Now what?"

"Peppermint patties, pinwheel cookies, and fudge!"

Finally a soft "wow" as she found her Christmas card and check to buy the coat she had admired. By the time we hung up, her dismal mood had vanished.

God bless the phone circuit that keeps our family circle from unraveling!

Lord, on this Christmas Day, bless with comfort
those separated from their loved ones.
—GAIL THORELL SCHILLING

DECEMBER 26

T've often wondered just how Mary felt after the heavenly host had returned to the Father, the shepherds and the Three Kings to their flocks and thrones, and the throngs in Bethlehem to their own abodes. How did she feel after everyone was gone?

It was just last week that our house echoed with voices: "Honey, run to the store for whipping cream!" "Kids, stay out of the candy until after we eat!" "Somebody get Jimmy out of the packages under the tree!"

Now the house is empty and quiet—the excitement dissipated into slamming car doors and revving engines. What's left behind are leftovers, copying new addresses brought on by a swarm of greetings, half-price sales on cards, gift wrap, and tree decorations, plus overflowing wastebaskets and empty freezers.

Did Mary also have a hard time retaining the thrill of the preceding days? Or was she wise enough to know that life is always a series of peaks and valleys, that you can't stay on the mountaintop, that you have to come back down to the valleys where life is lived and work is done. Surely that's what Mary did when she went back to Nazareth to be a wife and mother. And that's what we must do too, when the excitement of Christmas is over, keeping in our hearts the knowledge that as the earth turns, the gladness of Christmas will come again— as it always has and always will.

> *Father, help me get through the little feelings of depression
> that come when a happy time is over. And thank You
> for the knowledge that such times will come again.*
> —ISABEL CHAMP.

DECEMBER 27

On the Sabbath day he went into the synagogue, as was his custom.
—LUKE 4:16 NIV

I had been trying to listen more closely to God, but as I entered church on Sunday, I thought, Nothing dramatic has come to me this week. Everything's the same old routine. I followed my husband Gordon and our nine-year-old John into the sanctuary and scooted down the pew to save two seats—one for my teenage son Chris and one for his girlfriend. In a few moments they arrived, and the service began.

The oddest thing happened, though, when I opened my eyes after the morning prayer. I saw our family sitting in the pew together as if I were seeing them for the first time. A startling thought came to me: Chris brings his girlfriend to church. She didn't attend regularly anywhere until he invited her, and now she comes. Then another startling thought came: The same thing happened with Jeff, who's off at college. His girlfriend began attending church with our family and became quite active in the youth group.

In that moment of clarity, I saw that I had underestimated the importance of a good, ordinary routine. We had made it a simple habit to go to church each Sunday. We expected our boys to continue coming with us during their teenage years and on any Sunday when they were home from college. It was low-key, simple, and unremarkable, yet God had done something quite remarkable with it. Every time our hands opened the church door, it made it easier for someone else to come in and join us.

I settled back, knowing that I had been hearing from God more often than I had imagined, for every Sunday our family had answered His invitation, "Let us go to the house of the Lord" (Psalm 122:1, NIV).

> *Lord, help me to get into such a good, deep rut of Sunday worship*
> *that others can't help but follow the well-worn path.*
> —KAREN BARBER

And you will always give thanks for everything.
—EPHESIANS 5:20 NLT

That's what my mother used to say: "You *will* write thank-you letters for your Christmas gifts." Doing so almost canceled out the excitement of whatever had been in the wrapped boxes mere days before. I still recall the agony of gripping a stubby pencil in sweaty hands, chewing its eraser end, and asking, "What shall I say?"

Probably since the beginning of time, mothers have required the same etiquette of their offspring. My own sons didn't escape either. So I've come up with a solution for my grandchildren and for you. Make as many copies of this form as there are gifts, cut on the dotted lines, check the appropriate boxes, fill in the blanks, mail. Done! It may not be ideal, but it's better than nothing.

Dear Mom Dad Grandma Grandpa Aunt Uncle Cousin Friend Sweetheart (Other)

_____,

Thank you for the_____. It is beautiful handy just what I need my size not my size the right color not the right color something I can't wait to use a gift that will be good for me something I really like (other)_____.
Our Christmas was fun happy blessed busy disastrous (other)_____.
We had ham turkey meatloaf pizza vegetarian (other)_____.
Love, Blessings, Cordially, Warmly, Sincerely, Yours, Best, (Other)_____
(Signature)_____

And now, here's an already prepared thank-you prayer, but it must be said wholeheartedly and with sincere gratitude:

Thank You, God, for sending Your Son, Jesus—our Savior,
Redeemer, Blessed Hope—Christ, the center of CHRISTmas!
Only You could give Your children this perfect gift!
—ISABEL WOLSELEY

*"He will be great, and will be called the Son of the Most High...
and of his kingdom there will be no end."*

—LUKE 1:32–33 RSV

*T*he journey that began the December night I received my child's frightening medical news continued into the next summer. One evening I was sitting at the end of a dock beside a clear mountain lake. A few last rays from the setting sun tinted the scattered clouds, which earlier had brought a light rain. I was praying yet again for my child. Suddenly, I flung my open arms to the sky and spoke to Jesus with complete conviction: "If You have allowed it, then I can trust it." It was my way of giving up my child to Him—of giving up my desire to say how this should end.

No sooner had I spoken than a magnificent rainbow formed right before my eyes, filling the sky with color. I wanted to leap into the air and run under that rainbow, treading the clouds. I still had no answer for our family's crisis, but I had hope.

Six months later, after another Christmas celebration of the miracle of the Christ Child, our own child received miraculous news of perfect health!

Even in the dark times, Mary had a hope anchored in that first angelic promise, "Of his kingdom there shall be no end." I believe this hope supported her from the flight into Egypt clear to the foot of the cross. For all her joy in holding her Bethlehem baby, I picture her most keenly—even at Christmas—rushing into the outstretched arms of her risen Son.

Jesus, You give such hope and power and purpose to Your people! The tiny flailing fists of Bethlehem have become the strong arms of my salvation.

—CAROL KNAPP

There, in the presence of the Lord your God, you and your families
shall eat and shall rejoice in everything you have put your hand to,
because the Lord your God has blessed you.

—DEUTERONOMY 12:7 NIV

"Does anyone else have something to share?" Sean Bates, the best man, angled the microphone toward the tables where a hundred and fifty faces, softened by candlelight and glorious fall-color flowers, remained silent after his moving toast to our son John and his bride Courtney.

"I think I do," I said quietly. He handed me the mike as I rose.

Around the dance floor I saw husband and sons—Peter safe from Afghanistan and David just home from Iraq; Tom, newly married himself—and our new daughters Matti and Susan. There sat brother and nieces and nephews, cousins on both sides, friends I'd known for thirty years and some I'd known just thirty months. There were Courtney's parents, grandparents, aunts, uncles, brother, friends, neighbors. Oh, if only I could stop it all right here—all of us safe and whole and together, laughing, dancing, rejoicing.

"I want to tell you a 'John' story that I think is for all of us here tonight," I began. "One Christmas when he was about seven, Bill and I noticed John wandering from room to room where his brothers were playing and his grandmother and great-aunt were dozing. Then he found his dad and me and tugged us into the kitchen. In his wonderfully earnest way he looked up at us, paused, and said slowly and succinctly, 'This house is full of people I love.'

"Tonight, I think we can all say, 'This house is full of people I love!'"

I leaned over and kissed my newest daughter.

Giver of family and friends, help me to stop in the frantic pace
of the holidays and thank You for a moment full of people I love.

—ROBERTA ROGERS

DECEMBER 31

Forgetting those things which are behind, and reaching
forth unto those things which are before.
—PHILIPPIANS 3:13

*M*y children and grandchildren, who spent the early evening with me, have left to celebrate the new year with their friends. The lovely silence of the house nestles around me like a warm blanket as I settle into my prayer chair for a ritual I've practiced for several years. I turn off the lamp on the end table so that I can fully enjoy the Christmas tree lights and the lovely angel with silken hair who adorns its top. Then I light a candle and think back over the year, month by month.

What comes to mind is a mixture of things. I find that I still feel strong emotions as I recall the things that marred the year—arguments, tears and losses, hurricanes, wars of greed, and a relationship that ended. It's hard to let the pain go. But there are also happy memories I want to cling to: the moment of my granddaughter's birth, a favored friendship, a fresh spiritual insight, a satisfying work project, a trip to California.

But life is change, and I need to remind myself that endings lead to beginnings, and that even good things must be held lightly in order to grow. So one by one I offer them up, the sad ones and the glad ones, knowing that forever and in all ways, these released events of the past year are safe with God.

Now, as the clock nears midnight, I sit quietly in the stillness, feeling lighter and freer. The future, still a mystery, glistens with the promise of a Light beyond time, a Light that shines in the darkness, a Light that cradles overflowing hope.

Loving Lord Jesus, Light of the world, You are the moon that shines
on the shadows of behind. You are the sun that illumines the path ahead.
Keep me walking in Your Light throughout the coming year.
—MARILYN MORGAN HELLEBERG